The Literate Mind

Reading,
Writing,
Critical Thinking

Thomas E. Porter
Charles Kneupper
Harry Reeder

The University of Texas at Arlington

KENDALL/HUNT PUBLISHING COMPANY
2460 Kerper Boulevard P.O. Box 539 Dubuque, Iowa 52004-0539

Contents

Contents

Preface

This book began as a series of Class Notes for CACTIP (Composition, Analysis of Texts, Critical Thinking Integrated Program). This program, initiated at The University of Texas at Arlington in the fall semester, 1985, is a sequence of three courses which integrate reading, writing, and critical thinking. These courses replace the two semesters of freshman composition traditionally offered, and the sophomore course, Introduction to Literature. The tripartite division of this book reflects the approach taken in each course in the sequence: Book One: Exposition: The World as Given; Book Two: Argumentation: The World as Problematic; Book Three: Self-Expression: The World as Artifact.

The number of contributors to this volume are legion. The members of the committee that developed the theoretical base and the original design of CACTIP are faculty at The University of Texas at Arlington from the division of rhetoric, the Departments of English and Philosophy. They tackled, with enormous energy and persistence, the difficult task of finding a common ground for reading, writing and critical thinking. They developed the reading lists and the syllabi for the three courses in the sequence. The members of this original CACTIP committee were:

John Kushma, History	Tom King, Philosophy
Lenore Langsdorf, Philosophy	Carolyn A. Barros, Liberal Arts
Luanne Frank, English	Victor Vitanza, Rhetoric
Harry Reeder, Philosophy	Charles Kneupper, Rhetoric

Sam Perez (now of The University of Oregon), Education

I am grateful not only for the suggestions, comments and criticisms of the rest of the members of this group, but also for the spirit of collegiality in which they were given.

Book Two, Argumentation: The World as Problematic, is largely the work of Harry Reeder and Charles Kneupper.

The initial CACTIP courses were directed and taught by teams of faculty from The University of Texas at Arlington, the Dallas Community College District, and Tarrant Junior College System and the Arlington Independent School District. This alliance among university, community college and high school faculty contributed significantly to the original design and to the refinement of the Program. Their contributions are incorporated in the presentations of this volume. The names of these faculty members and their affiliation appear below:

Directors
Carolyn Barros, Assistant Dean of Liberal Arts, UTA
Michael Feehan, Assistant Professor of English, UTA
Victor Vitanza, Associate Professor of English, UTA
Charles Kneupper, Associate Professor of English, UTA
Harry Reeder, Associate Professor of Philosophy, UTA

Instructors
Betty Ann Clark, English Department, South Campus, TCJC
Jack Covington, English Department, Arlington High School AISD
R. P. Dexter, English Department, Mountain View Community College, DCCCD
Emory Estes, English Department, UTA
Hannah Goolsby, English Department, Sam Houston High School, AISD
William McMurry, English Department, Northeast Campus, TCJC
Sue Milner, English Department, Northwest Campus, TCJC
Mollie Newcom, English Department, Northwest Campus, TCJC
Kenneth Roemer, English Department, UTA
Thomas Ryan, English Department, UTA
Marjorie Schuchat, English Department, Brookhaven Community College, DCCCD
Harryette Stover, English Department, Eastfield Community College, DCCCD
Tena Ward, English Department, Lamar High School, AISD
Audrey Wick, English Department, UTA

The professional expertise and cooperative spirit of the community college and high school team members were an inspiration to the university participants. This effort illustrated what an academic alliance encompassing these different educational levels can accomplish.

The authors are also grateful to those consultants who contributed valuable critiques on the original design: O. B. Hardison, Jr. of Georgetown University, Frank D'Angelo of Arizona State University, Ralph Johnson of the University of Windsor, Jonathan Warren of Research and Higher Learning, Berkeley.

In developing the theoretical bases for the Program and for the discussions in this volume the authors drew heavily upon the critical writings of Paul Ricoeur, James Kinneavey, Steven Toulmin and Kenneth Pike. Ricoeur's discussion of hermeneutics, Kinneavey's elaboration of rhetorical aims, Toulmin's general approach to argument and Kenneth Pike's tagmemic system contributed substantially to the theories articulated in this volume. These are the intellectual shoulders on which we stand.

The manuscript was prepared with the assistance of Susan Chiasson, Laurie Jacobs and Cindy Williams. Special thanks are due Dr. Carolyn Barros, Assistant Dean of Liberal Arts at The University of Texas at Arlington, who participated on the CACTIP Committee, taught in the Program and edited the manuscript.

Finally, we are indebted to the National Endowment for the Humanities for support and assistance in mounting the Program and producing this volume.

Thomas E. Porter
Arlington, Texas 1987

Book One

The Literate Mind and the World as Given: Reading and Writing from the Perspective of Exposition

Chapter 1
Toward the Literate Mind

Reading and Writing

Throughout our educational experience, from grammar school through college, the two words we hear most frequently in our work assignments are "read" and "write." "Read the next two chapters for tomorrow." "For Friday write an essay on the Battle of Bull Run." Doing well in our academic work depends chiefly on our ability to "read" the assigned material and to "write" clearly, correctly and concisely. If we have trouble reading and writing, we will have trouble learning. Moreover, we will have trouble demonstrating to our teachers and our peers that we have learned. So it is crucial to our progress as students that we be able to read and write effectively and to demonstrate to others that we can.

None of this is news. You come to the college classroom with considerable experience in both reading and writing. You have probably formed an opinion about your own ability in both these areas. "I can read pretty well if I'm interested and the book is not too hard." "I don't like to write very much." "When my teachers tell me what they want, I can give it back to them." "I'm a lousy writer; writing isn't very important anyway." Ask yourself, "How well do you think you can read and write?" Make up your own assessment of your ability and compare it with these statements.

However you feel about your ability to read a text or write a paper, it will help to test your capabilities in reading and writing. Knowing what you can do and how well you can do it gives you the confidence to try things that might otherwise seem too difficult. We want to explore what it means to be a good reader, what it means to be a good writer, and offer some suggestions about improving these abilities. We will try to build on what you already know, and to help you to recognize both your strengths and your weaknesses.

There is an old saying that good readers are good writers. This may well be true; it is not altogether clear *why* it is true. To make an obvious connection, good readers may be good writers because good readers and good writers are good thinkers, in short, that they have developed the characteristics of a literate mind. We propose to investigate that mind. We propose to offer ways of thinking about reading and writing which will help you organize your thoughts and express them effectively. If you master the methods that we present here, you will be able to read a book or write a paper with the confidence that comes from understanding the text and being able to articulate your ideas effectively.

We will begin by looking at what the literate mind *does*, what reading, writing and thinking have in common.

Interpretations and Signs

In the beginning chapter of *The Hound of the Baskervilles,* Mr. Sherlock Holmes finds a cane left by an anonymous visitor. He examines the walking stick, a fine, thick piece of wood, bulbous-headed, with a broad silver band across it. On the band is inscribed "To James Mortimer, M.R.C.S., from his friends of the C.C.H." He presents the stick to Dr. Watson, and asks what he makes of it. Watson's conclusions are "elementary," but erroneous. Holmes concludes, from his investigation of the stick, that its owner is "a young fellow under thirty, amiable, unambitious, absent-minded, and the possessor of a favorite dog, larger than a terrier and smaller than a mastiff." Watson, as is his habit, wonders at Holmes' powers. For the great detective it is simply a matter of observation and deduction, an interpretation of the signs presented by the walking stick.

Interpreting signs is so much a part of our experience that we take it for granted. We know that a red octagonal sign at an intersection means stop; we know that slight chills are an indication of an oncoming cold. There are times when reading signs is a matter of life and death, for instance, the surgeon reading an electrocardiogram, interpreting black wavy lines on a travelling sheet. Scientists read the data they accumulate in the laboratory; the weatherman reads computer print-outs describing the movement of the upper air. Reading signs, interpreting data is a principal and essential function for all of us.

Word as Sign

Of the signs that surround us the most common and the most relevant to human experience is the word. We become so accustomed to interpreting words that we hardly notice we are doing it. When a friend greets us in the corridor with "how are you?" we don't, if we are smart, talk about our indigestion. We know from the circumstances that the expression is a greeting, not a question. If, on the other hand, a doctor during a physical examination asks "How are you?" we understand that we are to describe our ailments. In ordinary conversation the process of interpretation goes on without our even adverting to it. In most situations, the circumstances and our experience help us to interpret correctly, but the words themselves always require interpretation.

Words and Polysemy

The reason for this is simple enough: words are ambiguous, polysemic. A given word can have many meanings; if you need a demonstration of this point, consult a dictionary. The dictionary will frequently list up to ten or twelve meanings for a single word. And sometimes, indeed, the dictionary is not enough. Consider, for instance, the following examples: 1) The stove is hot. 2) This diamond is hot. 3) The topic is hot. 4) That pilot is hot. Each one of these sentences needs interpretation if it is to make sense, and the dictionary will be minimally helpful. If we are to paraphrase, that is, explain the sense of each sentence, we will need to render four different and distinct meanings of the word "hot." "Hot" in the first sentence refers to the temperature of the object. "Hot" in the second sentence conveys the notions of "stolen," dangerous and illegal. In the third sentence "hot" carries the sense of "interesting," relevant." Referring to a pilot, "hot" indicates superior flying ability with a dash of a daredevil wrapped in a cool exterior. In this last explanation note that "cool" requires further interpretation. "Coffee," "jazz," and "property" can all be hot, but again "hot" means very different things. All are instances of the polysemy of the word "hot" which only appear when the word is used in a sentence. The word itself can have a multitude of meanings; those meanings are narrowed down and specified only by their use in a text.

There are all kinds of texts; we are surrounded by them. A text can be, for instance, a set of street signs or road markers, a word and a gesture used in conversation, a single sentence, a book, a whole series of books. And in every one of these cases interpretation is necessary to make sense of these "texts."

Here we are going to confine ourselves to what has been called the inscribed text, that is, a system of signs made up of words and set down in print or in writing. A book, a newspaper, a magazine, a letter from our Aunt Harriet are inscribed texts.

Any inscribed text differs from other kinds of texts by virtue of the fact that it is self-contained, autonomous, and relatively permanent. Once the inscribed texts leave the hands of their creators, they have their own existence in the world. If you want to check this out, visit a library. There the texts stand, on the shelves, between their covers, waiting for readers. They are self-contained and autonomous in that, if I need the author along with the book in order to understand it, the book defeats its own purpose. Presumably, the inscribed text itself, without any assistance, contains everything a reader needs to know in order to understand it. It is permanent in the sense that a conversation is not; the text of a conversation disappears when the conversationalists cease speaking. So an inscribed text, whether it is a set of instructions taped to the refrigerator or a large novel, is a self-contained unit that, because it is made up of words, requires interpretation.

Interpretation and Education

Much of our education, as we remarked above, depends on our ability to interpret inscribed texts. Very early in our academic careers we are faced with assignments like: "Read the next two chapters for tomorrow." What this assignment means, we soon come to understand, is not reading the chapters aloud to the cat or simply passing our eyes over the black words on the white page. It means, in fact, that we will be expected to interpret the text. Reading, then, means interpretation.

Interpreting the Text

Mr. Sherlock Holmes, by examining the cane his visitor left behind, was able to put together a description of its owner. From the clues the cane provided he was able to build, with the use of his reason and his imagination, a detailed description that proved to be generally accurate. The cane served as a text; it provided a collection of signs that could be put together into a picture. The inscribed text—a note, a letter or a book—provides the same kind of clues to interpreting a message or an idea. Just as the cane is not the person, so the words in a text are not the meaning of it.

Here is an inscribed text to be interpreted.

To get to the Medical Complex from Arlington, take I-30 east to the Hampton Road exit. Go north on Hampton until you pass under the Stemmons Freeway. The Medical Center will be on your right. Take the main entrance, stop at the guard booth, then turn left at the first intersection. Follow the curving road to the parking garage on your left. The main offices are in an eleven-story building directly across from the parking garage.

This text is like the cane the visitor left behind. It is our job to interpret it.

Inspectional Reading and Preliminary Understanding

A quick first reading of this text indicates that it is a set of directions. The indications that this is so are words like "east," "north," "right" and "left." Other expressions designate places: "Arlington," "Medical Center," "parking garage." The phrases "to get to" and "follow the curving road" indicate movement and direction. Presumably, this inscribed text provides a way of getting from Point A (Arlington) to Point B (the Medical Complex). You probably did not have to go through anything like the explicit analysis above to conclude that you were reading a set of directions. As quickly as your eye took in the words, you were able to establish a preliminary understanding of what the text was about, namely, directions from Arlington to a Medical Complex.

This is the way interpretation of an inscribed text begins. We do an inspectional reading and, from our previous experience, we get a general idea of what the text is about. When we classify this text, for instance, as a set of directions, we establish the criteria for discovering what it means: directions must be read in sequences; no part can be omitted; directions are specific to the lay of the land and to landmarks.

To proceed further with our interpretation, we want to examine closely what the text says. If we are acquainted with the territory or if we have a road map at our disposal, very little explanation may be needed. Natives of North Texas might well understand that I-30 is the old Dallas-Fort Worth Turnpike. They would also know that the Stemmons Freeway is I-35. The Medical Center has a full title which the native might know: the Dallas Health Science Medical Center. These pieces of information, available to the native reader or to someone with a detailed road map, explain the words in the text.

The final test of any interpretation of directions is whether or not they actually take you to the destination they promise. And, it is important to notice, a correct interpretation of the text requires a correct interpretation of the whole text. That is to say, if we misunderstand any part of the directions, we will probably not get to the Medical Center. We have to correctly interpret all the parts in order to achieve the objective described in the text. Getting there is the final criterion for a correct understanding of this text.

Imagine for a moment that in the year 4000 A.D. an anthropologist discovers this set of directions to the Medical Center in a pile of rubble. The anthropologist, if she knew the language, would bring the same kind of preunderstanding that we bring to reading the text. That is, she would recognize it as a set of directions. Unless everything in the neighborhood had remained exactly the same for 2,000 years, her major problems would be locating the sites in order to reconstruct a map of the places mentioned. The principal value of the text in this dim future might be its indications of the kind of civilization that produced it. To understand the whole text, in the year 4000, might well be to understand the ground transportation system, a map of the Arlington/ Dallas area, a picture of an institution committed to health science and medical delivery systems. The same text can have different meanings to different readers; the text itself, its words, their order and arrangement, and their relationships to each other, does not change.

Even a simple text like a set of directions requires interpretation; it must be explained in order to be understood.

Another Example

Another example will help to illustrate how the same principles of explanation and understanding work in a more complicated text.

The Big Bull Market

The Big Bull Market was dead. Billions of dollars worth of profits—and paper profits—had disappeared. The grocer, the window-cleaner, and the seamstress had lost their capital. In every town there were families which had suddenly dropped from showy affluence into debt. Investors who had dreamed of retiring to live on their fortunes now found themselves back once more at the very beginning of the long road to riches. Day by day the newspapers printed the grim reports of suicides.

Coolidge-Hoover Prosperity was not yet dead, but it was dying. Under the impact of the shock of panic, a multitude of ills which hitherto had passed unnoticed or had been offset by stock-market optimism began to beset the body economic, as poisons seep through the human system when a vital organ has ceased to function normally. Although the liquidation of nearly three billion dollars of brokers' loans contracted credit, and the Reserve Banks lowered the rediscount rate, and the way in which the larger banks and corporations of the country had survived the emergency without a single failure of large proportions offered real encouragement, nevertheless the poisons were there: overproduction of capital; overambitious expansion of business concerns; overproduction of commodities under the stimulus of installment buying and buying with stock-market profits; the maintenance of an artificial price level for many commodities; the depressed condition of European trade. No matter how many soothsayers of high finance proclaimed that all was well, no matter how earnestly the President set to work to repair the damage with soft words and White House conferences, a major depression was inevitably under way.

Nor was that all. Prosperity is more than an economic condition; it is a state of mind. The Big Bull Market had been more than the climax of a business cycle; it had been the climax of a cycle in American mass thinking and mass emotion. There was hardly a man or woman in the country whose attitude toward life had not been affected by it in some degree and was not now affected by the sudden and brutal shattering of hope. With the Big Bull Market gone and prosperity going, Americans were soon to find themselves living in an altered world which called for new adjustments, new ideas, new habits of thought, and a new order of values. The psychological climate was changing; the ever-shifting currents of American life were turning into new channels.

The Post-war Decade had come to its close. An era had ended.

"The Big Bull Market" from ONLY YESTERDAY by Frederick Lewis Allen. Renewed 1959 by Agnes Rogers Allen. Reprinted by permission of Harper & Row, Publishers, Inc.

Inspectional Reading and Preliminary Understandings

You have just done an inspectional reading of this inscribed text entitled "The Big Bull Market." As a result of this inspectional reading, you have a few preliminary understandings of what this text is about. In the first instance, you might recognize, from the title, that it refers to Wall Street and the stock market. You might also see that it is referring to a particular time in American history. You came to these understandings, if you did, by virtue of seeing the title as a topic which the author is presenting in detail, by recognizing certain key words in the text: "profits," "capital," "stock market," "depression" and "post-war." On the basis of this evidence you can say that this text is about the stock market crash in the post-World War I decade. You can classify the text roughly as "historical." You can view it as "expository" since it describes an event in detail.

Explanation

Once you have a general set of understandings about the topic with which the text is dealing, you can proceed to examine and explain the parts. The phrase "bull market" might need explanation; a bull market is a buyer's market, characterized in the text by the word "optimism." In a bull market the investor assumes that the prices of stock will continue to rise. "Coolidge-Hoover Prosperity" might also need some explanation. The reference here is to two Presidents whose terms of office spanned the latter half of the 1920s. It might also be useful to understand how "over-production of capital," "over-ambitious expansion of business concerns," "overproduction of commodities" make the collapse of a bull market inevitable. Finally, it might be necessary to explain how "prosperity" is a state of mind.

In the second paragraph the writer talks about "the body economic." Explaining the second paragraph involves being able to describe the sense of this term. How does the author describe it and what purpose does his description have in the paragraph? At the end of the paragraph he talks about "soothsayers"; how would you define "soothsayer" and what words could be appropriately substituted for it? What are the possible meanings of the word "depression" and how does one arrive at the principal meaning of this word in this context?

In the third paragraph the text speaks of "American mass thinking." How does the text describe this concept and why does the text introduce it at this point? Finally, what war is being referred to in the expression "post-war decade"?

Answering these questions provides an explanation of significant parts of the text. There are methodologies which we will consider shortly that can help us explain the individual parts and especially their relationship to one another. These methodologies provide us with ways of classifying the parts of the text and their relationships. We will consider them in more detail at a later point.

Understanding the Text

Explaining a text is not the end of the process. When we explain the features of a text, we are stating what the text *says,* not what the text *means.* We began by looking at what kind of text we were reading and what the text was about. We needed some general understandings in order to begin explaining. We said this text was about a period of America history, that it dealt with the stock market, that it dealt with the beginning of the Great Depression. Those understandings were enough to get us *started,* but they did not exhaust the meaning of the text. The next question was: what is the author saying about this period of American history, the stock market, the Great Depression? By answering the questions raised in the previous paragraphs, we got some notion of the parts of the text, that is, what the text says. Now we want to consider what the text *means,* what the text is about specifically.

A typical definition of economics would state that economics studies the production and distribution of material goods. This text is about the way economics is part of people's attitudes toward their way of life. It sees the bull market as founded on optimism and an unlimited potential for wealth and growth. It sees the stock market crash as the end of that vision. It insists, finally, that Americans now live in a new world where that optimistic vision is impossible.

There are other understandings or insights that might be derived from this text; you may have come to some of them. With what you know now about the text, you can read it again and perhaps discover new insights that the text offers. Any new insights will build on the ones you already have and may require further explanation. For instance, in rereading the text, the word "poison" might jump out at you. What are the poisons that "seep through" the economic body, and how does one determine that they are poisons? Explaining this word and its use in the text might well lead to further insights.

Interpretation of the Text

When we have gone through our inspectional reading, come to some general preliminary understandings of what the text is about, examined and explained what the text says, and arrived at specific insights as to the meaning of the text (what the text is about specifically), we have developed an *interpretation* of the text. This is the process we go through whenever we read a text, whether it be a set of directions, a brief essay, a how-to manual, or a novel. Understanding this process of interpretation is key to getting control of the reading enterprise.

One More Example

Perhaps our approach to interpretation works for some texts and not for others. We will take one more instance and see how the cycle of preliminary understanding-explanation-new understanding works.

Little Red-Cap

Once upon a time there was a dear little girl who was loved by every one who looked at her, but most of all by her grandmother, and there was nothing that she would not have given to the child. Once she gave her a little cap of red velvet, which suited her so well that she would never wear anything else; so she was always called "Little Red-Cap."

One day her mother said to her, "Come, Little Red-Cap, here is a piece of cake and a bottle of wine; take them to your grandmother, she is ill and weak, and they will do her good. Set out before it gets hot, and when you are going walk nicely and quietly and do not run off the path, or you may fall and break the bottle, and then your grandmother will get nothing; and when you go into her room, don't forget to say, 'Good-morning,' and don't peep into every corner before you do it."

"Little Red-Cap" from *Folk-lore and Fable* by Jakob and Wilhelm Grimm. P. F. Collier Publishing Company, 1909.

"I will take great care," said Little Red-Cap to her mother, and gave her hand on it.

The grandmother lived out in the wood, half a league from the village, and just as Little Red-Cap entered the wood, a wolf met her. Red-Cap did not know what a wicked creature he was, and was not at all afraid of him.

"Good-day, Little Red-Cap," said he.

"Thank you kindly, wolf."

"Whither away so early, Little Red-Cap?"

"To my grandmother's."

"What have you got in your apron?"

"Cake and wine; yesterday was baking-day, so poor sick grandmother is to have something good, to make her stronger."

"Where does your grandmother live, Little Red-Cap?"

"A good quarter of a league farther on in the wood; her house stands under the three large oak-trees, the nut-trees are just below; you surely must know it," replied Little Red-Cap.

The wolf thought to himself, "What a tender young creature! what a nice plump mouthful—she will be better to eat than the old woman. I must act craftily, so as to catch both." So he walked for a short time by the side of Littel Red-Cap, and then he said, "See, Little Red-Cap, how pretty the flowers are about here—why do you not look round? I believe, too, that you do not hear how sweetly the little birds are singing; you walk gravely along as if you were going to school, while everything else out here in the wood is merry."

Little Red-Cap raised her eyes, and when she saw the sunbeams dancing here and there through the trees, and pretty flowers growing everywhere, she thought, "Suppose I take grandmother a fresh nosegay; that would please her too. It is so early in the day that I shall still get there in good time"; and so she ran from the path into the wood to look for flowers. And whenever she had picked one, she fancied that she saw a still prettier one farther on, and ran after it, and so got deeper and deeper into the wood.

Meanwhile the wolf ran straight to the grandmother's house and knocked at the door.

"Who is there?"

"Little Red-Cap," replied the wolf. "She is bringing cake and wine; open the door."

"Lift the latch," called out the grandmother, "I am too weak, and cannot get up."

The wolf lifted the latch, the door flew open, and without saying a word he went straight to the grandmother's bed, and devoured her. Then he put on her clothes, dressed himself in her cap, laid himself in bed and drew the curtains.

Little Red-Cap, however, had been running about picking flowers, and when she had gathered so many that she could carry no more, she remembered her grandmother, and set out on the way to her.

She was surprised to find the cottage-door standing open, and when she went into the room, she had such a strange feeling that she said to herself, "Oh dear! how uneasy I feel to-day, and at other times I like being with grandmother so much." She called out, "Good morning," but received no answer; so she went to the bed and drew back the curtains. There lay her grandmother with her cap pulled far over her face and looking very strange.

"Oh! grandmother," she said, "what big ears you have!"

"The better to hear you with, my child," was the reply.

"But, grandmother, what big eyes you have!" she said.

"The better to see you with, my dear."

"But, grandmother, what large hands you have!"

"The better to hug you with."

"Oh!, but grandmother, what a terrible big mouth you have!"

"The better to eat you with!"

And scarcely had the wolf said this, than with one bound he was out of bed and swallowed up Red-Cap.

When the wolf had appeased his appetite, he lay down again in the bed, fell asleep and began to snore very loud. The huntsman was just passing the house, and thought to himself, "How the old woman is snoring! I must just see if she wants anything." So he went into the room, and when he came to the bed, he saw that the wolf was lying in it. "Do I find thee here, thou old sinner!" said he. "I have long sought thee!" Then just as he was going to fire at him, it occurred to him that the wolf might have devoured the grandmother, and that she might still be saved, so he did not fire, but took a pair of scissors, and began to cut open the stomach of the sleeping wolf. When he had made two snips, he saw the little Red-Cap shining, and then he made two snips more, and the little girl sprang out, crying, "Ah, how frightened I have been! How dark it was inside the wolf"; and after that the aged grandmother came out alive also, but scarcely able to breathe. Red-Cap, however, quickly fetched great stones with which they filled the wolf's body, and when he awoke, he wanted to run away, but the stones were so heavy that he fell down at once, and fell dead.

Then all three were delighted. The huntsman drew off the wolf's skin and went home with it; the grandmother ate the cake and drank the wine which Red-Cap had brought, and revived, but Red-Cap thought to herself, "As long as I live, I will never by myself leave the path, to run into the wood, when my mother has forbidden me to do so."

You have just done a quick inspectional reading of this text. It may have sounded very familiar. Let us see, first, what sorts of preliminary understandings we garnered from the text.

Preliminary Understandings of Little Red-Cap

The title may itself have sounded suspiciously familiar, and you may have identified "Little Red-Cap" as "Little Red Riding Hood." If you didn't, the text would soon persuade you that this is the same story you heard as a child. The text itself offers broad hints about the kind of text you are reading. The text begins "Once upon a time." This is the conventional and agreed-upon opening of a folktale or a fairytale. As you progress through the story, you encounter a talking animal, astounding transformations, a happy ending. We have learned to identify stories with these features as "folktales." So our inspectional reading tells us that 1) we are reading a story, a piece of fiction; 2) the elements of this story are not going to conform to everyday experience; 3) all will be well at the conclusion of the story. With these preliminary understandings, we can consider then what the story says.

Explanation of Little Red-Cap

Because our preliminary general understandings of this text indicate that it is a story, a narrative, the major task in explanation will be to summarize the sequence of events. In a story, things happen and they happen in a given order. What happens and in what sequence is crucial to an explanation of the story.

What Happens in Little Red-Cap

When you have read a good story or seen a good film (a film is often a narrative, too) and you want to tell your friends about it, you tell them first what happened in the story or the film. If you have ten minutes to give a summary because the bus is leaving or you know that your friends will not sit still any longer than that, you try to condense the action as tightly as you can. If you had four hours, you could read them the story and talk about it, or take them to see the film. A summary of the action requires more selectivity; you have to pick the parts of the action that are significant.

A summary of "Little Red-Cap" might go as follows. A little girl, on her mother's directions, takes cakes and wine to her sick grandmother who lives in the woods. On her way she encounters a wolf who sidetracks her into the forest, where she plays happily for a time. The wolf hurries to the grandmother's house and devours the old lady. He then puts on her nightdress and climbs into bed. When the little girl finally arrives, the wolf invites her in and, after a brief discussion, devours her also. A woodsman passing by hears the wolf snoring and decides to investigate. When he discovers the wolf asleep on the bed, he cuts the animal open, frees grandmother and the little girl, and the duo celebrate their escape. If necessary we can boil this summary down this way: Red-Cap sets out to deliver cakes and wine to grandmother. She meets the wolf. The wolf devours grandmother. The wolf devours Little Red-Cap. A woodsman saves grandmother and Little Red-Cap.

This summary tells us what the story says. It is an explanation of the principal events in the folktale. It does not, however, indicate in any way what the folktale is *about,* that is, what it *means.*

Once we have lined up the principal events in the story, we will want to consider how these events are related to one another. Some questions that we may want to try to answer: Why does the wolf not simply devour Little Red-Cap when he first meets her? Why does he go through the charade of disguising himself as her grandmother before he devours Little Red-Cap? Why is the woodsman the appropriate character to free grandmother and Little Red-Cap from the wolf's belly? Why does he fill the wolf's body with stones before skinning him? Answers to these questions are explanations of the arrangement of the events in the story and how the events relate to one another.

Understandings of Little Red-Cap

A story, a fictive narrative, deals with human actions in an imaginary or possible world created by the text. Even when the world of the text looks very much like one we are familiar with, it is still imaginary. We will not be able to locate Little Red-Cap's village or the forest where grandmother and the wolf live on any map. The human actions we are dealing with are not simply movements, physical activity, but moments of discovery and decision. The tale, the short story, the novel, the play or the poem, all deal with real human actions in an imaginary context. Not all the actions in the story have equal significance. For instance, Little Red-Cap's picking flowers is not as central an event in the story as the wolf's devouring her. It is a physical activity which relates to what went before as an instance of Little Red-Cap's believing the wolf and disobeying her mother's directive. The activity itself is less important; Little Red-Cap could have sat under the tree and gone to sleep and something of the same effect would have been produced. What the story offers in terms of understanding relates to the human actions—to the knowledge, emotions and decisions of the personae. So our understandings of the story grasp the significance of the human actions in it.

Note that there are a number of different understandings which the reader can draw from the story. A simple and obvious meaning relates to Little Red-Cap's actions with regard to her mother's instructions. The mother says: "Do not run off the path." Little Red-Cap ignores this instruction and goes picking flowers in the woods. At the end of the tale Little Red-Cap thinks to herself, "As long as I live, I will never by myself leave the path, to run into the wood, when my mother has forbidden me to do so." So one meaning of the tale might be: Don't talk to strangers;

obey your mother. It is clear, however, that other meanings too are available in the story. The little girl's encounter with the wolf, disguised as grandmother, might trigger the insight that things are not always as they appear. On viewing the disguised wolf, Little Red-Cap remarks on her changed appearance. "Grandmother, what a big mouth you have." So the tale is also about the way in which appearances can deceive us.

If you read through the story again, you will notice that nowhere in the story does it say: "Obey your mother," or "Appearances are deceiving." We take both these meanings from the story, but they are not explicitly stated in the story. *Understandings, then, are ideas or insights that the text generates in our minds in fairly mysterious ways.* This story offers us a little girl and a wolf and a grandmother and a woodsman and the things they do; our mind grasps the significance of these events and their arrangement by formulating the statements: "Obey your mother" and "Appearances are deceiving." Explanation of what the story says is different from understanding what the story means in precisely this way: *explanation talks about the parts of the story* and what these parts contain whereas *understanding grasps the story as a whole and deals with what it means.*

We ought also to notice that the two meanings we have found in the story—"Obey your mother" and "Appearances are deceiving"—do not exclude one another. The story contains both meanings and we do not have to choose one or the other. In fact, we can consider how these two meanings might be related to one another. This consideration could lead us to yet another examination of the text.

Little Red-Cap, when she meets the wolf, forgets her mother's admonition not to leave the path. She is also deceived by the appearance of the wolf and suggests that the forest would be a delightful place to play in. The story says flatly: "Red-Cap did not know what a wicked creature he was and was not at all afraid of him." When she looks at the woods she sees "sunbeams dancing here and there through the trees" and "pretty flowers growing everywhere." She does not recognize the danger represented by the woods and the wolf until it is too late. Her failure to identify the wolf as wicked and the forest as dangerous causes her to disregard her mother's advice.

Putting these two meanings together, then, we discover that the story is about a naive innocent who discovers, the hard way, that, under the appearance of good, evil and destructive forces may lurk. We may here find an answer to the question we asked above, "Why does the wolf disguise himself as grandmother in order to devour the little girl?" It often happens, in our own experience, that we do not recognize evil for what it is until we have suffered its consequences. Especially for the inexperienced, what appears good may be a mask for evil. And the wolf in this tale is one such instance. So little Red-Cap ventures into a world with which she is unfamiliar and discovers that everything is not what it seems to be, that even the familiar figure of grandmother can conceal a malevolent force.

Reading: Interpreting a Text

To summarize: good detectives and good readers are good interpreters. A good detective gathers all the clues, explains how the clues fit together to make a pattern and so discovers the criminal. The good interpreter of texts works in much the same way.

Inspectional Reading

We begin with an inspectional reading. Our clues to what the text is about appear in 1) the title, 2) key words and phrases, 3) the type of text: for example, directions, history, folktale. These preunderstandings of what the text is about provide clues that direct our explanation in specific paths.

Explanation

Our explanations deal with various parts of the text and their interrelationships to one another. In the next section of this book we will consider methodologies for explaining a written text.

Understanding

Our explanations lead us to specific understandings of what the text is about. These understandings often come in a flash, a burst of discovery, in which we say "Aha! so that's what it means." Sometimes these understandings (and there are often a number of them) come thick and fast. Sometimes they come slowly and painfully. The explanations prepare our minds for grasping what the text is about. Often we must return to the text and reread it in order to develop further explanations that lead, hopefully, to further understandings.

Writing: Creating a Text

We said at the beginning of this chapter that good readers are good writers. We have looked at what reading a text entails and we have seen that reading is a process of explanation and understanding. We now want to consider the process of writing and what writing has in common with reading. Reading is interpreting a text; writing, on the other hand, is creating a text.

We do not, however, create our text out of nothing. As we bring preunderstandings to the reading enterprise, so we bring data, experience and insight to the writing enterprise. That enterprise is generally defined for us in broad terms: 1. Our mother says, "Aren't you going to write Aunt Harriet and thank her for her Christmas present?" 2. Your roommate says, "When are you going to write the landlord and complain about the plumbing?" 3. The history instructor says, "For Friday write an essay on 'One Cause of the Great Depression' "; 4. In a literature class, the syllabus says, "Write a ten- to twelve-page paper on a short story of your own choosing. This paper is due on the last day of class." Each one of these writing assignments presents a topic on which a text is to be created.

You might summarize the topics as follows: 1. gratitude for Aunt Harriet's gift, 2. an urgent need for plumbing repairs, 3. a cause of the Great Depression, 4. a selected story. These general topics provide us with a point of departure; they roughly define the subject about which we wish to write. Each one of them requires development, but the last two will demand more attention and reflection, in all probability, than numbers one and two. In any event, creating a text requires in the first instance that we describe, however roughly, the topic about which we wish to write.

The general topic, then, initiates our preunderstanding. We may need to examine it at more or less length in order to begin creating our text. For instance, if we have put off thanking Aunt Harriet, we might want to include an apology and an explanation for our tardiness. If the gift was a useful one, like money, we might want to detail how we spent it. On the other hand, a simple note: "Thank you, Aunt Harriet, for the thoughtful gift" might be enough to turn the trick. A letter to our landlord about the plumbing presents a similar challenge. If we have already made contact and gotten no effective response, we might want to meditate on the most effective way of stating our case. We might even consider a mild, somewhat veiled threat as part of our text. What we note about the first two topics—Aunt Harriet's gift, the need to repair the plumbing—is that we can explore them in the light of our own experience; we have the necessary data at hand. The latter two topics present a challenge of a different order.

In the first instance, we recognize that these general topics (the Depression; a short story) require further definition. Even in the most simple of historical treatments, the causes of the Great Depression are various, for example, a boundless optimism about continuing prosperity, the stock market boom and buying on margin, over-exploitation of foreign markets, insufficient federal controls on the economy. Within the general topic of "causes of the Depression," the assignment makes it necessary to select one particular cause for further examination. With regard to the fourth topic, the assignment makes it clear that we must select a story from those listed for the course that will be the subject of our examination. Once we have selected, on the basis of our knowledge or special interest, a particular cause of the Depression or a specific literary work, we are faced with discovering what we have to say about it.

Explanation and Invention

Our explanation of a written text involves an examination of the parts of the text and their relationship with one another. When we begin work on a topic, it is our job to "invent" the parts which we want to discuss. In the case of our letter to Aunt Harriet, we have already touched on "invention" in enumerating 1. an apology for our tardiness. 2. an expression of gratitude for the gift, 3. a description of the uses to which the gift was put. In inventing the parts of our letter to the landlord about the plumbing, we might consider 1. an enumeration of our attempted contacts with him, 2. a description of the difficulties with the plumbing, 3. presentiments of the disasters that might follow if the plumbing is not repaired, 4. a description of our course of action if he does not reply. With these efforts, each of which relates in a different way to the topic, we are well on our way to creating a text.

Inventing parts for our other two topics will require a little more effort. The stock market crash as a cause of the Great Depression is not a matter of our own experience and it will probably be necessary to gather some data on the subject. The excerpt on "The Big Bull Market" discussed above (p. 7) would provide a source of information and possible insights about that topic. Based on our reading of that text, we might want to explore 1. the condition of the stock market in September 1929; 2. the immediate economic consequences of the crash; 3. the long term economic consequences of the crash; 4. the psychological consequences of the crash; 5. the relationship between the economic and psychological consequences. Each one of these points can be explained in relationship to the other points as they come to bear on the topic as a whole.

To fulfill the fourth assignment, we select "Little Red-Cap." Again, our job of work would be to invent an explanation of the tale that elaborates an insight about its meaning. Our investigation of the text of "Little Red-Cap" (p. 9) turns up a number of understandings about the meaning of the story, for instance, "obey your mother," "appearances are deceiving." If we were to invent ways of exploring this insight in a text of our own making, we might divide the story into its principal events and consider how appearances deceive at each stage of the narrative, e.g., 1. Little Red-Cap is deceived by the apparent simplicity of her mission; 2. she is deceived by the courtly manners of the wolf; 3. although she is suspicious, she is catastrophically deceived by the wolf's disguise; 4. when she is saved by the woodsman, she recognizes the consequences (more or less) of her naivete. This is a simple invention which divides the story chronologically and applies a basic understanding ("appearances are deceiving") to each part. We might consider developing our text by enumerating the types of deception which the story includes. The types of appearances that deceive, e.g., 1. physical appearances that are deceiving, 2, psychological appearances that are deceiving, 3. moral appearances that are deceiving. Discovering ways of getting at the topic, that is, invention, is a significant step in the writing process which provides us with the means of explaining the topic to ourselves and to our prospective readers. To review:

Reading: Explaining the Parts to Discover What the Text Says

1. A little girl, on her mother's directions, takes cakes and wine to her sick grandmother who lives in the woods.
2. On her way she encounters a wolf who sidetracks her into the forest, where she plays happily for a time.
3. The wolf hurries to the grandmother's house and devours the old lady.
4. He then puts on her nightdress and climbs into bed.
5. When the little girl finally arrives, the wolf invites her in and, after a brief discussion, devours her also.
6. A woodsman passing by hears the wolf snoring and decides to investigate.
7. When he discovers the wolf asleep in the bed, he cuts the animal open, frees grandmother and the little girl, and the duo celebrate their escape.

or:

1. Red-Cap sets out to deliver cakes and wine to grandmother.
2. She meets the wolf.
3. The wolf devours grandmother.
4. The wolf devours Little Red-Cap.
5. A woodsman saves grandmother and Little Red-Cap.

Writing: Inventing the Parts from What the Text Means—Deception

Appearances deceive at each stage of the narrative, e.g.,

1. Little Red-Cap is deceived by the apparent simplicity of her mission.
2. She is deceived by the courtly manners of the wolf.
3. Although she is suspicious, she is catastrophically deceived by the wolf's disguise.
4. When she is saved by the woodsman, she recognizes the consequences (more or less) of her naivete.

This is a simple invention which divides the story chronologically and applies a basic understanding ("appearances are deceiving") to each.

or:

The types of appearances that deceive, e.g.,

1. physical appearances that are deceiving,
2. psychological appearances that are deceiving,
3. moral appearances that are deceiving.

But, you might object, we haven't begun writing yet. In effect, we began writing when we began thinking about choosing a topic. The subsequent process of invention, of discovering ways to explain the topic, required that we compose, at least in our heads, the divisions of the text we are creating. So before we have written the first sentence of our first paragraph, we have been deeply engaged in writing.

As we begin to actually set words down on paper, as we follow the inventional scheme that we have devised to explain our topic, we will, in all likelihood, come to new insights about the topic. As we explain what the written text says, we set up the conditions for our understanding of what the text means. As we struggle with the creation of our own text, the odds are good we will have the same experience. We are always somewhat in the situation of the fellow who does not know what he is going to say until he says it. The discipline of explaining the parts of the topic as we have organized them may well lead us to new understandings that further illuminate the subject matter. So it might occur to us, as we are developing the relation between the economic and the psychological situation in the aftermath of the stock market crash, that "depression" is a term that economics has in common with psychology. This might lead us off in a different direction as we reflect on the implications of that coincidence. Or it might come to us in a flash that the wolf does not get fair treatment in "Little Red-Cap." The tale has to tell us explicitly that the wolf is "a wicked creature." We might wonder why it is necessary to level this moral judgment. This discovery, again, might lead us in a new direction. So the writing enterprise is not simply laying out what we have already discovered, but the explanation that writing embodies can itself be grounds for fresh understandings or new discoveries.

So the topic we select becomes the subject for preunderstanding as we invent ways of developing it. Those ways of organizing the parts of the topic move us on to its detailed explanation in our actual writing. The versions we produce help us to discover further insights about the topic which we can incorporate into our revisions. When we have come to a stopping point, when we have explained the topic to our own satisfaction, we can look at the text which we have created as a whole.

Topic to Thesis

We will also have discovered in what we *say* about the topic what the topic *means* in our text. One way of focusing the meaning of the topic is to articulate it in a thesis. The topic is our subject in both senses: 1. it is the subject matter we are writing about and 2. it is the subject of the sentence which constitutes our thesis. So we might summarize the meaning of our explanation of "the stock market crash as a cause of the Depression" in a sentence such as: "The stock market crash contributed to the Depression by creating self-doubt, anger and fear in the American psyche." This thesis sentence enunciates in summary form the understanding that our paper on a cause of the Depression explains. In the case of our writing on "Little Red-Cap," the topic was "deceptive appearances." The thesis sentence which encapsulates our understanding about the topic might read: "The deceptive appearances in 'Little Red Cap' illustrate a naif's inability to cope with unfamiliar situations." The thesis puts a predicate to the noun or noun-phrase that is the topic and so sums up the insight of the text as a whole.

Reading, Writing and Thinking

At the beginning of this chapter, we said that good readers are good writers. The reason for this is that both reading and writing require good thinking. The process of thinking that engages us in both the reading and the writing enterprise is the cycle of preunderstanding, explanation, and understanding. We interpret a text by taking what we know about it and then explaining what the text says so that we can come to further understanding of what the text means. When we set up to create a text of our own, we chose a topic that encapsulates our subject for preunderstanding. Then we proceed to discover or invent ways of organizing our explanation of that topic which we can finally articulate in a thesis. This thesis encapsulates our understanding about the topic. Whether we are interpreting a text or creating one, we are drawing on the same arsenal of intellectual capabilities: preunderstanding, explanation, understanding.

Practice, Practice, Practice

Like learning the piano or playing short-stop, becoming a good reader and a good writer requires practice. We will be exercising our abilities by reading texts and writing about them. We will be learning specific methodologies that will help us both explain the texts we read and the topics we wish to explore. In the next chapter we will describe methodologies for examining written texts and for inventing ways of organizing our writing. Practice in applying these methodologies will sharpen those mental capabilities which we wish to bring to bear on the reading and writing enterprises. Reading and rereading, writing and rewriting are keys to developing this potential.

Chapter 2
Methodologies

In the head of the book it is written: understanding may come out of the blue, but explanation can be worked at consciously and systematically. If we can pursue explanation systematically, there are, then, systems or methods for arriving at consistent explanations of inscribed texts. What do we mean by "method" and what specifically are these methods for explanation?

The word "method" comes from two Greek words, *meta* and *hodos*. *Meta* means "according to" and *hodos* means "road." So a method is like a road; it provides us a way of getting to our destination; if we follow the right road, we get to the goal of our journey. Our objective is interpretation and there are methods, roads, that lead us to our goal. To avoid paralysis and to escape confusion, we need the organizational and directional help of good methodology.

As we were discussing the directions to the Medical Center, the Bull Market and Little Red-Cap, we put certain questions to the text. In asking these questions we drew, without specifying them, on certain methods. As we discussed writing, we invented ways of organizing explanations of the topic. Again, without naming them, we used the same methods. These methods show us ways of asking significant questions of the text or the topic and of organizing the answers to those questions. We begin our discussion of method by looking at two different methodological types.

Algorithms and Heuristics

The first type of method is called "algorithmic." If applied properly, it guarantees an adequately correct answer to a problem. We find algorithmic methods to be the common types in mathematics and science. If you are asked to multiply 345 by 273, and you understand the process of multiplication and you follow the procedure step by step, you will inevitably get the right answer. A pocket calculator can follow the rules for multiplication built into its transistors and so produce the proper product. If we follow the proper method for combining hydrogen and sulfur and oxygen, we inevitably get sulfuric acid. We tend to be very comfortable with algorithmic methods; they assure us of reaching a reasonably correct answer to a given problem.

Another type of method, the one with which we are concerned, does not ensure this kind of outcome. This type of method is called "heuristic." Again, the word comes from the Greek *heurisko* which means "to search out." (*Eureka* comes from *heurisko* and means "I have found it.") In approaching the interpretation or creation of texts, the procedures we use are heuristic; they provide ways of explaining the words, sentences, paragraphs of the text. Because words are not numbers or measurable quantities, because sentences and paragraphs can be explained in different ways, different people using the same heuristic procedures may come to different explanations and understandings. Sometimes, though we struggle with the explanation of a given text, we may come to no understanding at all. But if we are stuck and the text we are reading or the topic we are examining makes no sense to us, applying heuristic methods is a way to begin. Heuristic procedures lead us down the path of explanation in search of understanding.

We divided method into two types—algorithmic and heuristic; heuristic procedures themselves may be divided into two classes. The first class is general heuristics, that is, heuristic procedures that can be applied to any sort of text on any subject matter in any mode of expression. They can be used to analyze a history book, a scientific article, a work on philosophy, a novel and, if you like, an editorial in the college newspaper. We will study two methods of general heuristics: topoi and tagmemics.

The other class of heuristics is specific to a given subject matter or mode of expression. When we come to deal with argumentation, we will learn a method for analyzing arguments devised by a logician named Stephen Toulmin. This method applies to the analysis of texts insofar as they argue a case or an issue.

If we can use these methods in reading inscribed texts, and since we claim that good readers are good writers, we can also use these methods to organize our own writing. When we have a topic we want to explain and have trouble in setting out a coherent explanation of it, the topoi and tagmemics can help us organize our material. If we are attempting to argue a case, the Toulmin model can suggest ways of doing it effectively. So in mastering these methods, we are mastering a two-edged sword; it works both in our reading and our writing.

General Heuristic Method: The Topoi

If a heuristic method is a roadmap for the discovery of ideas in a text, the topoi are places along the road. *Topos,* from the Greek, literally means "place." The topoi are signposts or markers which the reader or writer may use in analyzing or developing a text. You are already familiar with some of the topoi. For instance, you have probably been asked to write an essay using comparison and contrast. These are places, two of the topoi. The key thing to remember is that topoi can be used as a system of explanation.

The common topoi, which we will use in reading and writing, are the following:

    I. Definition and Division

    II. Comparison
        a. Similarity
        b. Difference
        c. Degree

    III. Relation
        a. Contradictories
        b. Contraries
        c. Cause and Effect
        d. Antecedent and Consequence

These topoi require some explanation.

Definition

Oddly enough, beginning to deal with the notion of definition requires us to define it. The literal sense of the word "definition" (from the Latin *finis*, "end or boundary") is "to set limits." To define a word is to set it apart from other words, according to its sense. To define a thing, in words, is "to set it apart from other things by reason of its nature, its distinctive quality or features, and its functions."

The dictionary provides us with definitions of words and, as we noted above, often a number of different definitions for the same word. If we consult Webster's Dictionary about the word "definition" we find the following:

1: an act of determining or settling: as **a:** Roman catholicism: an official ecclesiastical statement concerning a matter of faith or morals as pertaining to faith; **b:** a proscribed or official standard for a commercial product; **c:** the fixing or determination of social character; **2:** a word or phrase expressing the essential nature of a person or thing or class of persons or of things: an answer to the question "What is x?" or "What is an x?"; **3a:** a statement of a meaning of a word or word group; **b:** the action or process of stating the meaning of a word or word group; **4a:** a determination of the real nature of the species by indicating both the genus that includes it and the specific differences or distinguishing marks; **b1:** an equation between a single symbol and combination of symbols for which it is an abbreviation; **5a:** the action or power of making definite or clear or bringing into sharp relief; **b:** distinctness of outlines or detail: clarity, especially of musical sound in reproduction; **c:** a sharp demarcation of outlines or limits.

All these definitions of "definition" depend very much on context, on the way the word is used in a given text. If we do not understand the kind of text we are reading, we will have difficulty lighting on the correct meaning of the word. So the dictionary does not give us *the* meaning of a word; rather, it gives us a number of *possible* meanings. The specific meaning is determined by the use of the word in the text.

Some examples: the word "hot," as we remarked above, changes meaning when it is applied to 1) a stove, 2) a diamond, 3) a topic, 4) a pilot. The expression "bull market" means something different when applied to the stock market or to the stockyards. (We have a similar problem with the word "stock.") If we were asked to define "wolf" in "Little Red-Cap" we should probably not begin by describing a ferocious quadruped in the class *Canis*. More likely, we would begin by describing a fictional character who was a wicked and dissembling creature.

Definition asks the question: "What does this word mean *in this text?*" It forces us to consider what precisely we are talking about. For example: what we know from reading the text is that the Big Bull Market may be defined as a period of economic prosperity. It was the climax of a business cycle which had included overproduction of capital, overambitious expansion, overproduction, artificial price levels, and depressed European trade. Also, the text defines this period as the climax of a cycle in American mass thinking and mass emotion. Ordinary people seemed to be enjoying prosperity as they lived with showy affluence and blindly optimistic attitudes.

Division

The topos *division* is a sub-category of definition. This topos divides a word or idea or thing into its parts so that we can consider what makes it up. We saw, for instance, that the word "method" comes from two Greek words meaning "according to" and "road." We also saw that "method" has the general meaning of "an organizing procedure or set of procedures"; we learned that we can divide that general meaning into two specific senses: 1) algorithmic and 2) heuristic. In "The Big Bull Market" the market has two parts or aspects: 1) an economic condition and 2) a state of mind. In the directions to the Medical Complex there are three parts mentioned: 1) the guard booth, 2) the parking garage and 3) an eleven-story building. In the setting of "Little Red-Cap" there are two distinct parts: 1) the wood and 2) the village. Division, whether of a word, an idea or a text, lays out parts for our inspection.

Definition describes the limits of what we are reading or writing about. It asks the question of the text: What is the sense of this word in the text? What is the content of this idea? What is the nature or function of this thing? The questions which the topos of division poses are: What are the specific senses of this general term?" What are the parts or aspects of this idea? How are the parts of this thing organized? In putting such questions to the text or to our own ideas, we have ways of explaining what the text says or what we mean to say.

Comparison

The second major topos with which we are concerned is *comparison*. In comparison we use familiar things or actions to explain unfamiliar things or unfamiliar actions. "A multitude of ills beset the body economic, as poisons seep through the human system." This assessment uses comparison to make the point. Economic problems in the state are like infections in the body. We can find certain similarities in things that are quite different as well as differences in things that seem quite similar. Comparison is a topos that puts together the familiar and the unfamiliar and explains the one in terms of the other.

There are three kinds of comparison: comparisons of similarities, of differences, of degree. (You might note that we are using the topos of division to explain the idea of comparison.)

Similarity

A heuristic method is like a road. The practices of the big bull market were like poison. Each of these comparisons put two things side by side in order to explain one by the other. In each of these examples, it is important to explain how the second term is like the first. Method is like a road in that it provides an objective and direction towards it. The over-extension of resources in the big bull market acted like a poison on the economic system. Another comparison was drawn by Will Rogers when he said: "I tell you folks, all politics is applesauce." This comparison is a bit more directly stated, yet it is presented without qualification. We are left to imagine what possible similarities and differences may exist between politics and applesauce.

Difference

Comparison can also involve differences in that we can come to understand what a thing *is* by understanding what it *is not*. Little Red-Cap notes that there are certain differences in Grandma's appearance. Grandma has bigger eyes, ears and teeth than Little Red-Cap remembers. These differences add up to a realization, which occurs to Red-Cap too late, that perhaps the figure in bed is not Grandma at all. When we spoke about "method," we noted that there are real differences between an algorithmic method and a heuristic method. The algorithmic guarantees one reasonably correct answer; the heuristic method leads to a number of reasonable explanations that may be quite different, one from the other. Algorithms will work for a physics problem, but not for a poem or a folktale.

Degree

A comparison of degree deals with things that fall in the same general category. A temperature of minus 10 degrees Fahrenheit and a temperature of 100 degrees Fahrenheit are both temperatures. They differ in degree, but belong on the same thermometer. A dog, a fox, a wolf differ from each other in specific ways, but all belong to the same biological class. Note that the question of degree is related to the question of similarity and difference. Human beings and elephants are both animals and mammals, but they are different in that human beings have reflective self-consciousness and elephants do not. The difference of degree relates to the way in which each of these animals knows. In using comparison by degree, it is necessary to specify the class or categories you are using.

Relations

Comparisons obviously involve relations, but the relations we consider under this heading deal with statements in opposition and with consequence. A relation of opposition sees statements as irreconcilably adverse to each other, for instance, hot and cold, black and white, powerful and impotent, finite and infinite. These oppositions can be characterized as either contraries (hot/cold) or contradictories (powerful/impotent; finite/infinite).

Contradictories

The term "contradictory" means, literally, "to speak in opposition" so contradictories always deal with the relation between two statements or propositions. In the case of contradictory statements, the opposition between them is always absolute: if the first statement is true, then the contradictory statement must be false; if the first statement is false, then the second contradictory statement must be true. So "John is powerful" and "John is impotent (not powerful)" are contradictory statements; only one of them can be true. Our minds cannot entertain the possibility that John can be powerful and not powerful at the same time in the same way. Of course, John may be powerful on the football field and powerless in the classroom. But he cannot be powerful and powerless at the same time on the football field. So if the context of these two statements about John is the same, they absolutely exclude one another; only one of them can be true. So when we read the text of "The Big Bull Market" we know that the statements "the country is prosperous (Coolidge-Hoover prosperity)" and "the country is not prosperous (in the grip of a major depression)" are mutually exclusive; they are contradictories.

Contraries

Statements can be, however, in opposition to one another without being contradictory. For instance, the statements "John is black" and "John is white" are contraries. Both statements cannot be true, but both statements conceivably could be false; that is, John might be red or yellow. (Contrast these two statements with the statements "John is black" and John is not black"; these statements exclude any third possibility and so are contradictories.) In "Little Red Cap" we can formulate two statements about the wolf's identity: "the wolf is a wild beast" and "the wolf is a human being." Notice that these statements as they stand are contraries, not contradictories. There is a third possibility, namely, that the wolf is a theriamorph, a beast with human characteristics. *Logically* there is no contradiction between these two statements and so the *possibility* exists that a wolf can be a beast with human characteristics. The fact that we have never encountered such a beast does not deny the logical possibility of its existence. The fictional world of "Little Red Cap" takes advantage of this possibility.

The questions that this set of topoi put to the text are: is the topic addressed in terms of opposites? Is this opposition noted in statements that present us with contradictories or with contraries? Does the text make a point of excluding one part of this opposition as impossible (contradictory) or as improbable (contrary)?

Cause and Effect

The other set of relations under this heading have to do with consequences. One word or idea follows on another; this "following on" can indicate a relation of 1) cause and effect or 2) antecedent and consequent. For instance, father and son, night and day, fire and smoke, wind and storm. These pairs each indicate a sequence. The sequence can be causal or simply temporal.

Cause and effect postulates a necessary connection between the two members of the relation. That is to say, if the one member is present, the other member follows necessarily. If we refer to "father," it is necessary that this male has produced children. If there is a child, it is necessary that the child have parents. Where there is smoke, there is ordinarily fire. This statement requires qualifications (dry ice, under certain conditions, can give off smoke), but by and large, a fire produces smoke. There is a necessary connection between the fire and the production of smoke. In "The Big Bull Market" essay, there are a number of conditions cited relative to the stock market crash: overproduction of capital; overambitious expansion of business concerns; overproduction of commodities, among others. These conditions are presented as *causes* for the collapse of the bull market. In "Little Red-Cap" the woodsman and Red-Cap fill the wolf's body with great stones which are so heavy that he falls down dead. This is a cause-effect relationship. When we see or use a cause-and-effect relationship, we are insisting that, where we have the cause functioning as cause, it will *inevitably* produce its effect.

Antecedent and Consequent

The relationship of antecedent and consequent does not require the same kind of necessity. For instance, we assume, on good evidence, that night follows day and that when the night is over, day will return. On the other hand, we do not insist that day causes night or night day. Often, when a storm is approaching, the wind rises. And indeed high winds might well be a sign that it is about to storm. We would not, however, insist that the wind causes the storm. In "The Big Bull Market" a major depression follows Coolidge-Hoover Prosperity. The text does not provide evidence to prove a cause-effect relation. One simply follows the other. Deciding whether we are dealing with cause-and-effect or antecedent-consequent is often a difficult matter. Does the full moon cause the change in tides or does it simply accompany that change? And often the difference between these two kinds of relationships is not spelled out in the text. But these topoi help us to explain what sorts of relations the terms or ideas of a text imply.

The questions that the relation of consequence suggests we put to the text are these: Is there a necessary (causal) relation between two or more words or ideas? Is a term or an idea a sign that precedes another term or idea?

Topoi As a Method of Explanation

The topoi provide a systematic way of organizing the parts of a text. They help us to take the text apart and see how the various pieces of it relate to one another. When we have applied the topoi systematically, we have explained the text, laid out its features methodologically. The topoi do not, repeat: *do not* tell us what the text *means,* but they do help us describe what the text *says.* Questions that the topoi inspire provide us with a way of getting at the text. We lay out the parts so that we can arrive at some understanding of what the text means. But explanation and understanding are related as antecedent and consequent, not as cause and effect. No amount of topological investigation guarantees an insight about the meaning of the text. On the other hand, explanation is often a condition without which we can make no sense of either what the text says or what it means.

The following summary is a topical analysis of what we have said about "method" in the above pages. It illustrates how the topoi can be used to examine the parts of "method" and so lead, hopefully, to some understanding of what a method is and how it works.

Summary: A Topological Exploration of Method

I. **Definition:** method is a way of organizing parts to comprehend the whole.

II. **Division:** there are two types of methods: algorithmic and heuristic; there are two types of heuristic methods: general and specific.

III. **Comparison**
   A. *Similarity:* method is like organizing bricks into a wall; method is like a road that provides definition and direction.
   B. *Difference:* heuristic method is different from algorithmic method; heuristic method provides a *direction* for discovery; algorithmic method assures a precise answer.
   C. *Degree:* the difference between general and specific heuristics is one of degree.

IV. **Relationship**
   A. *Contradictories:* the statements "one can apply method" and "one cannot apply method" cannot both be true at the same time in the same way.
   B. *Contraries:* the statements "the meaning of the text is clear" and "the meaning of the text is ambiguous" can both be false (the text could be, for instance, incoherent).
   C. *Cause and Effect:* the application of method is the cause of the organization of data; the effect is the organized data.
   D. *Antecedent and Consequence:* coming to an explanation of a text through the application of method *may* lead to insight, but explanation is only a condition, not a cause, of insight.

25

Tagmemics

The topoi provide us with one heuristic method for analyzing and constructing texts. Another method which can be used for the same purposes is called tagmemics. This method provides another way of looking at objects, ideas, and events that make up the content of texts.

The term "tagmemics" is a made word. *Tagma,* in Greek, means "something that is organized" and comes to mean "an army." "Emic" is taken from the last syllable of "phonemic" and comes to mean "an inside view." Taken together these syllables add up to "tagmemics" and the word means "an insider's view of an organized whole."

In an African folktale a trickster god walked down the road between two villages. An observer on the right side of the road insisted that the god was wearing a black hat whereas an observer on the left side of the road insisted the god was wearing a white hat. It was not until a third observer saw the god from a hilltop that he realized the god was wearing a hat that was half black and half white. All three observers were right about the hat, but only the third observer could explain why the first two differed about the color of the hat. Viewing an object like the hat, or an idea, or an event, involves perspective, that is, a selective angle from which the observer views the matter.

The tagmemic method insists that we acknowledge different perspectives on the same reality. To take another example: what is a tear? A chemist will tell you that a tear is a compound made up of H_2O with a trace of $NaCl$ and some potassium ions. A psychologist will tell you that a tear is a physical manifestation of some psychic disturbance. A poet might describe the tear as a "pearl from the heart." We do not have to choose among these definitions. Each one, in its own way, is true and each one adds another perspective to our understanding of the object. Tagmemics provide us with a systematic way of varying our perspectives on any given subject.

Tagmemic Perspectives

Tagmemics presents three basic perspectives on the way we think about things.

First Perspective: The Condition of the Unit

We can look at any object, idea or event as if it were *static* and unchanging. We can also look at any object, idea or event as if it were *dynamic,* that is, changing. For instance, take the classroom eraser. We can look at the eraser as a single unit, as a given, as a thing in itself. "This is an eraser," and hold one up. We can also look at the eraser as a unit that changes. "Here is one that is losing part of its paper backing, that is beginning to show signs of wear on the right hand edge, the layers of felt are beginning to come apart." In this perspective, we see the eraser 1) as a unit which is given and 2) as a unit which is changing.

Second Perspective: Part and Whole

We consider the unit (object, idea or event) from the *perspectives of part and whole.* The unit can be viewed as a whole with its own parts; it can also be viewed as a part of a larger whole. For instance, I can consider the eraser as a system made up of parts: it is constructed of six pieces of felt in three inch strips, a cardboard backing, thread, glue and paper. We can disassemble the eraser and consider all the parts that make it up or we can view these parts as working together in removing chalk marks from the blackboard. We can see the change in the various parts which comes from use.

The unit is itself a system, a whole; it is also a part of a larger system. For instance, we can consider the eraser in its context: chalk, the blackboard, the classroom, the school system. In this view of the eraser, it is a working feature of a system of visual communication. Again, we can consider the eraser and the system in which we find it as either static or in process. The eraser belongs to this system when it is simply sitting in the chalk tray; it belongs to this system in process when it is being used to clean the board. We might also note that the eraser has other uses within this system. It can also be used as a projectile; an irate teacher loses his patience and throws the eraser at an offending student. This is another process view of the eraser within the classroom system. Your imagination can supply other instance of uses to which the eraser can be put within its context.

Third Perspective: Relationships with Other Units

The unit under consideration can be related to other units by comparison or contrast. We can take any perspective on the unit (static or dynamic, unit-as-system or unit-in-system) and compare it or contrast it to other units. The eraser as unit-in-system is like the overhead projector; it is part of a visual system of communication. We can compare it as a static unit to the eraser on the end of a pencil. We can compare it as a unit in process to the delete key on a computer. Such simple comparisons illustrate the nature and the use of the eraser in itself and in its own system.

Tagmemic Diagrams

Tagmemics as a system allows us to lay out these perspectives graphically to show how we can use the tagmemic categories of conceptualization systematically to analyze and construct texts. The figure below shows the directions or vectors of these perspectives.

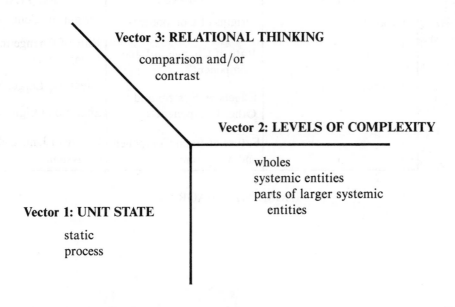

Vector 3: RELATIONAL THINKING

comparison and/or
contrast

Vector 2: LEVELS OF COMPLEXITY

wholes
systemic entities
parts of larger systemic
entities

Vector 1: UNIT STATE

static
process

If we put these directions together in a large scheme or matrix, they would look like this.

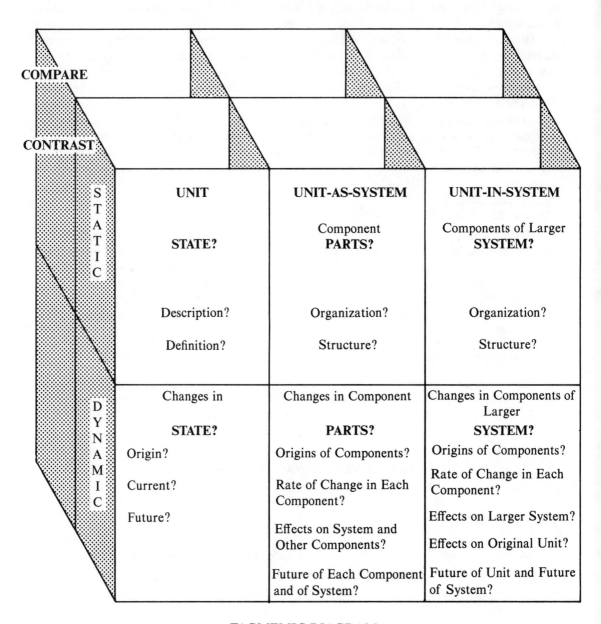

STATIC	UNIT	UNIT-AS-SYSTEM	UNIT-IN-SYSTEM
	STATE?	Component **PARTS?**	Components of Larger **SYSTEM?**
	Description?	Organization?	Organization?
	Definition?	Structure?	Structure?
DYNAMIC	Changes in **STATE?**	Changes in Component **PARTS?**	Changes in Components of Larger **SYSTEM?**
	Origin?	Origins of Components?	Origins of Components?
	Current?	Rate of Change in Each Component?	Rate of Change in Each Component?
	Future?	Effects on System and Other Components?	Effects on Larger System?
			Effects on Original Unit?
		Future of Each Component and of System?	Future of Unit and Future of System?

COMPARE

CONTRAST

TAGMEMIC DIAGRAM

This tagmemic cube shows the relationship among the three perspectives. It allows you to see at a glance different ways of looking at the unit. It proposes different questions which you can put to the unit in order to come to understandings about it. Like the topoi, tagmemics provides a way of analyzing and constructing texts. Unlike the topoi, it puts you, the observer, in the picture; that is, you choose to look at the unit *as* unit-as-system or unit-in-system.

Units and Systems

We said above that a unit for investigation can be an object, idea or event. When we used "eraser" as an example, we used a word that directly signified an object. You could, if you wished, take the analysis of "eraser" and write an essay on that topic. When we begin to examine a text, you select the unit you want to investigate. It is your preliminary understanding that provides a guide to the selection of the unit. So, for example, we might look at "The Big Bull Market" as a unit for investigation. To refresh your memory on this text, here it is again.

The Big Bull Market

The Big Bull Market was dead. Billions of dollars worth of profits—and paper profits—had disappeared. The grocer, the window-cleaner, and the seamstress had lost their capital. In every town there were families which had suddenly dropped from showy affluence into debt. Investors who had dreamed of retiring to live on their fortunes now found themselves back once more at the very beginning of the long road to riches. Day by day the newspapers printed the grim reports of suicides.

Coolidge-Hoover Prosperity was not yet dead, but it was dying. Under the impact of the shock of panic, a multitude of ills which hitherto had passed unnoticed or had been offset by stock-market optimism began to beset the body economic, as poisons seep through the human system when a vital organ has ceased to function normally. Although the liquidation of nearly three billion dollars of brokers' loans contracted credit, and the Reserve Banks lowered the rediscount rate, and the way in which the larger banks and corporations of the country had survived the emergency without a single failure of large proportions offered real encouragement, nevertheless the poisons were there: overproduction of capital; overambitious expansion of business concerns; overproduction of commodities under the stimulus of installment buying and buying with stock-market profits; the maintenance of an artificial price level for many commodities; the depressed condition of European trade. No matter how many soothsayers of high finance proclaimed that all was well, no matter how earnestly the President set to work to repair the damage with soft words and White House conferences, a major depression was inevitably under way.

Nor was that all. Prosperity is more than an economic condition; it is a state of mind. The Big Bull Market had been more than the climax of a business cycle; it had been the climax of a cycle in American mass thinking and mass emotion. There was hardly a man or woman in the country whose attitude toward life had not been affected by it in some degree and was not now affected by the sudden and brutal shattering of hope. With the Big Bull Market gone and prosperity going, Americans were soon to find themselves living in an altered world which called for new adjustments, new ideas, new habits of thought, and a new order of values. The psychological climate was changing; the ever-shifting currents of American life were turning into new channels.

The Post-war Decade had come to its close. An era had ended.

"The Big Bull Market" from *ONLY YESTERDAY* by Frederick Lewis Allen. Renewed 1959 by Agnes Rogers Allen. Reprinted by permission of Harper & Row, Publishers, Inc.

Unit: Big Bull Market

We select "bull market" as our unit to be analyzed. First we view it as static. The bull market is any economic situation in which investors buy stock in companies on the grounds that the stock will continue to gain in value. It represents an optimistic view of the economy.

Unit-in-Process

The post-war decade and its spirit of exansionism created the bull market and the over-production which resulted have led to the collapse of this situation. The bull market is dying and is never likely to revive.

Unit-as-System Static

The parts of the big bull market include: capital, big business concerns, commodities, stock market profits, maintenance of a high price level. These are the elements that comprise the bull market, that make for a buyer's market in the Stock Exchange.

Unit-as-System Process

All the elements in this system, at the end of the Hoover administration, were changing significantly so that over-production and over-ambitious expansion and an artificial price level were leading to the stock market crash. The bull market, as the system, required a real assessment of economic potential and the actual assessment was too optimistic.

Unit-in-System Static

The bull market was an economic condition in the larger picture of American life of the nineteen-twenties. It reflected American optimism after World War I, the possibility that everyone, the grocer, the window-cleaner, and the seamstress, could become rich along with the country. American leadership and American know-how made the sky the limit.

Unit-in-System Process

The stock market crash produced a substantial change in the American way of life. The prospects of prosperity and of "get rich quick" schemes collapsed along with the market. Investors who thought themselves on the road to riches found themselves back at the beginning and some opted out by suicide.

Under each of the six perspectives on "The Big Bull Market" we can locate comparisons. The market itself is compared to an organism in the opening sentence of the text: "The Big Bull Market was dead." The market as process is poisoned by overproduction and overbuying. Each part of the market contributes its own particular poison to the infection. If we consider the market as part of the system, American life is compared to a river with shifting currents turning into new channels. These comparisons relate the unit and perspectives on the unit to other realities like "body," "poison," "river."

Tagmemic Analysis

"The Big Bull Market"

	Unit	Unit-as-System	Unit-in-System

S T A T I C	Bull Market
	    Economic situation
	    Stock overbuying
	    Optimistic view
	    Paper profits
	    Big investors
		Bull Market Components
		    Capital
		    Big business concerns
		    Commodities
		    Stock market profits
		    Maintenance of high
		    prices
			American life in the 1920's
			American optimism
			American dream of wealth
			for all
			World Economy
			World Trade

P R O C E S S	Created by post-war expansionism and overproduction Prosperity is waning Bull Market is dying Market is likely never to recover	At end of Hoover's Administration all elements were changing Over-production and ambitious expansionism leading toward new thoughts about economy Assessment of change inevitable	Change in American life America's idealism fades World trade and economy changes Depression is on the horizon

In analyzing this text, we could draw on our preliminary understandings to identify other units for analysis. For instance, we might select the unit "prosperity" and follow that idea across the tagmemic categories. Choosing this unit would provide a different emphasis on our analysis of the text. As a static unit, for instance, prosperity is an economic condition and a state of mind. As it is in process, it depends on past history for its definition; to a nation without enough food to eat, a subsistence diet looks like prosperity. Considering prosperity as a system, the bull market is one of its parts. Viewed as a part of a larger system, prosperity is part of the nation's life which goes in cycles. The categories of the tagmemic matrix work for any unit and, in a given text, the unit you select—provided it is key—will shed light on what the text says.

So tagmemics provides us with another method for looking at a text or examining a topic. We can view the trickster's hat or the tear in our eye from a number of different points of view. The more perspectives we can get on a given object, idea or event, the more we know about it and about our relations to it.

Summary

Whenever we open a book or begin to write a paper, our purpose is understanding. We want to grasp the meaning of the text we are reading; we want to present effectively our ideas in writing so that our readers may understand them. No teacher, however brilliant, can guarantee that we will grasp the meaning of a text or generate a good idea for our paper. But these methods—the topoi, tagmemics—are ways of investigating texts and generating ideas that provide us with a way to start. We read a book and our reaction is "I have no idea what this book is about"; "I have a paper to write and I can only stare at the blank page before me." In these situations applying the methods we have described puts us on the way to understanding, to discovering what the text means and what we might want to say in our paper.

Understanding is not a one-time thing. We read a text like "Little Red-Cap" when we are ten years old and we get some meaning out of it. We read it again when we are twenty, and we come to different understandings of what it means. The text itself has not changed, but we have. As we acquire more experience and more knowledge, we are capable of greater and greater understanding. What we are able to grasp now depends on not only our natural ability, but also the fund of information we have gathered and all our previous understandings of it. We read a text and work at explaining it. Because of our explanation we come to new understandings of the text. We then can go back to the text with these new understandings and develop further explanations which lead us to discover still further meanings. This is the cycle of discovery that we experience as we move through our education.

The same cycle of development and discovery occurs when we write. In our first attempt at expressing our ideas on a given topic, we may not be able to express ourselves as clearly and as forcefully as we would like. By applying our methodologies, we can begin to see how our ideas can be better organized and better expressed. So through progressive drafts of the paper we not only clarify ideas for our readers, but we also clarify them for ourselves.

Francis Bacon remarks, "Knowledge maketh a bloody entrance." Any of us who have tried to struggle with new ideas, a challenging book, a difficult topic to explain, know what Bacon means. The application of our methods involves a struggle, an active engagement with a text, someone else's or our own. But the struggle is worth the price. Once we have mastered these methods, we can come to any text or topic, in school or on the job, confident that we will be able to make sense of it and to express ourselves effectively about it.

Chapter 3
The Reading Enterprise: Applying the Methodologies

We have discussed our aims: understanding; and the expression of understanding: we have examined our tools: the methodologies. Now we wish to examine how we apply these methodologies—the topoi, tagmemics—to reading texts.

Reading Levels

You come to college with a certain level of reading ability. You have been reading printed material from the first grade (and perhaps before). Everything we have said to this point in these notes assumes that you can read. If you have a driver's license, that means you could read well enough, for instance, to pass the written section of the Driver's Licensing Examination. You can, at the very least, retrieve basic information from printed matter and deal with ordinary (non-technical, non-obsolete) vocabulary with the aid of a dictionary. You can, then, at minimum, recognize and recall explicit statements in a printed text. You are also able to recognize and recall the order of details in a text and you are able to paraphrase the contents. This level of reading ability enables you to deal effectively with most of the situations you encounter in your everyday experience: shopping for groceries, reading instructions in a manual, filling out an application for a credit card, paying a traffic ticket. While this level of reading comprehension is a start, it will not sustain you very far in adult society, not to mention your college career.

When an instructor in a college class gives an assignment like, "For tomorrow, read Chapters Four and Five in the text," that directive may mean different things to each instructor who gives it and to each student who receives it. The least the instructor will expect is that you are able to bring some preliminary understanding to the text: that it is a history book, or a novel, or a biology text. The instructor will also assume that you can explain the words in the text, gather the information it presents and paraphrase its contents. In short, the instructor will expect you to know what the text says. In addition, the instructor may also want to know what the text is about, that is, what the text means. You may be asked to summarize the text, to state its main thesis, to explain its parts. When you are asked to summarize, to abstract the thesis, and to detail the parts, this assumes that you have some understanding of the text. Perhaps you have been used to a system in which, after reading a text, you waited for the instructor to tell you what it means. To get control of the reading enterprise, you need to be able to grasp the meaning of the text *on your own*. This is one objective we are pursuing: that you learn to learn from a text without depending on the instructor.

The texts that accompany *The Literate Mind* cover different disciplines—history, philosophy, science, literature—and come from different time periods. They are like the texts you will be asked to read in other phases of your college career. If you can master these texts, you will have little trouble with reading assignments as you go through your college programs.

Reading with a Perspective: Rhetorical Approaches to the Text

When we open a book, we enter a world, a universe of discourse. Just as the actual world of our experience can be viewed in different ways, so the world of the text can be viewed from different perspectives. We can, in the first instance, accept the actual world of our experience as given; we can accept and try to understand the structures and operations of its social, political and economic institutions. We can try to grasp the meaning of these institutions in our experience. We can also view this actual world with its institutions and strategies as problems to be addressed, as offering options. Finally, we can view the world and its institutions as organized by intelligence and imagination. In each of these cases the world we are considering is the same, the sum of our actual experiences. What changes is not the object of our regard, but the perspective with which we regard it.

The world of the text can be viewed from the same three perspectives. We can call these perspectives "rhetorical aims" because rhetoric organizes words into meaningful worlds or universes of discourse for these purposes. We can bring each of these perspectives to bear on any given text. As a text is organized in a definite and structured way, it is given; as it allows for different options, it is problematic; as it is the product of a creative intellect and imagination, it is self-expressive. We can, then, label these perspectives or rhetorical aims as 1) expository—viewing the world of the text as given; 2) argumentative—viewing the world of the text as problematic; 3) self-expressive—viewing the world of the text as artifact.

Exposition

The expository perspective or aim deals with the world of the text as given; it presents us with data and ideas that we choose to accept. For instance, when we consider an essay like "The Big Bull Market" as exposition, the text presents us a world in which there was a significant event called the Depression. It describes the causes for, and the effects of, that event. Banks failed, people jumped out of windows and the mood of America changed. So the text presents these events and our examination of them considers how they are explained and arranged. We engage the text on its own ground and in its own terms. The text "Directions to the Medical Center" assumes the world of Dallas and vicinity as a given. We also assume that, if we follow the directions, we will discover all the actual places the directions describe. From this expository perspective we view a text as presenting an organized view of a given world, its components and their interrelationships.

Argument

The argumentative perspective or aim views the world of the text as problematic. In this view the text makes a case for its assertions. We can argue with a text whenever we choose. This is to acknowledge that even the simplest issues raise problems on which we can take a position. We can, for instance, view "The Big Bull Market" as argumentative. The text claims that the Depression permanently changed the mood of Americans. We can examine the text to determine to what degree its details support this claim. What were givens in the text, then, become issues for discussion. Looked at as argument, this text assumes a different burden and offers the possibility of counter positions. Argument deals with the world as problematic, inviting discussion and debate.

Self-Expression

The self-expressive perspective or aim deals with the world of the text as artifact, a product of human intellect and imagination. Every piece of writing, even "Directions to the Medical Center," can be seen as self-expressive. Those directions select certain landmarks like the parking garage and describe the road as "curving." Another set of directions to the same place might select very different landmarks and use different descriptors. The point is that behind every text there is a "self," a mind and an imagination that is creating the text. When we use "self-expressive" in this context, as a rhetorical aim, the self is not the flesh-and-blood author, but rather the personal traces the organizing agent has left in the text. In some texts these traces are implicit and muted, but in others an "I" or "we" does appear in the text and testifies explicitly to the personalized world presented there. This perspective focuses on the self implicit or explicit in any text. It acknowledges that the text not only reflects, but also creates, a world.

We can, then, summarize these rhetorical aims this way: exposition deals with the world of the text as given, argumentation deals with the world of the text as problematic, self-expression deals with the world of the text as artifact. We may find that, for any given text, we are more comfortable using one of these rhetorical aims rather than another and that, in fact, a given text may seem to invite such a perspective. A driver's manual, for instance, encourages us to view it as exposition, whereas we might be drawn to consider the *Communist Manifesto* as argumentative or self-expressive. In any event we can approach any given text from each of these three perspectives. In this section of *The Literate Mind* we will treat texts as expository.

Approaching the Text

We are now equipped with some general preunderstandings relative to the reading enterprise. We have two sets of general heuristic methodologies for explanation: the topoi and tagmemics and three different perspectives or rhetorical aims that determine how we will view the text: as expository, as argumentative, as self-expressive. Now we are prepared to address a specific text in a specific reading situation. There are particular features of any given reading situation that we must now consider.

The Rhetorical Situation

The "rhetorical situation" defines a set of circumstances which occurs whenever we approach a specific text to be read or to be written. The features of the rhetorical situation are these: 1) exigence; 2) audience; 3) constraints; 4) self.

Exigence

We will not intentionally open a book to read it without some need to do so. This need can be an impulse from within or a responsibility imposed from without. We are, for example, looking for a way to kill time and our eye lights on a science fiction novel on our shelf. We pick up the book and begin to read. We are looking for some information on how to repair a carburetor and, while looking around the automotive parts store, a manual called *How to Repair Your Own Car* catches our eye. We pick it up and begin to read. On the first day of class the instructor says, "For next class read 'The Killers.'" At home, with a fine sense of doing our duty, we open the text and begin to read Hemingway's short story. We read the science fiction novel for enjoyment, we read the manual for information, we read the short story because it has been assigned. The exigency provides the motivation and determines the purpose for our reading.

Audience

Any text we set about to read is directed to some audience. The science fiction novel envisions entertaining a general audience. We may, on examining the book in the automotive store, discover that it is full of formulae and technical terminology and decide that this book is not intended for the general reader. We need a much simpler presentation of the subject matter to satisfy our need. On our first reading of Hemingway's short story, "The Killers," we may be puzzled and confused about certain aspects of the story and wonder, indeed, if this story is intended for a general audience. Deciding the level and kind of audience to which the text is directed generally involves deciding what kind of a text it is, whether it is history or philosophy or science or literature. When we come to that kind of decision about the text, we take a step toward placing ourselves in the audience the text envisions. In the classroom, for instance, we are ideally part of a critical audience bent on discovering the meaning of an assigned text through inspection, explanation and discussion.

Constraints

Every rhetorical situation imposes certain limitations on the reader or writer. The obvious constraints are limitations of time, energy, and knowledge in relation to the subject matter. If you are faced with a four hundred-page novel and four hours in which to read it, unless you are an exceptionally rapid reader, you can only get the sketchiest notion of its content. If you attempt to read the novel in a twelve-hour sitting, the odds are good that your energy will flag after a given period. If you set about reading a technical text, and your knowledge of technical terminology is exceedingly limited, the understandings you can expect to garner from that reading will be minimal. Other constraints focus your attention on aspects of the text; if you read the text as expository in order to gather information, your view of the text will be limited to this aspect. In order to deal effectively with these kinds of constraints, you have to make decisions at the outset about your objectives in the light of the given constraints within which you must work.

Self

You yourself are also a part of the rhetorical situation in that you bring a specific background, previous reading experience, formed ideas and attitudes to any given reading enterprise. If you have had, for instance, unpleasant experience with reading poetry, you might find that you approach any text which you identify as poetic with negative feelings. This will color your reading of the text and, most probably, your judgment about it. If you find history interesting, on the other hand, recognizing a piece as historical might put you in an enthusiastic frame of mind about tackling it. If your penchant is for the practical, you might find a work of philosophy dull and impenetrable. To do justice to a text, it is important that you recognize your own predispositions toward it and give the text a chance on its own terms.

Whenever we open a text, we encounter a rhetorical situation. Assessing these four elements—exigency, audience, constraints and self—establishes bases on which we can proceed with our reading.

Strategies for the Analysis of Texts

We begin our actual investigation of a text with a first reading which we may call "inspectional."

Inspectional Reading

An inspectional reading of the text, as the word implies, is an overview intended to help us come to a set of preliminary understandings about the text. The inspectional reading brings to bear our previous experience with texts and our understanding of audience. These two elements of the rhetorical situation will help us classify the work on a tentative basis. Classifications that will help us explain and understand the text: 1) a classification of the work as fiction or nonfiction—as a treatise or a short story or a poem or an essay; 2) classification according to discipline—historical or scientific or philosophical; 3) classification according to theoretical or practical emphasis—a cultural analysis or a computer manual. Such classifications overlap one another; they are also tentative and subject to revision as we read.

The inspectional reading may also help to locate the texts in time and space. If it contains words that are currently obsolete or which, on contextual grounds, have meanings which are different from contemporary usage, then the text can be located in the past. To illustrate from some texts which we are reading in the course, the excerpt from Gibbon's *The Decline and Fall of the Roman Empire*, "The Imperial Legion," is clearly not a twentieth-century account of this military organization. The sections on "Idols" from Bacon's *Novum Organum* contains terms and employs diction quite different from contemporary usage. Plato's *Apology*, by virtue of its content and the issue it treats, speaks of another culture and a set of institutions different from our own. You may not be able, simply from the text, to date Gibbon or Bacon accurately, but you ought to be aware that the text specifies a place remote in time and space and involves a cultural context that is not our own.

The title of a text often supplies major clues about the topic addressed in it and also indications about the disciplinary perspective and approach. Gibbon's work, for instance, from which "The Imperial Legion" is taken, is entitled *The Decline and Fall of the Roman Empire*. It does not take a lot of reading experience to recognize that this is a work about the past, that it is probably historical, that it deals with events relative to, and delineates causes of, the decline of the Roman Empire. Investigating the sense of the title, and, if we are dealing with a longer text, the Table of Contents will contribute to our preliminary understandings about the topic the work develops and the main issue it joins.

37

From an inspectional reading, then, we get a *general* set of preliminary understandings about the text. These understandings provide us with guidelines for approaching a closer reading and provide us with a basis for explaining the parts of the text and their relationships with one another.

An inspectional reading of "The Imperial Legion" might, for example, yield the following preliminary understandings. 1) The text provides a description of a Roman fighting force during the time of the Emperors. 2) The title indicates that this excerpt is about the Legion and that it deals with the makeup of this unit of the Roman Army. Though we could not be sure without a larger context, it is probable that 3) this text is nonfiction, 4) that it deals with history and 5) that it was not written in our century.

Note that none of these general statements about the text are found explicitly in the text. They are all inferences which we draw from looking at the title and quickly surveying the text. None of them tells us what the text is saying about the Roman Legion; none of them tells us, in any specific ways, about the meaning of the text. They do, however, provide us with general understandings we need to begin explaining the text.

Explanation

Our explanation of the text is really the way we proceed to answer those questions which were raised by our general preliminary understandings. What, for instance, does the text have to say about "The Imperial Legion"? What is the Imperial Legion and how is it made up? If it is part of the Roman Army, how central is it to that organization? These questions and others are presumably answered in the text. Our explanation of the text will answer them for us.

Our explanation will also test the validity of our preliminary general understandings. We might assume, quite properly, that a text beginning "Once upon a time" is a folktale like "Little Red-Cap." If we were to open a book entitled *A Portrait of the Artist as a Young Man,* we would discover that it begins "Once upon a time," and that it is not, indeed, a folktale. Further inspection of *A Portrait of the Artist as a Young Man* corrects our first impression. So our explanation leads us further into the text and provides a groundwork for *specific* understandings about it.

We noted in Chapter One that we can explain texts methodologically. In Chapter Two we discussed some general methodologies: the topoi and tagmemics. If we need help in analyzing the text, in discovering what the text says, this is the time to employ these methods. Here are examples of the application of these methods to the text we have been discussing, "The Imperial Legion."

Analysis of "The Imperial Legion" by Topoi

Definitions (implied):

Legion: principal organizational unit of Roman fighting army

Heavy infantry: principal strength of the Legion

Buckler: oblong, concave figure, 4 by 2½ feet, framed in light wood, covered with bull's hide, guarded by plates of brass

Pilum: heavy javelin, 6 feet long, triangular steel point

Sword: short, double-edged blade, suitable for striking or pushing

Division: Constitution of the legion
 Infantry: divided into ten cohorts
 First cohort: 1105 soldiers, elite fighters given custody of the eagle
 Nine other cohorts: 555 soldiers
 Total infantry unit: 6100 men

 Equipment:
 Defensive: helmet, breast-plate or chain-mail, graves, buckler
 Offensive: pilum, short sword

 Order of Battle:
 Ranks eight deep, three feet separating files as well as ranks

 Cavalry: Divided into ten troops
 First troop: 132 men
 Nine other troops: 66 men each
 Total cavalry unit: 726 men

 Equipment:
 Defensive: helmet, oblong shield, light boots, coat of mail
 Offensive: javelin, long broad sword

 Order of Battle:
 Coordinated with infantry, occasionally separated to form wings of army

Comparison/Contrast:
 Pilum with modern fire-arms (musketry): Pilum exhausted by single discharge at ten or twelve paces; extremely effective at that range against cavalry or infantry.

 Formation of legion with Greek/Macedonian phalanx: open, mobile formation of the legion superior to the sixteen ranks of long pikes, closely wedged, that formed the phalanx.

 Cavalry of Empire with cavalry of earlier Republic: cavalry of Republic formed of nobility, the "equestrian" order; no longer the case, rather formed from recruits from the provinces.

Relationships (antecedent/consequent; cause/effect):
 First cohort: formed of soldiers approved for valor and fidelity, so entrusted with post of honor and custody of the "eagle."

 Use of weapons: legionnaire launched his pilum, then drew his sword and closed with the enemy.

 Use of tactics: open-order formation with long front, so prepared to execute rapid manoeuver.

 Change of composition of cavalry: equestrian order occupied with administration of justice and taxes, so no longer engaged in actual combat.

Analysis by Tagmemics

UNIT: The Imperial Legion		Unit-as-System		Unit-in-System
S **The Roman** **T** **Fighting** **A** **Force** **T** **I** **C**		I. Heavy Armed Infantry "Principal Strength" Composed of 10 cohorts First Cohort Post of Honor Custody of Eagle 1105 Soldiers Other Nine Cohorts 555 Men Arms Uniform to All: Open Helmet Breast Plate Greaves Ample Buckler Lighter Spear Pilum Spanish Blade	II. Cavalry Composed of 10 squadrons/troops First Squadron Companion to First Cohort 132 Men Other Nine Squadrons 62 Men Arms Uniform to All: Helmet Oblong Shield Javelin Long Broad Sword Light Boots	I. Contrast to Greek and Macedonian 16 ranks of long pike wedged in close array II. Contrast between Imperial Cavalry and ancient Republic: No longer noblest youths Cavalry no longer preparation for offices of Senator or Consul
		Comparison of Pilum to Modern "Firearms": One Discharge at 10–12 feet; impact on cavalry due its "impetuosity of its weight."	Contrast: Roman despised the fuller armor which encumbered the cavalry of the East. Their weapons were more useful.	
D **Y** **N** **A** **M** **I** **C**		Process of Battle: Dart Pilum Draw Sword Rush and close with enemy Sword could strike or push Soldiers taught to push Organized into ranks eight deep with three feet between files and ranks resulted in flexible disposition, free space for use of arms and movement, and space for reinforcement to enter	Process of Battle: Usually connected with Legion; sometimes separated to act in line or as wings of army.	I. Greeks and Macedonian Phalanx Unable to contend with activity of the Legion II. Since Empire, the wealthy of the equestrian order administered justice or commanded a troop or cohort Bulk of cavalry manned from the provinces by the same class as the Legion Horses bred in Spain or Cappadocia

This analysis, using the topoi, lays out in specific detail the parts of the text. It tells us what the text says about the Roman Legion by putting the parts of the text in different topical categories. It shows how the parts of the text are organized into a single presentation.

Analysis of "The Imperial Legion" by Tagmemics

In applying the tagmemic method we will be dealing with the same text using a different approach. As you remember, the tagmemic approach allows us to view the text from a number of perspectives. The principal perspective that tagmemics shows us with regard to the Legion is as unit-as-system, with infantry and cavalry as parts within the system. It contrasts the Legion with other similar units like the Greek or Macedonian armies, and points out the differences between the Roman army of the ancient Republic and the Roman army of the Emperors.

Understandings

The analyses above provide us with ways of explaining the text. When we work through an analysis using these methods, we see the text in different lights. In fact, while we are doing this kind of analysis, ideas about the text have probably been popping into our heads. These ideas will ordinarily go beyond what the text says. In short, as we explain the text to ourselves, we are coming to insights about what the text means. It might be clear, for instance, that, the text presents the Imperial Legion as a well-organized and well-equipped fighting unit, superior to other forces in the field at the time. The analysis shows that the legion's organization, striking power and mobility make it the finest fighting force of its day. Nowhere in the text is this claim made, yet we get the clear impression that the text makes this claim.

Circling back to our explanations of the text, we can find a number of grounds for this claim. This is the way that explanations lead to understanding and provide evidence or grounds for supporting our interpretation. We might also note that, though the Legion is presented as a fine fighting force, there are indications in the text that it might not remain so. In the section on cavalry it is pointed out that the legionnaires are no longer drawn from the equestrian class of Roman citizens. The horses come from Spain or Cappodocia, two outlying provinces of the Empire, and it may be that the soldiers are drawn from those same regions. So planted in the last paragraph of the text is the notion that the personnel of the Legion might not reflect the ancient ideals that made it a superior fighting force. The understanding we have that the text proclaims the Legion first-class is qualified by the understanding that it might not remain so. You might have discovered other ideas or understandings about the text through your own analysis that can be tested in the same way, by further examination of the text.

Summary

The sum of our understandings and explanations amounts to an interpretation of the text. The reading enterprise is the process by which we arrive at this interpretation. We begin by assessing the rhetorical situation: why are we reading this text? how are we going to approach the text, that is, as expository or argumentative or self-expressive? We examine the title and the table of contents (if any) to gain some clues about the audience for which the work is intended. We then proceed to examine the constraints under which we have to work: the time limits we have for examining the text, the difficulties presented by the language, and the limitations imposed by our own past experience and knowledge. We consider our own biases, the predispositions with which we approach this particular text.

In our inspectional reading, we are concerned about classifying the work generally as fiction or non-fiction, as history or philosophy or science or literature, as theoretical or practical. The conclusions we come to by virtue of this preliminary investigation raise questions which we may want to settle by applying methodologies in order to explain to ourselves what the text says. We apply our general heuristic methodologies to the text—the topoi or tagmemics—in order to analyze the parts of the text and their relationships to one another. These explanations help provide answers to some of the questions we have raised in our preliminary understandings.

We then reflect on the analyses we have done, on the explanations these analyses embody. Through this process we come to understandings specific to the text, insights about the meaning of the text. If these insights are broad enough to comprehend the whole text, that is, if we are satisfied that we have grasped its meaning, then we have arrived at an interpretation of the text. The test of this interpretation is whether we can explain it successfully to ourselves and others.

The culmination of this process is an expansion of our knowledge and understanding about the text we have engaged. If we understand the process as well as the text, we have not only learned what the text means, we have also learned how to learn from a text.

Chapter 4
The Writing Enterprise:
Applying the Methodologies

Composition

A friend once asked a celebrated author how his latest novel was coming. The novelist replied, "It's all finished." The friend said, "Oh then, when can I expect to read it?" The novelist replied, "That will be a while. Now I have to write it down."

The novelist in this case has "composed" his text in his head. By thinking over his material, he has found ways of organizing it so that he knows what he wants to say. When we read a text in order to interpret it, we do much the same thing. We "compose" (that is, put together in an organized way) our explanations and understandings of the text. Like the novelist's organization of his story, this "composition" can be all in our heads. If we are extraordinarily skilled or extraordinarily lucky, then all we have to do is write it down. Expressing ourselves in writing, explaining our ideas to an audience, is ordinarily not quite as simple as that.

The point of the novelist's remark is this: any writing enterprise begins *before* we set words to paper. It begins when we discover what we want to write about, with a topic that we have found in a set of data—from our experience of reading a text or from a personal experience or from a set of statistics or from a conversation with friends. The topic we have chosen from any or all of these sources becomes the subject we wish to develop. It is the writer's job to explain the topic so that it can be grasped by a particular audience. In any writing enterprise we find ourselves in the same heuristic circle of preunderstanding, explanation and understanding that we discovered in reading; we bring preunderstandings on a topic from our experience and set out to explain it; from our attempts at explanation we discover new insights about the topic. The same methodologies that we used in reading texts can be used to explore topics in writing.

We have pointed out that the writing enterprise and the reading enterprise have features in common; it is also important to note how they are different. The data for the reading enterprise is the text itself. The data for the writing enterprise is chosen out of our experience with the data; before we begin to write, our options are theoretically infinite. If we received only one instruction and that instruction was to write, what would we do? What would we write about? Whom would we be writing to? What purpose would we want our writing to achieve? We can choose to write about anything to anyone for any purpose. But in fact, writing almost never happens this way. We write because the teacher has given us an assignment, or an employer has asked us for a report. Or we have to write a letter of complaint to our landlord, or a letter to our parents asking for money. In all these instances topic, data and style are all narrowed considerably by the situation.

The Rhetorical Situation

When writing is called for, we again have to deal with words, sentences, paragraphs, the ordering and arrangement of words and ideas in order to come to understanding. We are, in short, again faced with what we described above as "the rhetorical situation." Here we are not attempting to discover the meaning in a text, rather we wish to discover our own ideas about a topic and present them to a reader. Nonetheless, the features of the rhetorical situation are the same: 1) exigence; 2) audience; 3) constraints; 4) self.

Exigence

The rhetorical situation is generated by a need to write. This need or exigency can be internal or external. We may feel an impulse, a need, to write in our journal, to produce a short story, to write home. The exigency is external if we are given an assignment in class, asked to do a report by our boss, obliged to write a letter of complaint to our landlord. This need to write also includes a purpose. We write in our journals to have a record of our experiences, a short story to exercise our creative talent, a letter home to dispel our feelings of homesickness. We do our assignment for class in order to display our understanding of the material to the teacher; we write the report for the boss to enlighten her about the situation in our department; we write the letter of complaint to our landlord in order to get the plumbing fixed. Every rhetorical situation begins with some sort of exigency that specifies a purpose for our writing.

Audience

We are not only writing about something; we are writing to somebody. If, while fixing a car, our little sister asked us to explain what we were doing, we would reply on a very different level than we might if a friend of ours asked the same question. "Fixing my car" might be a completely adequate explanation to the four-year-old; we might wish to go into much greater detail with our friend.

The general audience we will be addressing while in college is the academic community. The representative of that community, for all practical purposes, is the course instructor. When the instructor directs, "Write a paper on the Peloponnesian War," he or she will expect us to be aware of the audience. The instructor will expect us to pick some aspect of the war, present an insight about it along with an explanation of our insight. He or she will expect an ordered presentation with a beginning, middle and end. Part of the expectation of this audience will also be that the paper is written in Standard English without errors in spelling or punctuation. If we are able to satisfy these expectations of the instructor, we will have no problem at all with written assignments.

Constraints

Any rhetorical situation imposes certain limitations on the writer. Sometimes the constraints are imposed because of the nature of the audience; an explanation to our little sister about the inner workings of the internal combustion engine would probably fail to interest her. A paper for a classroom assignment that simply summarized a chapter of the textbook would probably fail to hold the interest of the instructor. Writers themselves suffer certain limitations in terms of time, energy and knowledge in relation to the subject matter. To attempt a paper covering the entire scope of the Peloponnesian War would require considerably more time and energy than the ordinary college student could muster in a semester. Limiting a topic and the discussion of it to a reasonable length is a constraint that students must learn to manage. A severe constraint in the classroom situation is the time-graded essay examination; five short essays in fifty minutes requires careful budgeting of time. Learning to cope with this kind of constraint, the deadline, is essential to success in academe as well as in the business world.

Self

In any rhetorical situation, the self of the writer is obviously involved. Whatever we write reveals at the very least what we have chosen to say and the order in which we have chosen to say it. Whether the essay is deeply centered in a particular individual experience that affected us emotionally and personally or whether we are writing about inscribed texts we have read or about nuclear power or fiscal responsibility or budget deficits, whatever we write always says something about ourselves. Even if the word "I" never appears in the writing, the implicit message is that "I think that this is an important subject, I think I have something worthwhile to say about it, I think I am competent to say something about it, and I think you ought to read it."

Even when what we are writing is a "class exercise," the writing is a reflection of our thought, experience and personality. As such, it also conveys, at least implicitly, the writer's estimation of the reader. If the paper is full of broad generalizations, tired cliches, grammatical and syntactical errors, it indicates that we are either unimaginative and thoughtless or that our reader is not worthy of our best efforts. Neither impression is one we wish to go out of our way to create.

The writing enterprise, then, always occurs in a rhetorical situation. The exploration of the topic and the discovery of insights and understandings and their explanation in writing involves the application of methodologies to the topic we wish to present. Exigence, audience, constraints and our own personal bent sharpen and specify the way in which we develop any given topic. When we pay attention to these elements, we also develop better control of both the subject matter and our own explanation of it.

Rhetorical Aims

One way of sharpening our focus and gaining better control of the writing enterprise is to attend to the specific purpose of a writing assignment and to adapt the mode or way of writing to that purpose. You remember that we described three perspectives for analyzing a text: expository, argumentative, and self-expressive. We said then that every text could be approached in these three ways. We can divide ways of writing according to purpose into these same three categories. Just as any text includes to some degree all three, so any piece of writing may also contain all three. But in approaching a writing assignment, we can focus on one aim or the other, depending on our explicit purpose.

Expository Writing

Expository writing is principally enlightenment. Its purpose is primarily to inform, to share information and ideas with the reader. In exposition, we are not particularly concerned with changing the reader's mind or dealing with matters of controversy. The assumption we make is that our audience is open-minded on the topic and that we are simply to enlighten its members about that topic. The effective piece of expository writing explains clearly and coherently the topic to be treated. It deals with the world as given or taken "as is" and demonstrates how the elements of this given world work. If, for instance, we wish to explain the workings of the transmission in a car to a general audience (people with little knowledge of the workings of the gasoline engine), we would be doing an expository piece. The purpose would be to explain how the transmission works in the context of the engine. There would be no overt attempt to convert people to the appreciation of the wonders of a transmission or to explain our own emotional response to the piece of equipment. Essentially, in expository writing, the purpose is to describe the parts of a topic so that people understand how they constitute a whole. The principal virtues of a piece of expository writing are clarity, organization and completeness. After reading an exposition on the transmission, the reader should understand the function of that piece of equipment, the parts that make it up and the way in which the parts work together. If we are writing an expository piece on a written text, the reader should understand the thesis the text is presenting, the significant parts of its organization, and the way those parts relate to one another. In short, a good exposition of a written text would be a treatment of its thesis with an accurate and comprehensive explanation of the way the thesis is developed in the text.

Argumentative Writing

Argumentative writing is essentially persuasion. With this purpose in mind, the writer seeks to influence the audience to accept a position on the topic in question. The position taken is, obviously, controversial; if the audience accepts the position presented without question, there is no need for argument. The claim that American democracy is the best form of government is not likely to stir up much controversy among a typically American audience; an audience of Russians might find it highly controversial. Granted, then, that the position we put forward or the claim we make is problematic, that is, open to question, we proceed to support it by drawing on those principles and/or data which the audience is most likely to recognize as reasonable. In the classical tradition, we support our claims by a chain of logical reasoning on the grounds that our audience is most likely to be persuaded by right reason. We marshall those facts which best support our case for this audience. It is clear that, in putting together the facts of the argument, the presentation will involve considerable exposition. But we would be presenting the data in the case as we saw them in order to persuade the audience to accept the claim. In the argumentative essay, the data are not reported simply as information; they are used as grounds or evidence for a claim. The implications of the data are not left solely to the discretion of the reader, but the writer explicitly states how this evidence supports the claim and so suggests that the reader accept it. Argumentative writing views the world not as given, but as problematic, that is, as presenting problems to be resolved, issues to be explored and actions to be taken.

Self-Expressive Writing

In one sense, all writing is self-expressive. When we do an exposition or construct an argument, though the focus is on the material to be explained or the claim to be argued, we are making choices by selecting the topic, inventing the parts, arranging the material, ordering the evidence. But the emphasis, as we note above, falls on the explanation or on the claim rather than on the notion that *we* are doing the explaining or presenting the claim. In fact, if we are too obvious about our own reactions in a piece of expository writing or in argumentation, and draw too much attention to ourselves as writers, it can actually smudge the clarity of the exposition or dull the point of the argument. We want the ideas to stand out clearly in exposition; we want the claim to dominate in argument. The fact that it is *our* exposition or argument is not as important, in many cases, as the exposition or argument itself.

Explicitly self-expressive writing has a place when we consider the world as artifact. The writer of fiction, when doing a novel or poem, creates a world. Out of the images of experience, the novelist or the poet creates a world that, in some sort, resembles the one we live in. Though we may not be able to reconstruct the process by which the writer of fiction produces a written text, we have no doubt that it somehow reflects our own experience. In the same way, all our writing reflects our experience and we can set out to explain to the audience in an exposition or a piece of argumentation the specifics of that experience. In self-expressive writing, we are presenting to the reader those distinctive aspects of our experience, our way of thinking and our view of the world. This is typical of the writing of syndicated columnists like Russell Baker, William Buckley, Mike Royko, and Mary McCarthy. Readers the nation over listen to these voices giving them a unique view of the world. The famous columnist, scientist or literary critic may present his/her scientific or critical views in a way that emphasizes a personal understanding of an event, some scientific data or of a literary text. But the columnist, the scientist or the critic has earned the right to expect people to listen to his or her personal views. It is by our control of the data, the cogency of our reasoning and the distinctive perspective we bring to our subject that we earn the right to place our personal vision before the public.

Choosing a Topic

As we have inferred above, the rhetorical situation plays a large part in limiting the choice of topics. *A topic is what we will write about.* If we are writing our landlord about the rent or the plumbing, our topic, dictated by the exigency of the situation, is "the rise in rent for the apartment" or "the leak in the kitchen pipes." If we are given a class assignment to write about the causes of the Civil War, then this limits our choice of topic, but probably not sufficiently. Time constraints will indicate that we cannot cover all the causes unless we intend to write a book. So we might pare down our topic to "some economic causes of the War between the States." A more general assignment might leave us a wider choice; for instance, we might be asked to write about a personal experience. So we might choose to describe a trip to the hospital or a visit to grandmother's. Our topic might be "my fears about the hospital" or "summer days at grandmother's." Note that all these topics provide a starting point and a focus for a writing enterprise. They describe what we wish to write about in a nutshell. The topic encompasses the whole of one writing project; it encapsulates insights based on both the rhetorical situation and the data of our experience.

Approaches to the Topic

In selecting our topic and stating it in a phrase, we have probably also fixed on an approach, set ourselves a rhetorical aim. A topic like "some economic causes of the Civil War" we might treat as primarily exposition, to explain the differences between the industrial North and the agricultural South. If we are assigned a summary of "The Roman Legion," we may need to explain the parts of this text around a topic like "The Organization of the Legion." In the letter to our landlord we will most probably want to make an argument against a rise in the rent. So the approach we would take in our letter would be argumentative, emphasizing the reasons against the rise. The topics about the hospital or the visit to grandmother's lend themselves to a self-expressive approach in which we detail our feelings and reactions about these experiences. Some points of argument might creep into our presentation on economic causes of the Civil War; both the letter to our landlord and our essay on the hospital will undoubtedly involve some exposition. But our objective in the letter will be primarily to persuade the landlord not to raise the rent and our primary objective in the hospital essay will be to express our feelings and responses to these experiences. So in choosing a topic we consider the rhetorical situation and we choose a rhetorical aim or objective in the light of the effect we wish to have on the reader. Any choice of topic, then, should include an assessment of the rhetorical situation and an awareness of the purpose of a writing assignment. Getting control of audience factors, the constraints imposed by the assignment and of the purpose envisioned is essential to becoming an effective writer.

The Development of a Topic: Invention

"Invention" comes from a Latin root (*in-venire*) which means "to come upon." Invention is a discovery and, in this case and for our purposes, it means discovering ways of explaining our topic effectively. What we need to discover about a topic is what we have to say about it. We already have some data and some insights about the topic or we would not have chosen it. If we are writing about a text like "The Roman Legion" or "The Big Bull Market" or "Little Red Cap," we have analyzed these texts to determine what they say and what they mean. We found our topic among the insights we had while reading these texts. So then our development of the topic comes out of our experience with and our insights about the text. Now we are faced with finding ways and means of explaining our topic by organizing the data around our insights.

There is only one way of discovering what we have to say on paper about a topic: write it down. And the only way to begin writing is—to begin. And the question we put to ourselves that triggers this writing process is simply: what do I have to say about the topic? Because we have studied the text about which we are going to write and because we have considered the rhetorical situation, our first draft will have direction and content. We know what Gibbons' text says about the Roman Legion, we know what "The Big Bull Market" says about the Depression and we know the details of the narrative in "Little Red Cap." So we can begin writing to discover what we have to say about these texts.

Drafting

And so we begin. Consider the following opening statements.

1. What I want to talk about in this paper is "Little Red Cap."
2. "Little Red Cap" is a story about a little girl who disobeys her mother.
3. The most interesting character in the folktale "Little Red Cap" is the wolf.

We could grade each one of these sentences in terms of their effectiveness and focus, but each one of them gets the ball rolling. The first one is the equivalent of clearing our throat before speaking; in a subsequent draft we could scratch it out because it simply announces the topic. Sentence number two focuses on the little girl as principal character in the tale and provides a base for retelling the story. The third sentence offers a discovery perspective; the topic shifts from the tale or the principal character to the wolf, a different perspective from the first two. But, as we have said, each one serves the purpose: to start us writing. We are probably well advised to keep writing through the first draft. The point is to get our insights on paper.

Once we have committed our insights to writing in this first draft, we can critically examine what we have said. The tools we used to examine the reading text—topoi, tagmemics—are now available to analyze our own composition. Are the terms we have used clear or do we need to define them? Have we divided the topic into its component parts? What kind of connections have we made among the parts? Are we explaining our topic as a unit-as-system or as a unit-in-system or both? Have we organized our writing in terms of cause and effect or in terms of antecedent-consequent? These are questions we can put to our text to see how cogently we have explained the topic for ourselves and others. The methodologies help us clarify our ideas and their expression.

Suppose we have written through a draft which begins with opening sentence three above: "The wolf is the most interesting character in 'Little Red Cap.'" We have set out to explain to the reader why the wolf is "the most interesting character" in the tale. In our draft we make the following points:

When the wolf meets Little Red Cap, he does not act like a wild beast, but speaks to her like a gentleman.
Having persuaded Little Red Cap not to hurry to grandmother's, he rushes to the old woman's house and devours her.
Instead of simply pouncing on the little girl, the wolf disguises himself as grandmother and carries on a conversation before gobbling her up.
After the woodsman cuts the wolf open and releases the girl and her grandmother, he fills the wolf's carcass with stones.
The wolf is an interesting character because he has human qualities without ceasing to be a wild beast.

Our first draft calls attention to those events in the narrative which catch our interest because of the two aspects of the wolf's behavior—the human and the bestial. At this point we have "defined" the wolf in a unique way: he has the characteristics of a human but the instincts and appetite of a wild beast. Now we are faced with explaining why this "interesting character" has these qualities and how they work in the tale. If we are stuck at this point, we can try applying the methodologies.

Because the wolf addresses the little girl in gentlemanly fasion, she takes him to be one of her own kind. So at least from Little Red Cap's point of view, she and the wolf are similar, that is, they have human qualities in common. The wolf also resembles grandmother, at least to the extent that he assumes her clothes as a disguise. The woodman, on the other hand, contrasts sharply with the wolf; he is not deceived by the "old sinner" and he sees the wolf as his enemy. The topos of similarity-contrast allows us to line up the characters in the tale in terms of their relationships. We might then see how these relationships are organized by applying tagmemics. If we have sketched out the relationships in the story by developing the tagmemic cube, we can check unit-in-system, viewing the wolf as our unit. Our sketch might look something like this:

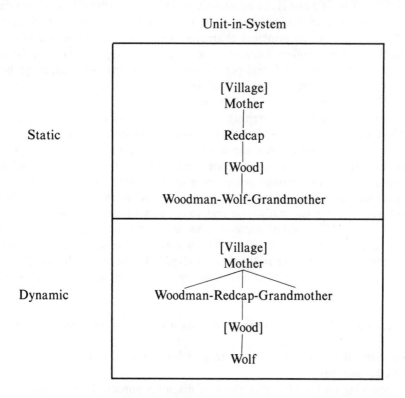

Unit-in-System

Static

[Village]
Mother
|
Redcap
|
[Wood]
|
Woodman-Wolf-Grandmother

Dynamic

[Village]
Mother
|
Woodman-Redcap-Grandmother
|
[Wood]
|
Wolf

Looking at this system we discover that the relationships change according to the characters' identification with either the village or the wood. The little girl does not deal with the wolf as a stranger or an enemy because in fact he acts like the adults of her village in talking with her. The wolf relates to the grandmother because, although she has connections with the village, like the wolf, she lives in the woods; the woodsman, also a wood-dweller, is identified with the villagers because he kills the wolf. The final situation of the characters which is configured in the dynamic unit-in-system reveals that the coalition of the villagers has destroyed the only figure totally identified with the wood. So we might decide that the "interest" that the wolf draws in the tale might derive from our discovery that the wolf represents a threat to the village and its values and that this threat is destroyed by the woodsman. We can write another draft in which we highlight the meaning of the tale as a conflict between the values of the village ("civilization," mutual help, community) and the threat that the wolf poses to those values.

50

Figures of Speech

Another feature of our draft which can be very revealing is our use of figurative comparisons. We note such usage in "The Big Bull Market" text we have considered; for instance, the poison that seeps through the body economic at the start of the Depression. A comparison of the economic system to the human body and the defects of that system as poison certainly illustrate the impact of those defects on the citizenry. In our own drafts it is often very helpful to note what sort of comparisons we have used, what similies or metaphors are at work in our text. For instance, as we attempt to develop the topic "some economic causes of the Civil War," we might discover a sentence like "the cotton bales of the South could not compete with the cannons of the North." "Cotton" makes a strong contrast with "cannons" and these images represent, on the one hand, the agrarian society of the South and, on the other, the industrial character of the North. Cotton must be traded for arms; cannons are immediate instruments of war. Pelting the invaders with cotton bolls is no response to the shot and shell of the cannon. Our topic, then, can be wrapped up in these two contrasting images. Even the expression "gentleman" relative to the wolf conjurs up the image of a dapper dresser who is sauve and well-spoken, a striking contrast with the image conjured up by the word "wolf." These comparisons, similies or metaphors—have implications that help explain our understanding of the topic. Applying the topos of comparison noting figures of speech also helps us discover ways of furthering our development of it.

Topic and Thesis

The topic is what we are writing about: *the wolf in "Little Red Cap"* or *Cotton and Cannons;* the thesis is *what we wish to say about the topic.* The thesis with which we approach writing our first draft is always exploratory and provisional; we may discover as we proceed through our drafting and rethinking that the thesis has changed noticeably. If we were, for instance, to take our original statement about the wolf as an interesting character as our thesis, by the time we have finished exploring it, we would have a different thesis statement: for instance, "the most interesting character in 'Little Red Cap' the wolf represents a selfish isolationism which threatens the altruistic solidarity of the villagers." *Notice that our thesis finds a predicate for the subject-topic.* There may be no reason in the world for including the thesis statement as such in our composition. But forcing ourselves to generate this kind of summary statement allows us to see 1) whether we have made our point clearly and 2) whether our point is worth making. We know that, if we can summarize a text we have read in such a thesis statement, that we have control of what the text says and what the text means. Similarly, if we can summarize our own text this way, we have explained our topic in a meaningful way. The final draft of our paper should relate through all its parts to our thesis statement and, if it passes this test, our composition is a clear and comprehensive treatment of the topic.

Revision

Throughout the drafting process we have been revising our composition. Revision, literally, means "seeing again," "taking another look." In our first draft we got our ideas down on paper; we tried to explain our topic as clearly and interestingly as we could. Then we looked at this first draft to see how effectively we accomplished our purpose. At this point we become a reader of our own text. We take a look at what we have written and evaluate it. We are, effectively, rethinking our topic. Have we bitten off more than we can chew? Have we started out on one topic and have we slid into dealing with another? We may have started out talking about our fear of the hospital and, in the middle of our piece, shifted to talking about the experience of the anesthesia. We may find that, halfway through our essay on "Cotton and Cannons" that we are talking about naval blockades of Southern ports by the Union forces. We may then decide that our topic in the hospital essay is "my experience with anesthesia" and that our essay on economic causes of the Civil War is really about "the South and naval power." A look at what we have done in the first draft may lead to rethinking of a topic and so redesigning our explanation of it.

Rethinking frequently, as we have seen above, involves applying the methodologies where we need them. Rethinking almost always involves rewriting, either in whole or in part. It may be necessary to rewrite a whole passage or to produce a whole new draft. It is seldom that we will produce an acceptable piece of work in the first draft. "Easy writing is vile hard reading."

Revision also includes repairing. This activity looks to smaller sections of writing: sentences or words that do not effectively carry our meaning. When we change a word or a sentence, we are not altering the basic organization of our piece. Choosing a more precise word or framing a more intelligible sentence will not remedy organizational problems, but it will refine or sharpen our meaning. Sometimes repairing will involve simplification, saying what we mean more directly. A sentence like "the feline creature crouched upon the mural edifice" can be less effective than "the cat sat on the fence." It helps, when we are stuck for the appropriate sentence or word, to say what we mean as simply as we can. Rethinking and rewriting require that we let the language flow as we write our drafts, that we do not hesitate over every word. We can always return and repair once we have established the general direction we wish our writing to go.

Rethinking, rewriting and repairing go on together as we struggle to express ourselves more clearly, more concisely and more imaginatively. Revision allows us to turn the experience of writing to our own benefit and to the benefit of our readers as we enlarge our own understandings and convey that understanding to our readers. The writing enterprise is both ordered and imaginative revision. By careful rethinking, rewriting and repairing we turn our unformed and unshaped understandings into clear, comprehensive and intelligible language—expository, argumentative, or self-expressive essays.

Editing

The final "look" we wish to take involves editing our work. We have been concerned, to this point, about generating, arranging, and specifying our understandings. Before we are finished with the process of revision, we must consider the mechanics of our presentation: punctuation, syntax, spelling. The conventions of standard edited written English also make a statement to our reader. Following the rules indicates concern about clarity, about intelligibility, and about consideration for the sensibilities of the reader. If my speling is arbetary and I don't do nothing about puntuation and I go running with my santenses the reeder begin to think that mabe my idees are as slopy as my grammer. It might be, in special cases, that non-standard English is appropriate; on the other hand, we should have control of the rules and the conventions of grammar and spelling so that we have a choice. Generally, for most audiences, standard English is the norm.

Summary: A Model of the Writing Enterprise

This model of the writing enterprise (see below) draws on our description of the process to this point. It is an attempt to present in static units what is essentially a dynamic process. But it will provide a visual summary of the way in which the writing process moves towards a final product.

Whether we set ourselves to writing a paragraph in an examination or a twenty-page term paper, we go through the same process in getting our thoughts on paper. It may be, that in answering an examination question, we do the planning and generating in our heads and, as we are getting our ideas down on paper, we also edit them. To do an acceptable twenty-page paper, on the other hand, we may have to move through a number of different drafts, return to our plan, generate new ideas, rewrite and repair in each successive draft. In either case, if our writing is to be effective, we move through the process the model outlines. With practice, we acquire the craft of writing well and create a paper which is worth the reading.

Preliminary Resources	Planning	Generating	Expressing	Editing
1. Data about the topic	1. Reflection on the topic, audience, self	1. Invention of parts to explain the topic	1. Production of first draft	1. Corrections of grammar and usages
2. Preliminary insights about the topic	2. Reflection on constraints, resources, outcome	2. Organization of explanation	2. Rethinking	2. Changes for more appropriate reader reaction
3. Heuristic methods		3. Articulation of tentative thesis	3. Rewriting	
4. Elements of the rhetorical situation.				4. Repairing

Integrating Reading and Writing through the Critical Thinking Methodologies/Heuristics

What you may have discovered as you read the chapters on the reading and writing enterprises or as you performed these operations is that, whether "vile" or "easy," we constantly move back and forth between the two enterprises. Whether reading or writing, whether analyzing or inventing, we utilize the critical thinking methodologies of topoi and tagmemics to integrate the processes. As we use the topoi or tagmemics to invent the parts of our topic or thesis for writing, we are forced back to the reading enterprise to see if we have included all the parts we perceived to be significant in the earlier reading. As we are involved in this rereading, we may discover new relationships, comparisons that will support our thesis in another way. As we apply the critical thinking methodologies to our reading, we are beginning to write. As we write, we read and analyze. It is through these heuristic methodologies—topoi, tagmemics—that reading and writing are integrated.

In the university we must read and write; there is no getting around it. Many of us move from the reading of an assigned text to the writing of a new text of our own with great difficulty. And most of us never take the time or realize the benefits of rereading and rewriting. With the aid of the critical thinking methodologies we can make the transit from reading to writing much more easily. The methodologies *initiate* this transition as they provoke insights worth writing about. They *foster* the transition as they beg to be used for both analysis and invention, and they *facilitate* the transition by providing both ongoing and back-up systems for the two enterprises: when the reading and writing are moving smoothly, the methodologies enhance and extend the transition by dredging materials to the surface for further understanding and expanded explanation; when a problem is encountered in either the reading or the writing (and this is more often the case) topoi or tagmemics applied to the problem can help to break up a knot in the understanding or help a writer explain a difficult part of the thesis. The methodologies initiate, foster and facilitate the movement from reading to writing. They serve as link between these enterprises by providing instrumentation toward understanding.

The Hermeneutic Circle

At the beginning of our discussion, we cited the old saying that good readers are good writers. We then added quickly that good readers and good writers are good thinkers. We also noted that, though these statements may well be true, it is not altogether clear why they are true. We have discovered, however, that the methodologies with which we have been working apply to both the reading and the writing enterprises; they are common instruments which the literate mind has at its beck and call for analysis and invention. We would now like to suggest that there is an underlying activity of the mind which makes use of these instruments. This activity is the process of explanation and understanding which has been called "the hermeneutic circle."

The process of explanation and understanding is 1) integrative and 2) mysterious. It is integrative in that the mind takes the parts of a given problem or text and makes wholes of meaning from them. Sometimes this integrative act of understanding occurs in a flash; we suddenly have an insight into the parts which organizes them into a whole. A classic instance of this experience is the story of Archimedes and the crown of the King of Syracuse. The King had given a goldsmith a mass of pure gold from which the artisan was to produce a crown. When the crown was delivered, the king suspected that the artisan had used an alloy in its construction and had kept some of the gold for himself. So he summoned Archimedes, a philosopher by trade, and asked him to determine whether the crown was pure gold or not. Since melting the crown down was not a viable alternative, Archimedes had to solve the problem some other way. Shortly after, sitting in his bath, he noticed that his body displaced a certain amount of water. The solution to the problem flashed into his head and, in his excitement, he rushed out of his bath down the street, shouting "Eureka, (I have found it)." Gold would displace more water than an alloy and by submerging the crown, its composition could be discovered. Archimedes was able to make a whole out of the parts; he was able to put the problem of the king's crown together with the principle of the displacement of water by dense bodies. We have all had comparable experiences of our own. We have puzzled over a problem, examining it from different perspectives, applying (consciously or unconsciously) a number of methodologies and suddenly—eureka!—we saw the solution; we grasped the meaning of the whole.

This process is mysterious in that we cannot anticipate when an insight will occur. A hundred explanations do not add up to an understanding because explanations deal with parts and understandings with the meaning of the whole. Nonetheless, investigation of the parts, explanation of the elements in a text, inventional procedures applied to a topic are the ordinary ways we prepare for these flashes of understanding. It is also the case that not every understanding is as dramatic as that of Archimedes. We may indeed start with relatively simple understandings that seem obvious once they have occurred to us (they may also seem obvious to those around us). But they are understandings and they are our own, and therefore to be treasured. Moreover, any understanding of the whole can become the basis for further explanation and larger understanding.

This last observation explains the notion of *hermeneutic circle*. Every process of understanding builds on previous understanding. And every explanation that we make is supported by the grasp of the whole that our preunderstanding gives us. Our inspectional reading yields some understanding of what the text is about; on the basis of this preunderstanding we can begin to examine the parts, using the methodologies at hand. Out of that examination we may well arrive at a fuller understanding of the text. If we have begun writing on a topic, we may, as we noted above, have to return to the text for another turn around the hermeneutic circle. Each time our understanding becomes fuller and we integrate more parts into the meaning of the whole. From our preunderstandings, we move to explanations of the parts out of which (hopefully) come new understandings. These new understandings become preunderstandings for further explanation which provides the grounds for a set of deeper understandings and so forth. Each time we return to the text or the topic, we move around the circle and so our understanding grows and our interpretation becomes more comprehensive. Here are three diagrams that, in different ways represent the way the hermeneutic circle works. Each one supplies a slightly different perspective on the process of understanding.

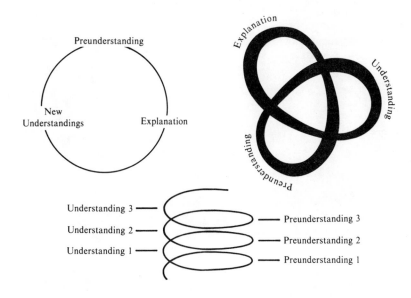

The circular diagram emphasizes the continuity of the process; the spiral diagram indicates how the circle moves interpretation forward; the Mobius knot underscores the recursiveness of the process.

We have seen how the hermeneutic circle leads us to understandings of the world as given, how the methodologies serve as instrumentation for our explanations of texts from that perspective. We are now ready to move on to consider the interpretation of texts as problematic, as they engage issues in argument.

Book Two

The Literate Mind and the World as Problematic: Reading and Writing from the Perspective of Argumentation

Chapter 5
Text as Argument

Overheard in a bar:

Joe: (after his second beer) They don't make ball players like they used to. All the great ones are gone. Ty Cobb and Babe Ruth, them guys was ball players.

Pete: Hey, wait a minute. Look at the record book. Maris broke Ruth's record for season homers; Hank Aaron broke his record for lifetime four-baggers. Pete Rose got more hits than Cobb; Lou Brock stole more bases. Today's athletes are bigger and stronger and faster than those old guys.

Joe: Them records don't mean nothin. Roger Maris, who was he? He's hittin a rabbit ball and he played in more games that season than Ruth. And it took Rose a lot more games to beat Cobb's record.

Pete: Yea, but the pitching is so much better these days. They didn't use relief pitchers back then; you started a game, you were expected to finish it. Pitchers throw faster and they got more stuff and when one tires out, they bring on a fresh one.

Joe: Yea, when the going gets tough, today's ball players get goin'—right out of the game. You didn't hear the old-timers hollerin help. Today all we got is a bunch of cry babies. They're makin' a fortune and every little ache or pain takes 'em out of the lineup. The old-timers played hurt or well, drunk or sober.

Pete: They didn't have to deal with the pressures, either. Night games, artificial turf, television, living in a giant fish bowl. Today's players deserve every penny they can get.

And so forth.

We have all seen a simple statement turn into a heated argument. In the discussion above, Joe makes an assertion and gives reasons for it. Pete takes a counter-position and presents his reasons. What began as a presentation of views and an explanation of them becomes a controversy.

If you are an actual discussant with Joe and Pete, you can press your own position, ask them questions, respond to their arguments. This kind of interchange can go on until closing time and after. As we read the discussion above, Joe and Pete are not available for questioning. What we have is a written text. As we learned in the first book, we can read the discussion above as exposition, that is, we can determine what the text says and what the text is about; we can describe Joe's position and Pete's position. We can also see those positions as claims that the discussants wish to support. When we see their statements as claims, we are treating the text as argument.

Toulmin Model

Special jobs need special tools. To cut a piece of string, to sharpen a pencil, to slice an apple, a jack knife will serve; a surgeon, however, needs a special cutting instrument—a scalpel. The topoi and tagmemics will do to slice a text into its parts and these methods will work for any text. When, however, we need to assess a text from a special perspective, we need a special method. When we want to read a text as an argument, to view it as problematic, we need a special heuristic. The special heuristic for argument we shall examine here is called the Toulmin Model.

Argumentation and Argument

Eavesdrop in the local bar or the student union and you will overhear discussions like the one between Pete and Joe. "The old-time baseball players were better than today's stars." "Rock-n-roll is dead (or ought to be)." "We should nuke the Russians before they nuke us" or "We ought to dismantle all our atomic weapons unilaterally." In a live situation where such topics are being discussed, the process is argumentation. That is, an argument is being presented live in order to persuade someone to accept or believe or do something. Argumentation is the living process by which people exchange insights, reasons, and points of view in order to create a consensus. If, however, we decide to present our position in written form, what we write down is an argument. What we produce will, hopefully, be a presentation of our position that is reasonable and acceptable to our audience. We take into consideration the circumstances of our readers, their beliefs and their relationships to us. By and large, we wish to present a written argument which is reasonable, acceptable to our audience and stated in an orderly way.

The model developed by Professor Toulmin provides a framework for analyzing and constructing arguments in writing. Like the topoi and tagmemics, it is a way of explaining the text that shows the relations existing between and among the parts of a given argument. It does not, as such, deal with elements like the nature of audience, or the beliefs of the writer, but only with the terms of the argument in the text.

Claim, Grounds and Warrant

In Toulmin's system, the structure of any argument has three major elements: claim, warrant, and evidence or grounds. The claim is an assertion which the text attempts to establish as true. "Old-time baseball greats are better than today's stars" makes a claim to be argued. The assumption here is that the person or persons addressed do not accept that this assertion is true. If the entire audience to which a claim is addressed is fully convinced that it is so, no argument is necessary. Any claim, to be bona fide, will be controversial.

The second element in the structure of an argument is evidence or grounds. The evidence or grounds is the data which, in the view of the arguer, supports the claim. The data can be strictly factual or inferential based on the facts. The kind of evidence adduced by Pete and Joe relates to performance records of players and the conditions under which those records were compiled. The discussants raise the issue of motivation and draw inferences about motivation from players' salaries and performance with physical disabilities. This kind of data provides reasonable grounds for supporting the claim.

The third element in the structure of any argument is the warrant. The warrant has as its purpose bringing the evidence to bear on the claim; it connects the claim with the data that grounds it. Facts, of themselves, do not prove anything. That Ty Cobb batted over .400 in his career is a fact; it does not, in isolation, say anything about Cobb's superiority over Pete Rose. We need a warrant to connect the assertion that Cobb was better with the assertion that he batted .400. If we agree on the general principle that batting averages are a significant criterion for discriminating among ball players, then the fact bears on and supports the claim. The process of argumentation in every day life includes many arguments which leave out one or another of these elements. Very often the warrant is implicit rather than expressed. For instance, we might make the assertion that Mr. X killed an innocent person and so he should suffer the death penalty. The claim here is straight forward: Mr. X should be punished by death; the evidence here is equally patent: he murdered an innocent person. The warrant for this assertion is implicit: anyone who kills an innocent party should be punished to the full extent of the law. Whether explicit or implicit, these three elements—claim, grounds and warrant—will be contained in any reasonable argument.

Backing, Qualifiers, Rebuttal

If all claims were undeniable and all evidence irrefutable and every warrant incontestable, then our three elements—claim, grounds, warrant—would be sufficient for the analysis of any argument. In fact, however, any one of the three may be challenged. So, to complete the picture, we need three further categories: backing, qualifiers and rebuttal.

We may not want to make a claim which is absolute or unconditioned. In the case of our murderer, Mr. X, we may want to add this qualification: "if he was not insane at the time of the murder." When we qualify a claim, we put conditions on its applicability. In checking claims that are made in a written text, we should be on the lookout for words like "possibly," "likely," "to some degree."

It may also be that our warrant is not self-evident, that it needs further substantiation. If, in the case of our murderer, Mr. X, "the full extent of the law" does not include capital punishment, then our warrant will not support our claim that Mr. X should suffer the death penalty. So we may wish to provide an argument in favor of capital punishment in order to back our warrant. In this case, the warrant would become the claim of another argument, namely, the full extent of the law should include capital punishment. We would then provide further evidence and another warrant to support the original warrant.

We may also wish to explain our qualifications and backing by the use of rebuttal. Here we might account for exceptional circumstances, evidence to the contrary, or the like. For instance, in the case of Mr. X, we may want to avert to the fact that Mr. X did not kill this innocent party during a state of war. In supporting the case for the old-timers against contemporary ball players, we may want to point out that the old-timers did not enjoy the benefits of sophisticated training methods and advanced medical technology. Rebuttals allow us to support our claim or warrant or evidence by anticipating objections and answering them.

The Toulmin Model can deal with simple arguments like the ones above or with more complex arguments. In a long and complex presentation, we might encounter a series of arguments that support a single claim or a chain of arguments that are interdependent and that stretch to five, ten or more claims with grounds, warrants, backings, qualifications and rebuttals. No matter how long the chain or extensive the series of arguments, the three major components—claim, ground, warrant—and three subordinate components—backing, qualification, rebuttal—provide a method for charting its development. The Toulmin Model, then, is a specific heuristic instrument for analyzing texts as argument and for composing argumentative texts.

Applying the Toulmin Method

Viewing a text as argument requires that, first, we have control of what the text *says* and what the text as given *means*. We may begin, then, by analyzing the text as exposition. After examining Thoreau's essay, *Civil Disobedience,* for instance, we discover that the text is about the individual's relationship to government, and that the individual as moral agent has an obligation to evaluate governmental decisions and, if they are destructive, to refuse to accept them. We can simply stand pat with this understanding of Thoreau's presentation; we have come to know what the text is about as an expository piece. Or we can take a further step and see the statement about the individual and society as *a claim that Thoreau's text is making.* In taking this step, we view *Civil Disobedience* as controversial, that is, as dealing with a set of problematic statements to be examined as argument. Such an examination supposes that the text, in saying and meaning what it does, offers statements that are debatable.

Note that our consideration of the text as argument assumes that we have already determined what the text is about, that we have arrived at a specific set of understandings about the text. Our general heuristic procedures, topoi and tagmemics, are the methods by which we examine the text in hopes of arriving at these understandings. We moved from our general and preliminary preunderstandings of the text, through explanation to (hopefully) a specific set of insights. Those insights or understandings, now that we are viewing the text as argument, become *our preliminary understandings for a new trip around the hermeneutic circle of explanation and understanding.* This is why we need a *special,* as well as a general, method. Neither topoi nor tagmemics deal precisely with the problematic aspects of the text. We have already used, if we needed them, the general heuristics to grasp what the text says. Then, after we have formulated insights about the meaning of the text, we can consider our formulation of those insights as a claim. This is the first step in the application of a special method for dealing with the text as argument.

The details of our analysis we now take to be grounds or evidence for the claim. Definition, division, comparison and contrast are not only ways of explaining the parts of the text; from the point of view of argument, they are *ways of organizing the evidence to support the claim.* When *Civil Disobedience* speaks to the question of the relationship between the individual and the government, it includes data about slavery in the United States, the war against Mexico and building roads. All these activities of the government are supported by taxes. In support of its claim, the text presents slavery and the Mexican War as immoral and destructive activities in which the conscientious citizen should not participate. By contrast, road-building is a good and useful activity which the conscientious citizen should support. The parts of the essay that we discovered through application of the general methods we now consider not only as explanations, but as evidence in support of a claim.

The third element in the Toulmin Model, the warrant, connects the evidence with the claim. It provides the reason for viewing the evidence as evidence, rather than as a series of explanatory facts or assertions. For instance, it may well be true that the Mexican War is immoral, but it does not immediately follow that therefore citizens should not pay their taxes in support of that war.

It may be that, as Thomas Hobbes suggests in *Leviathan,* the citizen's principal responsibility is to support the government which alone can guarantee order in the state. *Civil Disobedience* suggests that the individual conscience is the highest court in moral matters, and that individual conscience takes precedence over governmental authority. When we understand that the individual has a moral obligation to make a judgment about governmental action, then it follows that, if a citizen concluded that the government is acting immorally, the citizen is obliged to refuse cooperation. Our understanding of the warrant, which may be stated explicitly in the text or may be left unstated, completes the structure of the argument.

In coming to understand the text as argument, we have made yet another turn around the hermeneutic circle of preunderstanding, explanation and understanding. Our insights about the text which we discovered by using the general heuristics of topoi and/or tagmemics become the preunderstanding of our treatment of the text as argument. Our specific understandings about the meaning of the text stated in a thesis become the claim we wish to investigate. We then examine what the text says in the light of this claim, discovering the evidence which is presented to support it. The evidence might involve, as we have seen, other subordinate claims with backing and qualifiers, for which further evidence is presented. Our explanations of the evidence for the principal claim may also involve understandings about subordinate claims and further evidence. One insight or understanding that emerges fresh from our consideration of an argument or arguments in the text is the warrant. If we have identified the claim and detailed the evidence, and we see the connection between them, we have discovered the warrant and so understand the argument. Our judgment about the strength or weakness of the argument will depend in part on the way the evidence supports the claim by means of the warrant. There will be more on the bases for this judgment in the following chapters.

Intertextuality: The Reading Texts as Argument

The texts we have already read as exposition cover a wide range of disciplinary genres: history, philosophy, autobiography, science; and a wide range of topics: the Roman Legion, Jungian psychology, Plato's *Apology.* The texts to be read as argument (see *Reading Texts, Volume II*) cover much the same range of disciplinary genres, but they share a common topic: the relationship between the individual and the state. Each of these texts can be read as arguing for a definition of individual liberty and a description of how the individual's liberty is limited by membership in society. Not all of the positions taken in these texts, not all the arguments presented, are compatible with one another. The views on individual liberty have varied in different periods of history, in different societies.

Since this is the case, we can view these works intertextually, as *argumentation,* an ongoing discussion among the texts themselves about the nature of liberty and the nature of society. It would be interesting to get John Stuart Mill and Martin Luther and Thomas Hobbes and Martin Luther King in the same room exchanging their views on this matter. Though this personal interchange is obviously impossible, we do have their arguments on the subject and can engage these arguments through the texts they have written. We can, then, not only consider the individual arguments of the individual texts, but we can consider how these different sets of arguments reinforce, modify, or even contradict one another. We can evaluate John Stuart Mill's arguments in *On Liberty* for their strength and their weaknesses, and we compare and contrast these arguments and our evaluations of them with Thomas Hobbes' view of liberty in *Leviathan*. This sort of critical activity allows us to form our own understandings of what liberty means in the context of society and provides us with data for our own arguments on the subject.

So we can, as it were, enter into the discussion with these texts by stating our own claims, drawing on our explanations of the texts and our own experience to make our own arguments. Just as the Toulmin Model served to help us analyze the texts as argument, so it can serve to help us build our own case. By checking the evidence to see that it supports our claim and by stating the warrant we see connecting the evidence with the claim, we have conscious control of the argument we are making. The result is an understanding of the position we take and of our reasons for taking it.

Argument as Persuasion

Much of the writing we do and which we will do involves an attempt to persuade our audience to accept our claim. We want our parents to send us more money to cover our expenses, we want the landlord to fix our plumbing, we want the insurance company to give us a refund, we want our client to favor our proposal over that of our competition, we want the employer to hire us rather than other candidates, we want our boss to promote us, we want our instructor to give us an "A." All these "wants" amount to claims we are making. Marshaling the appropriate evidence and presenting or implying a reasonable warrant allows us to make our case persuasively.

We are all aware that a rigorously logical argument is not necessarily persuasive. Logic may not be enough. Because persuasion depends on more than just the structure of the argument, we must also consider the rhetorical situation. As we noted in the first book, the features which define a rhetorical situation are: (1) exigence; (2) audience; (3) constraints; (4) self. We now apply these features to an argumentative rhetorical situation.

Exigence

When writing about a controversial topic, our purpose is to make an argument in order to persuade our audience. We are not just presenting "facts"; we are presenting evidence in support of our claim. In all the cases mentioned above, the need to write coincides with the need to persuade.

Audience

In considering our audience with regard to persuasion, we will want to select the evidence and the warrant which is most likely to move our readership to accept our claim. If we are writing our landlord to persuade him to fix the plumbing, we will want to present that evidence most likely to move him to prompt action. The leak, if unattended, is likely to do serious damage to the carpet and the drywall; delay in fixing the leak will increase the damage and so the expense for repair. The inconvenience the leak causes us is a good reason in itself for repairing the problem, but it might not inspire the landlord to take immediate action. His concern for his property, on the other hand, would provide a stronger motive. The warrant for connecting the evidence and the claim might be the landlord's responsibility in law for maintaining his property. A tactful reminder that this is the case establishes the claim.

In writing a class assignment, persuading the instructor to accept the thesis we are arguing would involve different strategies than those we use with the landlord. We take care, in presenting our evidence, to show that we have read the assigned material. We make sure that the evidence we are presenting is accurate. It is probably a good idea to make our warrant explicit and it will not hurt our case if we choose a warrant with which we know the instructor agrees. Using the methodologies of the discipline, which the instructor has emphasized, in organizing our material will also support our case. In argument, as in other rhetorical situations, keeping the concerns of our audience in focus is key to effective writing.

Constraints

The basic constraints in this rhetorical situation are those we encounter in any writing enterprise: time, energy, our knowledge of the subject matter, the nature of our audience. A fifteen-page letter to our landlord detailing all the problems related to the leak in the plumbing will probably tell him more than he cares to know about our difficulty. On the other hand, a two-page paper on the American Civil War, its causes and consequences, would probably be too short to make an effective argument. For written assignments in our college courses a limited, properly qualified claim will generally be much more manageable in terms of time, energy, and evidence than a broad general claim. Our ability to limit our claim and define our terms will handle the principal constraints of papers assigned for class.

Self

In any rhetorical situation, the self of the writer is obviously involved. When we are writing a persuasive piece, the most important characteristic of the writer is credibility. We want our argument believed by the reader and the self-image we want to project is that of someone who can be trusted. The kind of credibility we wish to establish depends on the situation. In the first letter to our landlord, we may want to appear fair and reasonable and so trustworthy in our report of the evidence. In our fourth letter to the landlord, we may want to insist on our rights and convince him that we can be trusted to take the case to court if necessary. The kind of credibility we may wish to establish in papers written for class will be based on a careful reasonableness. We want to show the results of our efforts, to be careful in our use of evidence, to be clear in our presentation, and to be logical in our reasoning. A paper that shows carelessness in grammar, spelling and punctuation does not present the kind of image of the writer that inspires trust on the part of the instructor. If we are sloppy about details, the implication (true or not) is that we will be slipshod in our use of evidence and in our reasoning from it. The old, tired question "Do you take off for spelling?" can always be answered in the affirmative. Even if the instructor does not consciously penalize us for incorrect spelling, the impression we make is not favorable. Establishing credibility is central for the writer whose purpose is to persuade.

The World as Problematic

The old saw states: "There are two sides to every question." The first proposition of Murphy's Law is "Nothing is as simple as it looks." When we view the world as problematic, we acknowledge the truth of these two propositions. The age-old questions that recur in our personal and social history always involve controversy. "What is the good life?" "How is the opposition between the rights of the individual and the rights of society to be resolved?" "What does it mean to be human?" "What does it mean that anything exists?" These questions have been debated since the dawn of history; each age and every civilization have formulated their own answers to them. Even if we think that we have adequate answers, there will always be people out there who disagree with us. If we are going to live amicably with others, we need to be able to state our case and argue it effectively. Understanding other people's arguments, understanding and explaining our own position effectively is the way of making progress for ourselves and for society.

In reading texts, whether they are the classic texts of Western civilization or editorials in the morning paper, we have the methodologies of topoi and tagmemics to help us grasp the claims these texts are making and the specific methodology of the Toulmin Model to help us explain the structure of the arguments. As we use these methods to promote our understanding of what the texts say and what the texts mean, we can grasp the arguments that are being made on either side of important issues. As we try to explain our own position in writing, we come to understand its strengths and its weaknesses and the way in which our warrant connects our evidence to our claim. So we have the equipment to deal with a world which often seems thoroughly muddled and with problems that seem hopelessly confused. And if we are finally unable to convince everyone that we are right in our answers, we will at least be able to organize the questions and our own responses to them.

Chapter 6
General Heuristics and Argument

In the first book we dealt with the classical topoi and tagmemics. These general heuristics can be applied to any reading of a text: as expository, as argumentative or as self-expressive. However, the primary focus was on grasping the meaning of the texts as expository. Here the focus shifts to reading texts as argumentative. The general heuristics, as we have noted, are not designed to reveal the structure of an argument. The *Toulmin Model* is the *special heuristic* helpful for that purpose. Before dealing at length with the Toulmin Model, we will need to consider additional topoi which are specially helpful in dealing with argumentative texts.

The common topoi which we examined above were:

I. Definition and Division

II. Comparison
    A. Similarity
    B. Difference
    C. Degree

III. Relationship
    A. Contradictories
    B. Contraries
    C. Cause and Effect
    D. Antecedent and Consequent

Another major category of the classical topoi can work as grounds or evidence in argument. It is:

IV. Testimony
    A. Authoritative Testimonial
    B. Non-Authority Testimonial
    C. Maxims
    D. Laws
    E. Precedents or Examples
    F. Statistics

In this chapter, we will look at these additional topoi in somewhat greater detail.

IV. Testimony

The topoi we have just reviewed are all wholly contained within the text under consideration. We are talking about the definition of words as they are used in the text; we consider the divisions of the text itself; we look at the relationships among words, ideas and events specific to a given text. The topos of testimony differs from these topoi in that *it refers us outside the text under consideration, to other texts.* If we are writing, we draw on external sources for this topos. In fulfilling class assignments, our search for appropriate testimony will ordinarily take us to the library.

A. Authoritative Testimonials. When we come upon citations or quotations in a written text, the text is offering us information not on its own authority, but from an independent source. Generally, the text will vouch for this information as competent, fair, impartial and accurate. So on the topic of federal administration policy, a citation from a presidential address would be appropriate. A Harvard professor of economics would be an acceptable source on the topic of supply and demand, or a school superintendent on particular problems in public education. In creating arguments of our own, we will want to find sources which are creditable and reliable, which our readers will be inclined to accept without cavil.

B. Non-Authoritative Testimonials. Occasionally, we will come upon testimony not from an authoritative source. Very often, in such cases, the source is a celebrity venturing an opinion outside the realm of his or her expertise. For instance, Albert Einstein on theology, Frank Sinatra on politics, Tom Landry on credit cards. Though such testimonials are potentially persuasive because of high regard in which the public might hold these figures, most critical audiences would not accept such non-authoritative testimony as reliable evidence in an argument. When evaluating testimony, we should be careful to assess the credentials of the authority cited.

C. Maxims. Maxims are sayings which incapsulate or epitomize folk wisdom or community sentiment on a given issue. They can be quotations from literary sources or proverbial sayings: "You can't legislate morality" or "One bad apple spoils the barrel." Thoreau's *Civil Disobedience* begins with the maxim, "That government governs best which governs least." The text uses this maxim as a principle in developing the topic of *Civil Disobedience.* Use of a maxim always runs the risk of being easily countered by its contrary. For instance, "look before you leap" and "he who hesitates is lost" counterbalance each other. The trick, of course, is knowing which one to apply in a given situation. In the case Thoreau presents, the government that governs least must decide when to exercise its power or risk not governing at all. On the other hand, maxims do reflect common sentiments and can reveal cultural values which support an argument.

D. Laws. The testimony under "appeal to law" contains a variety of related notions. There are, for instance, laws of particular governments, that is, law as enacted legislation. The laws of the United States, of the State of Texas, international laws all exist as written texts. These laws testify authoritatively to society's view on a range of human actions.

In addition to particular legislation, there are natural laws such as the law of gravity. Physical laws provide authority for cause and effect arguments in the realm of science. Analogously, there are also laws of human behavior, laws of economics or of psychology. Although these laws are less able to fulfill rigorous tests of causality, they can be often used authoritatively in arguments on relevant topics.

E. Examples. An example is a particular instance that can illustrate or explain an idea or a principle. Often the example is an imbedded narrative or story that conveys the general idea through a set of particulars. When, in his *Autobiography,* Ben Franklin wants to illustrate the principle that achieving moral perfection requires effort, he tells the story of a man who wishes to grind a rusty axe to a high polish. The effort of turning the grindstone against the pressure of the metal requires too much labor and the man decides that he "likes a speckled axe best." In an argumentative perspective the example is testimonial evidence for the validity of the claim. Thus, when a scientist generalizes from a series of past experiments, each case in the series is an example of the general principle he is demonstrating. In legal cases, when a judge considers earlier decisions in similar cases, the examples serve as analogies. (For more on analogy, see pp. 117–119.) That is, they do not have the same testimonial weight as the scientific instances. The circumstances of each legal case are unique and so the lawyer or judge can only point to similarities with earlier cases. In using examples to demonstrate claims about human behavior, they highlight the relation between the example cited and the claim.

F. Statistics. Statistics can provide powerful testimony in explaining a topic or supporting a claim. Like any other instrument, however, statistics must be handled cautiously. There are three basic kinds of statistics: descriptive, converted, and inferential. Each one of these has a different function and so must be interpreted differently.

1. **Descriptive Statistics.** Statistics that are descriptive simply count units. There were 230 million Americans according to the 1980 census; there are 60 students in English 1302–005. Such statistics are easily aggregated and understood.
2. **Converted Statistics.** In this category statistics are converted into, for instance, percentages. Thus, in a class of 20 if 5 people are making A's, then 25% of the students are A students. Again, these percentage breakdowns are simply a matter of accuracy in counting and figuring.
3. **Inferential Statistics.** As the name implies, inferential statistics draw conclusions based on data and assumptions about the data. They attempt to determine whether observed differences in statistical data are significant.

In general, descriptive statistics are the safest and the easiest to use. When we look at converted statistics, the meaning can change drastically when compared to descriptive statistics. For example, if a town of 1,000 grew to 2,000 over a 10-year period, it would have 100% population growth, while a town of 100,000 that grew to 150,000 would have a growth of 50%. On percentages alone the smaller town would seem to have grown more even though its actual growth was 49,000 less. Similarly, when descriptive statistics are examined in relation to inferential statistics, the differences do not always seem particularly important. For example, in a test of educational methods a change in test scores might be found statistically significant at the .05 level. This means that the difference should occur by chance alone only five times in a hundred. So it is likely that the difference is due to teaching methods employed. But if the change in average score was a .20 difference, then it would occur twenty times in a hundred and we could ask whether that change was practically significant. Interpreting inferential statistics requires considerably more sophistication than interpreting descriptive or converted statistics. For those of us without a professional knowledge of statistics, citations using inferential statistics to support a claim depend very largely on the credibility of the statistician.

In summary, the topos of testimony cites sources external to the text in order to explain a topic or to support a claim. Given the relevance of the testimony cited, the effectiveness of the testimony will depend on the credentials and the credibility of the authority providing it. With the addition of testimony we have a set of topoi sufficient to deal with expository and argumentative texts. We want now to look closely at the way in which these general heuristics work in conjunction with the specific method, the Toulmin Model, for dealing with texts as argument.

Chapter 7
The Toulmin Model

The Toulmin Model is a *heuristic* for composing and interpreting arguments. Although it is "heuristic" in that it permits more than one interpretation of a specific argument, this model differs from general heuristics (topoi, tagmemics) in that arguments require a greater degree of agreement or univocity about the meaning of individual words and ideas than do interpretations of texts approached in other ways (for instance, as exposition or self-expression). The polysemy of language must be brought under more control in argumentation in order to be sure that the conclusions reached are *shared* conclusions. We have to be as clear as we can about the *terms* of our argument.

Before explaining the Toulmin Model in greater detail, let us look for a moment at the nature of arguments. People argue in order to persuade each other to accept, to believe, or to do something. Like the discussion in the bar at the beginning of Chapter Five, *argumentation* is the living process in which people exchange insights, reasons, and points of view in order to persuade. *Arguments* are the written or spoken texts which people present to others in order to persuade them. Thus an argument is a *text* abstracted from the living process of argumentation. In approaching and interpreting arguments, it is extremely important to remember the *references* which the text makes to other texts and to the world around us. This is a major factor in determining the *meaning* of words and ideas in argumentation.

To see how the Toulmin Model works, we will examine four simple arguments:

1. There's smoke coming out of that house, so it must be on fire.

2. He killed an innocent old woman, so he should be punished to the full extent of the law.

3. He ate the leaves of a tomato plant, so he must see a doctor.

4. Every little boy gets dirty, and Tom's a little boy, so you know what to expect.

Like all arguments, each of the above examples has a point or **Claim (C)** that the arguer is trying to persuade the reader to accept. In each of the arguments the Claim is introduced by the word "so":

C(1): that house must be on fire.

C(2): he should be punished to the full extent of the law.

C(3): he must see a doctor.

C(4): you know what to expect.

The Claims in Arguments 1–3 are straightforward enough, but the Claim in Argument 4 is left unstated and so must be *understood* by the reader: the audience is expected to "fill in" the proper **Implied or Unstated Claim (UC):**

UC(4): Tom will get dirty.

It is not uncommon to leave the Claim unstated: in fact, this can be a rhetorically effective strategy of argumentation, since it forces the members of the audience to think of the Claim on their own. Many arguments contain implicit or implied Claims, Grounds, or Warrants (especially Warrants). Sometimes these implied parts of argument are obvious, and sometimes they are hard to find. Let us see why this is so.

In order to find or "see" an implicit assertion in a text, we must have some insight or under-standing of the text as a whole. (Hence the need for previous examination.) The implied Claim in the above example was obvious because seeing the implication required only a quick grasp of the whole simple text, plus the kind of common knowledge which is part of our culturally shared *preunderstanding:* given half a chance, little boys will get dirty.

Once we have identified the Claim of an argument, we can begin to *assess* it. At this early stage of interpreting the argument, the most we can expect is that its Claim be clearly and un-ambiguously stated (or easily inferred). Of course, our assessment of the Claim at this point must be tentative. As we expand our grasp of the argument through our recursive process of explanation and understanding, we must continuously re-assess the argument in terms of new insights into its structure (the presence or absence of Claims, Grounds, Warrants), content (what the argument is *about*), and referential elements (the role this argument plays in addressing other texts and the world).

In practice, it is a good idea to spend enough time in identifying the form or structure of an argument (that is, finding its Claim, Grounds, Warrants, etc.) before attempting to assess fully the argument's *strength*. Without an identifiable Claim, Grounds, and Warrant there is simply no argument present. But the mere *presence* of these elements does not make an argument strong, or rationally persuasive. The process of interpreting an argument and assessing its strength is a holistic and recursive process, as we will see in this chapter.

In addition to a Claim each of the above simple arguments presents a reason or a piece of evidence which is supposed to persuade the reader to accept the Claim. In the Toulmin Model the principal evidence upon which Claims are based is called **Grounds (G).** The grounds will spell out the basic facts, rules, moral judgments, definitions which the argument provides in support of its Claim. In our sample arguments these Grounds seem clear:

G(1): There's smoke coming out of the house.

G(2): He killed an innocent old woman.

G(3): He ate the leaves of a tomato plant.

G(4): Tom is a little boy.

Having identified the Grounds of the argument, we can begin to assess their *relevance* and *sufficiency* in reference to the Claim. Are there enough Grounds provided to support the Claim? Are the Grounds cited relevant to the Claim? It should be noted at this point that the answers to these questions will depend in part on the presence (or absence) of relevant Warrants, Qualifiers, and Rebuttals, as well as on the referential elements of the argument.

In dealing with the referential elements of the argument, we rely upon clues in the text to refer us to the facts, issues and values which the text addresses. These facts, issues and values addressed in an argument may be present in another text (especially as a relevant argument), or in the world at large. Here the Toulmin Model and the use of topoi and tagmemics will help us to explore relevant issues and to deal with the questions of relevance, sufficiency and acceptability of the evidence grounding a Claim.

Grounds alone do not lead to a conclusion: the same data, definitions, divisions may be interpreted, and used, in different ways. Thus one or more **Warrants** are required to tie together the Grounds and the Claim. Warrants are often left unstated and must be understood by the reader (**UW**). Let us use our examples to help to explain the relationship between Grounds, Warrants, and Claims.

In Argument 1 only the Claim and Ground are stated:

C: The house is on fire.

G: There's smoke coming out of the house.

The *connection* between this Ground and Claim is, however, pretty clear. In fact, it is so obvious that the arguer did not state the Warrant (W) which connects the stated Ground to the Claim. The Warrant in this case is a maxim:

UW: Where there's smoke, there's fire.

This Warrant is an inductively established "sign" or "causal connection" statement. (We will return to these classifications of Warrants in Chapter Eight.)

Now consider the second argument: *He killed an innocent old woman, so he should be punished to the full extent of the law.* Again, the Ground and the Claim are clear:

C: He should be punished to the full extent of the law.

G: He killed an innocent old woman.

Here again, the Warrant, the connection between the Ground and the Claim, was probably thought to be too obvious to be worth stating; so the implicit warrant is:

UW: One who kills innocent old women should be punished to the full extent of the law.

This Warrant is a general moral or legal principle which is applied to the particular case cited as the Ground.

The third argument is perhaps less clear: *He ate the leaves of a tomato plant, so he must see a doctor.*

C: He must see a doctor.

G: He ate the leaves of a tomato plant.

The problem here might be summed up in the question, 'What is the connection between tomato leaves and doctors?' Here an understood Warrant, plus a further Ground, seem required:

UG: Tomato leaves are poisonous.

UW: One must see a doctor when poisoned.

These statements clarify the relation of the stated Ground to the argument's conclusion. Note, however, that the ability to spot the missing parts of this argument depend upon preunderstanding and some explanation of the argument. Our preunderstanding enabled us to identify the argumentative aspects of the text. Our knowledge of the explanatory power of the Toulmin Model helped us to use the clue-word "so" to interpret the two statements as Ground and Claim, and thus to expect an implicit or understood Warrant.

If, at this stage, our preunderstanding does not include the knowledge that the tomato plant is related to deadly nightshade and that its leaves are poisonous, the explanation thus far (dividing the argument into Claim and Ground) at least suggests how we could find out what we need to know to interpret the text further (to find the implied Warrant). This preunderstanding would indicate that there are two likely connections between eating a plant substance and needing to see a doctor: poisoning and choking. Our culturally shared preunderstanding also tells us that is problematic to seek a doctor for one who is choking, because of the time involved in getting medical help. Thus our preunderstanding and our explanation based in the Toulmin Model suggest the appropriate missing Warrant and Ground. We could check on this by consulting a book on botany. Thus the Toulmin Model can also help us to locate further information which we need for a fuller understanding of an argument.

The fourth argument is somewhat different: *Every little boy gets dirty, and Tom is a little boy, so you know what to expect.* This argument implies its Claim and states its Ground, but also states the Warrant connecting them:

UC: Tom will get dirty.

G: Tom is a little boy.

W: Every little boy gets dirty.

This Warrant is clearly a generalization from past experience.

Thus we have seen that the **Warrant** (**W**) provides the connection between the Grounds and the Claim, by showing the relevance and propriety of moving from the set of assertions in the Grounds to the assertion of the Claim. This feature of the Toulmin Model is very useful, since all too many arguers seem to think that Grounds alone substantiate Claims. The Warrant of the Toulmin Model displays the way *these* Grounds are tied to *this* Claim.

Once the Warrant(s) of an argument has been identified, we may begin to assess it. Is the statement connecting Grounds to the Claim acceptable or trustworthy? It may be very trustworthy, somewhat trustworthy, or trustworthy only in the presence (or absence) of certain limiting conditions. Thus an assessment of the Warrant(s) of an argument leads directly to a re-consideration of Grounds and Claim, as well as to a consideration of the remaining categories in the Toulmin Model: Backing, Qualifier, and Rebuttal.

When we do not expect our Warrant to be accepted by the audience, **Backing (B)** is necessary. This Backing essentially presents a further argument, now for the acceptability of the Warrant. Since backing is an argument within the main argument, it may be called a **sub-argument.** Again the Toulmin Model can be used to analyze the Backing. Here the **Warrant** of the original argument would be considered the **Claim** of the sub-argument, and the Grounds and Warrants for this new claim must be sought.

Qualifiers (Q) are often necessary because the evidence does not provide sufficiently strong support for an unqualified claim. If the evidence is sketchy or incomplete, we may wish to add "possibly" to the Claim statement. Other qualifiers are: "probably," "tentatively," "to some degree." Each of these indicates a different degree of firmness in asserting the Claim. "The world will end tomorrow" is a Claim that would require some qualification unless we had very special evidence.

Rebuttals (R) introduce possible circumstances which might require revision of an argument's Claim or Qualifier. If there are exceptional circumstances, alleviating or intervening factors, or relevant facts, which would require modification of the claim, these may (and in most cases should) be presented as a part of the argument. We might claim, for instance, that "President Reagan is the best man to lead the country" and then add "provided he does not succumb to senility" to cover an exceptional possibility.

We have now covered all the parts of the Toulmin Model. We can then visualize it in diagram form.

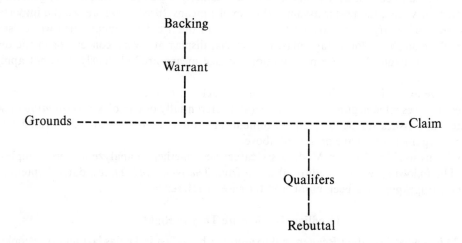

The simplest way to use this diagram is to list the parts of an argument under the headings of **C, G, W, B, Q, R,** as is done in this text.

Reading a written argument in order to *explain* it, we use the Toulmin Model's six categories of argumentative assertions: **Claim, Warrant, Grounds, Backing, Qualifier,** and **Rebuttal.** We begin to analyze the argument by making a preliminary classification of its statements under these headings. In this way, the Toulmin Model functions much like the *topoi* in helping us identify different parts of the argument.

Having identified **Claim, Grounds, Warrant,** we can check **Backing, Qualifier, Rebuttal** for further understanding of the argument. For instance, consider the (implied) Warrant in Argument 1: *Where there's smoke, there's fire.* This Warrant is so generally known and accepted that we are not surprised that no Backing is offered for it.

We might, however, recall that there are instances of "fireless" smoke (such as the vapor around dry ice). Therefore we can use the Toulmin Model's categories of Rebuttal and Qualifier to explain why the Claim that the house *must* (in all possible instances) be on fire is perhaps too strong to fit the Grounds provided. To be more proper (in some, but not all, circumstances), we might qualify the Claim this way:

Q: *Most probably,*

C: the house is on fire.

A Rebuttal (an exception or limiting case) might be added to justify or explain this new Qualifier.

R: [The house is on fire] unless, of course, it contains huge quantity of dry ice (or some other such "fireless" smoke-producing substance).

Notice further that ordinarily we accept the *presumption* of fire when we see smoke. This presumption is based in our culturally shared preunderstanding. Fire prevention posters generally do not mention "dry ice"; the poster assumes that smoke means "fire." Here we see the importance of the *referent* of an argumentative text: we do not call the fire department when we see smoke in the fireplace on the set of a stage play, in a special display at a rock concert, or in the disappearing act of a magic show; the presumption "smoke means fire" obviously does not apply to those situations.

The above examples show how the Toulmin Model can help to take us beyond a simple *explanation* of a presented argument to a fuller (and referentially oriented) *understanding* of some of the facts and issues surrounding the argument. A similar treatment can be provided for the other three arguments we have presented above.

Now let us use the Toulmin Model's six categories together to analyze a more complex argument. The following text is an editorial taken from *The New York Times,* dated September 9, 1984. The paragraphs have been numbered for ease of reference.

Headline: Oh So Sure They're Right

1 This is what President Reagan said to a prayer breakfast in Dallas last month: People who resist the imposition of prayer in public schools are "attacking religion" and frustrating the will "of the great majority of Americans."

2 This is what he said to a B'nai B'rith convention in Washington last week: The Constitution "makes sure that every single American is free to choose and practice his or her religious beliefs or to choose no religion at all. Their rights shall not be questioned or violated by the state."

We owe a debt of thanks to Research Assistant Renee Clark, who supplied this example.

3 There's a contradiction here, evident to those who in fact choose no religion at all, plus many Catholics, Jews, Protestants of varying persuasion and others. What would Mr. Reagan advise them to do when their children are ridiculed for not participating in "voluntary" school prayers? Does he, truly, think they're free to go out and resist such religious practice? Or does he think, as he said in Dallas, that if they do resist, it is *they* who are guilty of intolerance?

4 Intolerance: That's the word that's burning beneath all the smoke about religion and politics, a coupling that offends neither church nor state. There's plenty of religion in politics—and ought to be. People in a democracy should act on their social values, whether derived from their religious faith or from secular sources.

5 Churches have long preached the social gospel. They have been prominent in the civil rights movement, in the Vietnam resistance, in antinuclear campaigns, even in partisan campaigns like the Rev. Jesse Jackson's run for the Democratic nomination. It's no sacrilege against the Constitution that, in place of the social gospel, other churches now preach social Darwinism, inveigh on behalf of spending Federal billions for new weapons and against spending any Federal dollars for abortion.

6 The danger comes from people who are "oh so sure" they're right, who insist that they alone represent the one true political faith, who revile the other side as godless, intolerant obstructionists.

7 The President has come close to expressing just such certitude. Even though he seemed to moderate his views Thursday before the B'nai B'rith, just two days before, to the American Legion, he was still dividing the world into children of light and children of darkness: "What some would do is to twist the concept of freedom of religion to mean 'freedom against religion.' "

8 Religionists have every right to lobby for causes, to run for office, to criticize with vehemence—but not to misrepresent their opponents or ridicule their motives. Indeed, these rights carry with them a responsibility to respect other views. In short, tolerance: the vital insulator of democracy, the cushion that softens the sharp collisions between different views and faiths and enables all Americans to live together in reasonable harmony.

9 Mr. A may strongly support capital punishment yet feel passionately that abortion is murder. Mrs. B may disagree with equal passion on both counts and demand of Mr. A, "Death is death. Why can't you see the inconsistency in your positions?" There are times when devout practitioners of one creed, though completely sure they are right, confront equally tenacious believers of the opposite. In this free society, the practical, not to mention moral, mechanism is tolerance.

10 Did it ever occur to the President that opponents of school prayer might have worthy motives and are not out to frustrate "the great majority of Americans"? Did it ever occur to him that they might be right? And even if not, did it ever occur to him that their views deserve the President's respect?

11 That would be tolerance. Or, as Learned Hand, the legendary jurist said during the dark days of World War II: "The spirit of liberty is the spirit that's not too sure it's right."

The Claim of this argument seems to be stated at the start of Paragraph 7:

> C: The President has come close to expressing just such certitude.

The phrase "just such certitude" is not terribly clear when thus pulled out of context. We will use square brackets to *explain* what the phrase *means* by tying it to key concepts introduced in Paragraphs 4 and 6:

> C: The President has come close to expressing [a dangerously intolerant] certitude [which is a threat to freedom in America].

Note further that the editorial does not accuse Reagan of dangerous intolerance, but argues that his various speeches, when combined, seem to "come close to" such intolerance. Since this argument's Claim is an *interpretation* of the point of view behind various speeches to diverse audiences, it is quite proper so to qualify the Claim. (This particular precision in stating the Claim is especially important given the line of argument here: the argument would be self-contradictory if the author were to show intolerance himself.)

The principal **Grounds** which this argument offers to support its Claim seem to be the following:

G1: President Reagan has contradicted himself in two speeches. [Paragraph 3, supported by Paragraphs 1 through 3.]

G2: Intolerance is the basic issue in the church-state debate. [This seems to be implied by the first sentence in Paragraph 4 and the last sentence in Paragraph 9.]

G3: When addressing the American Legion, President Reagan divided the world into children of light and children of darkness.
[Supported by a quotation from the speech in Paragraph 7.]

G4: [It seems not to have occurred to President Reagan] that opponents of school prayer might have worthy motives and are not out to frustrate "the great majority of Americans." [This statement seems implied by the first rhetorical question in Paragraph 10.]

G5: [It seems not to have occurred to President Reagan] that they [opponents of school prayer] might be right. [This statement seems implied by the second rhetorical question in Paragraph 10.]

G6: [It seems not to have occurred to President Reagan] that the views [of opponents of school prayer] deserve respect. [This statement seems implied by the third rhetorical question in Paragraph 10.]

G7: The danger [to a democracy] comes from people who are "oh so sure" they're right, who insist that they alone represent the one true political faith, who revile the other side as godless, intolerant obstructionists. [Paragraph 6.]

Given these Grounds, what Warrant allows us to arrive at the Claim? There seem to be three major Warrants presented in the argument which connect the above Grounds to the Claim:

W1: The right to lobby for causes, to run for office, and to criticize with vehemence carry with them a responsibility to respect other views. [Paragraph 8.]

The first Warrant is backed up by the following Backing:

B(W1)1: Tolerance is the vital insulator of democracy, the cushion that softens the sharp collisions between different views and faiths and enables all Americans to live together in reasonable harmony. [Paragraph 8.] [Ground of sub-argument for W1.]

This Backing of the first Warrant is in fact the Ground of a **sub-argument.** As we noted, a sub-argument is an argument within a main argument. Most sub-arguments argue for the acceptability of a particular Ground or Warrant.

Since the sub-argument for W1 is a Backing for W1, that means that W1 is the Claim of this sub-argument. A sub-argument must also contain (at least) Claim, Grounds and Warrant. Thus, as we also noted above, any sub-argument may be analyzed utilizing the Toulmin Model. The obvious implied Warrant connecting **B(W1)1** and **W1** is:

UB(W1)2: The rights of democratic citizenship carry with them the responsibility to preserve and protect democracy. [Warrant of the sub-argument for W1.]

The second Warrant for the main Claim is:

W2: Tolerance is a practical as well as a moral attitude essential to a free society. [Paragraph 9.]

This Warrant is a principle which ties Reagan's statements (the Grounds) to the "danger" and "threat" implied in the Claim. It is backed by the whole of Paragraph 9, which will be summarized as follows:

B(W2)1: People in fact often hold firmly to opposite beliefs.

This Backing is once more the Ground of a sub-argument which has W2 as its Claim. This sub-argument seems to rely upon an implicit Warrant and implicit Ground:

UB(W2)2: The lack of tolerance can lead to tyranny. [This is a further Ground of the sub-argument.]

UB(W2)3: We should maintain democracy and avoid tyranny. [This is the Warrant of the sub-argument.]

The final Warrant is expressed in the last paragraph:

W3: The spirit of liberty is the spirit that's not so sure it's right. [Paragraph 11.]

This Warrant is backed by an appeal to the authority of the man who made the Claim:

B(W3)1: Learned Hand, the legendary jurist, made the statement which is used as W3. [Paragraph 11.]

The above interpretation of this argument is not the only one possible, but it is a plausible interpretation. The categories of the Toulmin Model are instrumental in *explaining* the functions of the various statements in this argument, which in turn leads to an *understanding* of the argument. This understanding is evident especially in those statements that bring out the *implications* of the argument and fill out the Toulmin Model categories.

Notice that, in the process of interpretation of a written argument, our preunderstandings are challenged and often changed. For instance, an editorial might turn out to be less an argumentative than a self-expressive epideictic text, that is, a text that celebrates an event or a person (we often encounter such editorials on the Fourth of July and at Christmas). Or, an argument which we at first take as straightforward might, at a later stage of explanation, be re-interpreted as ironic, and thus implying or *meaning* the *opposite* of what it explicitly *says*. An example of this is Jonathan Swift's *A Modest Proposal* which suggests that the Irish solve their food production problem by eating their babies.

Likewise, a particular explanation of a part of the text often needs to be re-evaluated after we reach a new understanding of the whole text. For instance, if a new insight moves us to decide that a statement we had interpreted as Claim is in fact support for an implicit Claim, we must now re-explain the role of that statement in the argument (is it Ground, Warrant, Backing, or Rebuttal?). This recursive process of examining a text as argument might be outlined as follows:

1. Read the text inspectionally.
2. Apply the general methods of topoi and/or tagmemics to discover what the text *says*.
3. State the thesis of the text either from the text or from your insight about it. This thesis is likely to be the **Claim (C).**
4. Re-read as often as necessary, to get a feel for the interrelation of the statements (in terms of the categories of the Toulmin Model).
5. Use surface clues such as "since," "for," "because," which introduce **Grounds (G)** or **Backing (B),** and "thus," "therefore," "so" which introduce **Claims** (including the Claims of sub-arguments, which may be Grounds, Warrants, Backings, or Rebuttals).
6. Once you have a plausible idea about the general structure of the text (**C, G, W),** look for *implications* which may be required for the argument to be rationally persuasive—this must be done because some Grounds or Warrants may be implicit, on the assumption that their audience will supply them.
7. Assess the argument (finding the relevance and sufficiency of the Grounds, the trustworthiness of Warrants, the appropriateness of Qualifiers, and the relevance and weight of Rebuttals—and, as we will see in Chapter Nine below, a knowledge of informal fallacies is also useful in assessing arguments).
8. After assessing the argument, re-assess your interpretation by re-reading the text, grounding each of your assertions in the surface features of the text—keeping in mind the *referential* elements (exigence, audience, constraints, self) of argumentation in which the argument appeared (or is to appear).

Writing and the Toulmin Model

The Toulmin Model may also function as a heuristic in composing arguments. If you think through your own arguments in terms of the Toulmin Model, you can develop a powerful framework for them. Your **Claim** should focus on a controversial issue. Remember: no controversy, no argument. Knowing that you must provide **Grounds** will often send you back to the text you are reading to gather evidence. Searching for a **Warrant**—a convincing way of explaining the relevance and propriety of the Grounds to support your Claim for a particular audience—centers your attention on the connections between your Claim and the sorts of Grounds which will be persuasive. **Backing** your Warrant, to make sure that you reach the audience you intend to persuade, will force you to face actual or possible opposing Warrants and Grounds, different interpretations of relevant Grounds and their related Claims. When examining the relations between Grounds, Warrants, and Claims the possibility (or actuality) of exceptions and limiting cases arises, and you must develop possible **Rebuttals** and **Qualifiers** for your Claim, again keeping your audience in mind.

This process of writing using the Toulmin Model is also recursive. As you read relevant arguments and information, you jot down notes. When you use heuristics to get ideas for your argument, you make more notes. Drafting sections of the argumentative essay is often interspersed with further research on the issue. This process may modify or change the Claim. Most often this change is a gradual limiting of the original Claim by the addition of Qualifiers and Rebuttals. Sometimes you may even make a complete about-face because more information on the matter may provide convincing arguments for an opposite view.

In describing the application of the Toulmin Model to the composing process, attention to *audience* has often been mentioned above. This is crucial to persuasive argumentation. As an audience changes (say, from a panel of experts to a general audience), the argument also changes. The need to provide Grounds, Warrants, Backings, Rebuttals and Qualifiers—and even to modify your Claim—will vary when you address the same (or a related) topic to different audiences. For instance, consider capital punishment as presented to: a group of lawyers, a police academy, a general audience. Knowing that each of these audiences has a different set of values, knowledge, and related beliefs could well cause you to create an argument with different Grounds, Claims, and Warrants for each group. A Warrant which is common knowledge to lawyers may be wholly unknown to a general audience, thus requiring Backing for the latter audience but not for the former. A Ground such as "Capital punishment has not been shown unequivocally to deter crime" may well be accepted by a group of lawyers and yet be rejected by the members of a police academy. Thus, in composing arguments (as with any other sort of composition) you should keep firmly in mind *for whom* you are writing.

Let us review the process of interpreting and assessing a text considered as argument. When we look for the Claim of an argument, how do we go about finding it? We begin with an inspectional reading of the text based in our preunderstanding. We then go to the topoi and/or tagmemics to explain the parts of the text. Locating the definitions, divisions, comparisons in the text enables us to decide upon an (at least preliminary) interpretation of what the Claim is. Likewise, in trying to classify assertions as Grounds, Warrants, we can draw upon a topological analysis. Tagmemic analysis is especially helpful in exploring the referential elements of an argument, by inviting us to examine the argument's concepts and referents from different points of view. Such an analysis will also help us to decide upon the argument's effective strength, by uncovering further relevant information.

We have looked at some general aspects of the Toulmin Model as an interpretive and compositional heuristic. In the next chapter we will examine one of the key elements in the model, the Warrant. It is on the basis of the Warrant that we can identify and classify types of argument.

Chapter 8
Classifications of Argument

When the high sheriff came beating at an English householder's door, the question ordinarily put to him was *quo warranto,* "What is your warrant?" Today the law officer, in making an arrest for a crime to which he was not a witness, presents a warrant. The officer's power in a given case depends on the warrant he possesses. It should be obvious, from our discussion in the last chapter, that the Warrant (of the argument) is equally important to securing a Claim. What we want to consider at this point are various kinds of Warrants as they specify various types of argument. Even when an argument fulfills all the requisites of the Toulmin Model, that is, it has a Claim, provides Grounds and establishes a Warrant, it is necessary to evaluate the strength of the argument. The strength of an argument is judged by its effectiveness in establishing or justifying the Claim. Complete arguments with accurate Grounds are not necessarily "correct" or "incorrect" or "logically valid" or "invalid." Rather, most arguments are better or worse—that is, they create a greater or lesser probability of the truth of the Claim—or are more or less persuasive to a critical audience. The strength of the argument depends, in great part, on the Warrant used and the degree of probability with which the Warrant connects the Claim and the Grounds. We want, then, to consider special types of arguments based on different kinds of Warrants.

In this chapter, we will treat six major classifications of argument: **Generalization, Analogy, Sign, Cause, Authority,** and **Principle (GASCAP).** Like all arguments, the six major classes can all be diagrammed using the Toulmin Model. These six types do not exhaust possible classifications; there are other ways to classify arguments. These six have been chosen because they are among the most likely to be encountered in reading and to be employed in writing.

The system used here, as we have remarked, classifies arguments on the basis of the Warrant utilized in the argument. Thus, as we come to understand better the classifications of argument and the more specific standards which apply to their evaluation, we will find that our understanding of the slippery concept of "Warrant" also improves. For each of the classifications, we will consider:

1. a definition and an example of the argument with the features of the Toulmin Model labeled;
2. a discussion of the major criteria upon which that type of argument is appropriately evaluated, and
3. a discussion of potential problems in the use of each type of argument.

Generalization

Generalization (or induction) occurs whenever we reason from a series of cases to a conclusion. Though the conclusion is frequently a summarizing generalization, it may also be particular. For example, when a zoologist notes:

Grounds: Observed swan 1 is white
               Observed swan 2 is white
               Observed swan 3 is white

either of two conclusions might be drawn inductively. One conclusion would be the generalization that (Qualifier) *probably* (Claim) *all swans are white.* An alternative particular conclusion might be that (Qualifier) *probably,* (Claim) *Swan 4 will be white.* The Warrant for either argument could be stated as "given that Swans 1, 2, and 3 are white, it follows by generalization or induction that. . ." or somewhat less redundantly stated: "Since all observed cases of swans have been white, then. . . ." Notice that in the second version the *since* statement is merely a summary of the Grounds and that "it follows by generalization" is implicit and unstated. Among argument types in which the Warrant is implicit, generalization ranks high. The presentation of a series of cases serves as the cue that generalization or inductive reasoning is being used.

Although many issues can be raised concerning claims warranted by generalization, there are always two major questions. First, **are there enough cases in the grounds?** Second, **are the cases representative?** In the abstract there are no exact or absolute answers to the question: how many cases are enough? In practical situations some audiences will demand more cases than others. How many cases are needed is also relative to how many cases exist. If there are four million swans, a critical audience would want more than three cases in order to conclude that "all swans are white," but might find three enough to establish some small degree of probability that the next observed swan would be white. Public opinion surveys make generalizations about 230 million Americans based on surveys which contain between 1000–2000 cases. Such surveys can be quite reliable if they use a sample that is representative of various ages, income, ethnic and sex distributions across the total population.

To strengthen an argument by generalization may mean providing more cases. To strengthen an argument by generalization may mean providing Backing showing either (1) that the grounds contain an adequate number of cases, or (2) that the cases are representative, or both. Depending on the specific Claim being made and the audience being addressed, there may be more specific standards for an adequate number of cases or selection of a representative set.

An argument whose Warrant is generalization *never* establishes a claim with absolute certainty. However, it can establish Claims with very high degrees of probability, so high that for practical purposes the degree of difference between probability and certainty is trivial. Thus, we may be practically certain on the basis of generalization that the sun will rise tomorrow. But generalizing arguments may also produce much weaker probabilities. Based on a generalized sense of the probabilities, the meteorologist advises us that "it will probably rain tomorrow." And we all know that this prediction may not prove accurate.

Among the key problems in assessing generalizing arguments is the issue of representativeness. Any text may include only those examples which seem to support the claim. If reflection and research reveals 40 examples of which only 10 support the claim, and only 5 of those 10 appear in the text, it is very clear that the examples are not representative. Sometimes the only available Backing a text provides for the representativeness of the cases presented is its own testimony that the cases reported are typical. If so, the Warrant depends on the weight of this testimony.

Analogy

An argument by analogy occurs when known likenesses between two things provide grounds that they are or should be alike in that respect which the claim seeks to establish.

For example, when attorneys argue in the courtroom on the basis of legal precedents, they attempt to show as grounds that the case being tried is similar to previous cases. The Warrant, which is usually implicit and unstated, would be something like "If the previous cases are similar, then a similar decision should be made in this case" or simply "It follows by analogy." Presentation of precedents in legal argument is likely to be biased in favor of the presenter's case, with the opposing attorney presenting conflicting precedents, and the judge is left to decide which case is the strongest. Often readers will get the idea that the reasoning is occurring by analogy when a series of comparisons are developed. However, the series of comparisons often resembles the series of cases in generalization, so some potential for confusion is possible.

On other occasions the Warrant will itself be a direct statement of likeness.

Thus, given as Grounds that
   "We face an economic recession today"

and the Warrant
   "which is like the economic recession which JFK dealt with effectively by tax reduction in 1960"

then the Claim
   "we should enact a similar tax reduction today."

When an argument from analogy takes this form of presentation, then the Backing should show how the 1960 recession and today's recession are alike.

In appraising the strength of an argument based on analogy, several questions are important. Are the two matters being compared similar in all or most crucial respects relevant to the claim? Are there differences between the two matters being compared which would support contrary or contradictory Claims? When both similarities and differences are compared to one another, which seems to bear the greatest weight?

Whenever two *different* things are being compared, they cannot be the *same* in all respects. Because this is true, at some point differences will occur which have the potential to weaken or destroy the analogy. Generally, literal analogies are considered to be stronger than figurative analogies. When a historian compares the situation before World War I to that before World War II, and from this comparison states that these three situations show similar characteristics, the comparison is considered to be literal; different historical periods are the basis for the analogy. The comparisons are substantive in that they deal with real historical situations which are in the same class. If a text were to compare human beings to plants stating that, like plants, a human being needs "nourishment," "stability," and "roots in the community," then the analogy is figurative.

Human beings are compared to plants. Substantively, the differences are so great as to render the analogy debatable. Figurative analogies are often better for illustrating or clarifying the Claim than for establishing it.

Analogies are an important but limited type of argument. Many important discoveries or insights develop from arguments by analogy. But then the Claim may be further supported using other types of argument. For example, in science where analogical argument is acceptable for use in formulating hypotheses, the Claim first elaborated through analogy will be verified by induction. The old saying applies: *omnis analogia claudicat.* "All analogies limp."

Sign

Sign arguments greatly resemble causal arguments; the difference is primarily that, while in causal arguments the "cause" is seen as producing the effect, a "sign" points to something else which may precede it, occur simultaneously with it, or follow it. When a sign relationship is established, it enables us to predict in roughly the same way that the causal relationship allows prediction.

For example, given the Warrant:
Being red in the face is a sign of embarrassment

given the Ground:
Joe is red in the face.

then the Qualified Claim:
(Probably) Joe is embarrassed.

Notice that being red in the face is not the cause of Joe's embarrassment, but only an indication that he is embarrassed. Redness of face is a sign of embarrassment because it often happens that embarrassed people do become red in the face. However, since some people do not blush when embarrassed, we cannot really even say that becoming red in the face is an infallible sign of embarrassment.

When attempting to back Warrants based on a sign relationship, the key issue is whether or not the sign is fallible or infallible. A fallible sign means that the matter indicated may occur or often occurs, but does not always occur. Joe may be embarrassed without turning red-faced. An infallible sign means that what the sign indicates *always* occurs in connection with the sign. For instance, iron glowing red is *always* hot. Whether a sign is fallible or infallible is ultimately a matter of observation and thus sign Warrants ultimately rest on generalization. When a sign Warrant is based only on a series of fallible signs, a very tenuous argument can result. The legal case based entirely on circumstantial evidence, which is used in a series of sign arguments to show that the accused is guilty, is sometimes persuasive, but, because each sign is itself fallible, there may be reasonable doubt. Arguments based on fallible signs cannot establish Claims beyond a degree of probability.

Cause

A causal argument relies on a Warrant which connects Claim and Ground by means of a causal relationship. In a causal relationship two "facts" relate in that one produces the other or makes the other occur. When a causal relationship is established, it becomes possible to infer the cause from the effect or the effect from the cause. For example, taking as our Warrant "gravity causes objects thrown into the air near the earth's surface to fall," we could apply it to the Ground that "an object is being thrown into the air near the earth's surface." And then we could make the Claim that "the object would fall." Causal Claims enable us to make predictions, presuming that causal relations are stable over time. When you go to your doctor's office with a fever, the doctor will interpret the fever as a symptom (an "effect") and seek to determine its cause. One possibility is that the fever is caused by infection. Antibiotics interact with the body's natural mechanisms to cure infection. And so the treatment is aimed at removing the cause of the symptom through the combined causal agency of the body's natural defenses and the prescribed antibiotics. Notions of causality are involved in both diagnosis and treatment.

Causes are notoriously difficult to prove because they are not directly observable and thus must be inferred from observation. When a causal Warrant is challenged, one approach to Backing the Warrant is to show that it meets appropriate tests. One such set of tests, developed by John Stuart Mill, is called **Mill's Canons.**

> **Canon of Agreement:** When the cause occurs, the effect follows invariably. When the effect occurs, the cause preceded it.
> **Canon of Difference:** If the cause occurs and the effect does not or if the effect occurs and the cause did not precede it, then the suspected cause is either not the cause or not the sole cause.
> **Canon of Correlation:** In general, the intensity of the effect varies in relation to the intensity of the cause. (More of the cause more of the effect or vice versa.)

Though causal Warrants are difficult to establish incontrovertibly, to the extent that we can show in all known cases that the cause and effect occurred invariably in sequence, that no known cases have appeared in which the cause was actively present and the effect did not occur, and that, when the intensity of the cause has increased, so has the intensity of the effect, we have strongly backed the causal Warrant.

Causal Warrants are often difficult to apply to many problems of human behavior. Causes can best be established in the natural sciences. In these sciences, physical or biological laws are essentially statements of causal relationships. Although we sometimes speak of the "causes" of human action, they are more difficult to establish as causal Warrants. For example, if I kick several different people, I can reliably predict the kick will cause pain, but I cannot predict how they will react—one person might cry, another might turn around and hit me, another might run away, another might call the police. Thus, when we read discussions about the causes of crime, child-abuse, drug addiction, war, we would be well advised to recall that human behavior is very complex and to apply the tests of Mill's Canons to any causal Warrants in such cases. We often are misled into thinking we are more sure about the causality of human action than any precise application of the term "cause" would allow.

Authority

An argument with authority as Warrant occurs whenever we support a claim by appealing to another's judgment. Arguments from authority are very simple. For example,

Given the Grounds:
John Doe, Professor of Economics at Harvard University says the federal deficit will produce inflation.

and the Warrant:
A Harvard Economics professor should be competent to make an economic judgment worthy of our belief.

we come to the Claim:
The federal deficit will produce inflation.

Notice that in arguments from authority the Grounds and the Claim are redundant in that *both* say the federal deficit will produce inflation. But the Grounds only say the *Professor says* so, the Claim says *it is* so. Generally speaking, fully explicit statements of Warrant for arguments from authority are rare. Rather, the tendency is to rely on attributions or titles to indicate the qualifications of the authority. Thus in the Grounds we know that the authority cited is a Professor of Economics at Harvard University. The attribution of the title "Professor" presumably establishes the competence of the authority. Stating simply "John Doe says" would not have the same effect.

The notion of authority is somewhat inflated these days. An "authority" does not necessarily have to be a highly credentialed academic or political expert. The term means precisely someone who is in a position to know. Thus, ordinary citizens who were eyewitnesses to a crime have authority to testify about what happened because they were in a position to know. The expert and the eyewitness are both authorities in their own areas. Since we cannot be sure that the reader will know why an authority is an authority, it is generally useful to refer to titles and credentials to signal qualifications.

Several key questions can be used in evaluating arguments from authority. The most important is whether the authority is qualified in relation to the Claim being made. When Jerry Falwell speaks on American foreign policy, questions can be raised whether he is competent to make authoritative judgments on this issue. Some audiences, such as members of the Moral Majority, might argue that he is competent. Other audiences might think differently.

Similar questions can be raised about whether the authority is only presenting his own personal view, or is stating a position held generally by most authorities in a particular field. The issue comes down to whether the authority is making a representative judgment. If other authorities in a field disagree on a given claim, it would weaken the force of the argument. Please note, however, that a lone dissenting authority might turn out to be right and the majority wrong.

Generally, it is desirable to go beyond a warrant from authority when possible and to attempt to discover the basis for the authority's argument. Of course, if we are successful in discovering and validating this argument, the Warrant ceases to be "authority." Often, however, the topic is too abstract, or complex, too densely embedded in preunderstandings to make the basis of the argument readily available and so we rely on the authority's judgment. When most people go to their medical doctor, they are interested in the diagnosis and prescription. Few ask for a full explanation of the doctor's reasons for the diagnosis or the prescription. If we should ask, our ignorance of medical terminology added to our unfamiliarity with biological and physiological and pharmacological processes will make it difficult for us to understand the explanation. The need for at least a primer course in medicine and medical terminology works to discourage patients from examining the doctor's reasons. In such specialized areas this results in a quite legitimate dependence on the authority of the experts.

Principle

Arguments using principle as Warrant are traditionally described as deductive. Although our treatment of argument from principle here looks very much like traditional deduction, there is an important difference. Advocates of deductive argument claim that, if they are validly reasoned and with true premises, the claims of deductive arguments follow of necessity and with certainty. Other critics point out that we cannot presume that claims warranted by principle are necessary or certain. This is the case in practical situations because 1) few principles can be known to be absolutely true or 2) because there may be inadequacies in either the Backing for the principle or in Rebuttals that support the application of the principle.

An argument using principle as warrant relies on a generalization for its backup. Generalizations may suggest universal distributions (all or none) or partial distributions (some, many, most, nearly all, a few, not many, almost none). Arguments based on principles with universal distributions are stronger than those based on partial distributions.

Thus, given the Ground:
    Socrates is a fish.

given the Warrant:
    All fish are mortal.

then the Claim:
    Socrates is mortal. (Qualifier) practically certain

Obviously, given the same Ground, if the Warrant had been that "most fish are mortal," then the Claim would require a greater Qualification from "practically certain" to "probably." Notice also that the Warrant (all fish are mortal) is ultimately backed up by generalization. Throughout human experience there are no reported cases of fish that have lived forever. However, we have noted that generalizing arguments cannot establish absolutely certain Claims. One immortal fish destroys the whole argument. The Claim can be no more certain than the Warrant upon which it is based. Since principles often are based on generalized Backing, they cannot produce certain Claims.

In evaluating an argument from principle, several questions need to be answered. First, is the principle an appropriate one to apply in the particular case? Second, is there adequate Backing for the content of the principle? Third, are there other relevant principles that might be considered?

For example, given the Ground that:
    Being a teacher pays less than being an accountant.

And given the Warranting principle that:
    Occupations should be chosen that provide for maximum economic reward.

Then, the Claim follows:
    Everyone should prefer being an accountant to being a teacher.

However, while few practical people would deny that economic considerations are a part of career choice, many people would deny that "maximum economic reward" is a justified principle and many would argue that other principles such as job satisfaction and potential for personal development are relevant considerations. Actually, a multitude of considerations seem to be relevant, and while an argument can be made from principle that appears "logical," unless audiences accept the principle, there is little persuasive impact. "Principles" are easy to invent and difficult to support, especially when they are not backed by valid generalization or by the traditional values of the audience.

Summary of Classification, Definitions, and Criteria for Appraisal

1. Generalization

From cases: Are there enough cases? Are they representative?

2. Analogy

From a series of comparisons or statement of likeness in the Warrant: Are the similarities important? Do the differences lead to contrary Claims? Are the similarities more or less important than the differences?

3. Sign

From knowledge of Indicator Relation: Is the sign fallible or infallible?

4. Cause

From knowledge of a Cause-and-Effect Relationship: Can the relationship meet the tests of Mill's Canons of Agreement, Difference, and Correlation?

5. Authority

From Competent or Expert Testimony: Is the authority competent or expert in relation to the Claim made? Is the competence accepted by the audience? Is the Claim representative of the individual authority or the field in which the person is acknowledged to be an authority?

6. Principle

From a general statement: What is the basis for the general statement? Is it appropriate? Do other principles apply?

Chapter 9
Counterfeiting: The Fallacies

The Use of Fallacies

A classic illustration of chutzpah (outrageous arrogance) is the man who murdered his mother and father and then threw himself on the mercy of the court because he is an orphan. When we recover from the effrontery of this argument, we recognize quickly enough that it is fallacious, an instance of counterfeit reasoning, but we may have difficulty explaining why. The claim here, that the judge should show mercy because the defendent is parentless, is supported on the obvious grounds that his parents are dead. The principle invoked to serve as Warrant may be stated: it is right and proper to show mercy to the disadvantaged. Implicit in this principle, however, is the condition "through no fault of their own." The defendent is totally responsible for his orphanhood and, moreover, is an emancipated adult. So the appeal *ad misericordiam,* to the principle of mercy, should not apply.

Not all fallacies are this obvious. Identifying types of fallacies protects us against accepting faulty arguments and allows us to explain to ourselves and others why they are faulty. A fallacious Warrant, for example, fails to perform as a Warrant should to connect the grounds with the claim.

In dealing with fallacies there are a few cautions which we ought to observe. 1) Simply putting a label on a fallacy is generally not sufficient. Because fallacies are informal, we must explain why a particular text or argument contains a fallacy. In order to do this effectively, we must mount an argument of our own to show that a fallacy has indeed been committed. Explaining the case of the homicidal orphan is crucial to labeling the Warrant fallacious. 2) We must be on guard against fallacy-hunting. Is there a way in which we can see a given claim, Ground or Warrant as legimate? For example, a patricide in a law court who was deprived and abused as a child by the father he murdered might reasonably enter a plea for mercy with the judge. We must exercise some degree of judgment about whether such a plea is admissible. 3) The knowledge of fallacies might tempt us to use one or another fallacy ourselves in order to make a persuasive case to the unenlightened. To use fallacies deliberately to dupe a reader or a listener is inexcusable. By the same token, we ought to be careful to check our own arguments in what we write for unintentional use of a fallacy to support our case. With these provisos we can examine a number of fallacies which occur frequently in argument. The list here is not all-inclusive or exhaustive, but it does cover frequently occurring instances.

Types of Fallacies

I. Begging the Question:

This fallacy occurs when an argument contains a statement which is based on a prior acceptance of the Claim.

> *Example:* (Background: a theological debate.) Of course God exists, for whence could have come the whole world, if not from an omnipotent Creator.

> *Analysis:* Claim: God exists.
> Ground: The world exists.
> Warrant: The world must have come from an omnipotent Creator.

While the Warrant is clearly necessary to get from the Ground of this "cosmological argument" to the Claim, no one would accept the world as coming from an "omnipotent Creator" if they didn't already accept the existence of God. Thus, this Warrant begs the question. The argument, then, assumes what it set out to prove.

2. Red Herring

This fallacy occurs when an argument "side-tracks" or strays from the relevant issues. It often occurs in debate when one participant wishes not to discuss an issue raised by another participant.

> *Example:* (Background: a debate during the health hazards of smoking.) Why should we worry about smoking and cancer? There are of more immediate hazards to our health, e.g., unsafe automobiles and the rising crime-rate.

> *Analysis:* Claim (implied): We should not waste time debating the health hazards of smoking.
> Ground: There are more immediate hazards to our health, such as unsafe automobiles and the rising crime-rate.
> Warrant (implied): We should expend all our efforts dealing with immediate or short-term hazards and ignore long-run hazards.

This argument is clearly questionable, and if we suspect that the person offering this argument is just trying to avoid the issue of the hazards of smoking, we should cite the arguer for committing the red herring fallacy.

3. Straw man

This fallacy occurs when an argument misrepresents another's argument or position and then attacks the misrepresentation, rather than the relevant argument or position.

> *Example:* (Background: a debate on welfare)
> **Mr. Smith:** "In hard economic times we must not forget those less fortunate in our society. Therefore, when inflation rises, we need to put more federal dollars into welfare programs."
> **Mr. Jones:** "Don't listen to Smith. He's just trying to give everyone a free ride!"

> *Analysis:* There is a notable difference between an expanded welfare program and a "free ride for everyone." Jones has attacked his own straw man, and not Smith's position.

4. Ad hominem

This fallacy occurs when an argument attacks an individual rather than a relevant issue. Slurs on a person's integrity or intelligence are common forms of the *ad hominem* fallacy.

Example: (Background: a political debate over capital punishment.) **Senator Snip:** "Of course Senator Stripe is opposed to capital punishment. What can you expect from a cowardly, knee-jerk liberal?"

Analysis: Here Senator Snip is attacking Senator Stripe personally ("cowardly," "knee-jerk") rather than addressing the relevant issues.

5. Improper appeal to popularity (or to common or past practice)

This fallacy occurs when mere popularity (or the fact that such a thing is or has been commonly done) is appealed to as a reason for adopting a particular conclusion or Claim, and this popularity (common or past practice) is inappropriate as a Ground for that Claim.

Example: (Background: a debate over the 1984 Presidential election.) Of course Reagan is the best candidate. After all, the overwhelming majority of Americans are behind him.

Analysis: Claim: Reagan is the best candidate.
Ground: The majority of Americans are behind him.
Warrant (implied): Any candidate who is popular is the best candidate.

Since, as Lincoln said, "you can fool all of the people some of the time," the implied Warrant commits the fallacy of popularity. Just because a candidate is popular, it doesn't follow that the candidate is the "best" (most politically astute, most concerned with common good, etc.) one.

6. Improper appeal to pity

This fallacy occurs when an argument appeals inappropriately to pity in order to support a Claim or conclusion. Examples of this fallacy occur earlier in this chapter.

7. Improper appeal to authority

This fallacy occurs when a Claim is supported by reference to some authority, and this authority is insufficient to Ground the Claim. Because appeals to authority are so important in argumentation, we must examine this fallacy in a bit more depth than most of the rest. No one knows everything—and cannot be expected to. Thus many arguments must rely upon the testimony of experts. Appeals to authority can be inappropriate for a variety of reasons. Some common instances of this fallacy can be uncovered by asking the following questions:

1. Is the authority cited really an authority? (Some form of peer recognition of the person's status as an authority is important here.)
2. Is the authority cited an authority in a relevant field? (When an advertisement shows us a football player recommending tires or underwear, we should be wary.)
3. Is the authority cited in a position of bias or conflict of interest relative to this argument? (We should always beware of possibly biased opinions. Someone being paid to recommend a product is always suspect.)
4. Is there a concensus among authorities in this field with respect to the Claim being supported? (If not, someone on the other side of the argument can appeal to *another* authority, and the credibility of both appeals in supporting competing Claims is weakened.)
5. Is the authority identified? (If not, we cannot follow up and assess the appeal.)

8. Hasty generalization

This fallacy occurs when an argument seeks to establish a Claim inductively, and there is insufficient evidence (Grounds) to establish that Claim. (This insufficiency is usually a lack of cases cited or a biased selection of cases.)

Example: (Background: a discussion of faculty at the University of X.) Faculty at the University of X are lazy. Why, I've seen many of them lounging around the faculty club every Friday afternoon.

> *Analysis:* Claim: Faculty at the University of X are lazy.
> Ground: Many faculty have been seen lounging around the faculty club every Friday afternoon.
> Warrant (implied): This group is (1) a large enough sampling of (2) representative cases, to warrant a generalization.

The evidence in the Grounds is anecdotal, and probably fails to satisfy both the conditions in the Warrant for the generalization.

9. Fallacy of accident

This fallacy occurs when an argument relies upon a general rule without considering whether the relevant circumstances of the argument might warrant the present case being considered as an *exception* to the rule (and thus a candidate for a **Rebuttal** in terms of the Toulmin Model).

Example: (Background: a discussion of a medical case.) Of course we must give Smith penicillin; he has pneumonia.

> *Analysis:* Claim: We must give Smith penicillin.
> Ground: Smith has pneumonia.
> Warrant (implied): Anyone who has pneumonia should be given penicillin.

The problem with this Warrant is that a sufficient number of people are allergic to penicillin that doctors must first test for the allergy before administering the drug. Otherwise, they run the risk of killing their patient rather than curing him or her.

10. False cause

This fallacy occurs when an argument mistakenly claims something to be the cause of something else. False cause fallacies may be divided into two types: confusion of temporal succession with causation, and mistaken cause.

Example: (Background: a hospital visit.) I'll tell you why you broke your leg. Remember that black cat that crossed your path yesterday?

> *Analysis:* Claim: The black cat's crossing your path was the cause of your breaking your leg.
> Ground 1: A black cat crossed your path yesterday.
> Ground 2: You broke your leg.
> Warrant (implied): A black cat's crossing one's path is the cause of bad luck.

Such superstitions as "if a black cat crosses your path, you'll have bad luck" are the result of confusing the mere temporal succession of two events with causation.

Example: (Background: a PTA meeting, in a debate over educational standards.) I'll tell you why kids aren't learning the basics anymore. It's leniency and lack of discipline in the home.

Analysis: Claim: Ground 1 is the cause of Ground 2.

        Ground 1: There is leniency and lack of discipline in the homes of our children.

        Ground 2: Our kids aren't learning the basics anymore.

        Warrant (implied): Leniency and lack of discipline in the homes makes children unwilling or unable to learn the basics.

Whatever the cause of the recent decline in standard test scores across the U.S.A., it is likely to be complex, involving many factors. Simply to single out one element of our complex social situation as being *the* cause of social change, as the above Warrant does, is too simplistic. During such debates as the one in this example, it is common to hear a number of "simplistic cause" fallacies (such as: it's the teachers; it's the decline of religion; it's the Democrats).

11. Faulty analogy

This fallacy occurs when an argument is based in a weak or non-existent analogy.

Example: (Background: a debate over a nuclear "freeze".) I don't see why everyone is so upset over the atomic bomb. When the crossbow was invented, everyone called it the ultimate weapon and thought there could be no defense against it. The same thing happened with the invention of firearms.

Analysis: Claim (implied): We should not be so upset over the atomic bomb.

        Ground 1: When the crossbow was invented, everyone called it the ultimate weapon and thought there could be no defense against it.

        Ground 2: The same thing (as G1) happened with the invention of firearms.

        Warrant (implied): The crossbow and the firearm are, as cases of "ultimate" weapons, sufficiently like the atomic bomb that we may, by analogy, establish the Claim.

While there may be a need to avoid hysteria about the atomic bomb, the power of atomic fission and fusion are of such an order of magnitude that the analogical application in the Warrant is highly questionable.

12. Poisoning the wells

This fallacy occurs when an argument does not take into consideration evidence which calls an assertion (usually a Warrant) into question. This fallacy might be called the "true believer syndrome," for it occurs when one holds blindly to one position. The True Believer will distort counter-evidence to make it appear to fit his or her argument or position.

Example: (Background: discussion of Freudian psychology in a debate over psychoanalytic techniques.) Of course the Behaviorists will offer you "evidence" that their techniques of psychotherapy are superior to Freudian analysis. But their "evidence" is merely the result of techniques developed by persons with underdeveloped super-egos.

Analysis: Claim (implied): The evidence offered by behaviorists to support the Claim that their method is superior to Freudian analysis is not to be trusted.

        Ground: Behavioral techniques were developed by persons with underdeveloped super-egos.

        Warrant (implied): Persons with underdeveloped super-egos are unreliable judges of psychological evidence.

Note that the Warrant implied here *presupposes* that the theoretical basis of Freudian analysis is somehow true. Notice further that the Ground discredits a competing theory—without evidence or argument. The "poisoning the wells" fallacy involves this sort of *pre*-judging and *pre*-sorting of relevant evidence so that it is never in fact seriously considered.

13. Equivocation

This fallacy occurs when a word or phrase is used in an argument in more than one sense, resulting in a confusion of meanings.

Example: (Background: a debate over prison reform.) Since Americans value freedom, we should free all the poor criminals locked up behind iron bars.

Analysis: Claim: We should free all the poor criminals locked up behind iron bars.
Warrant: Americans value freedom.
Ground (implied): Locking up criminals is incompatible with American values.

The implied Ground here makes it clear that the sense of "freedom" in the Claim and that in the Warrant are in fact different. Part of the freedom Americans value is the freedom from fear of attack; freeing all the criminals would deprive other citizens of this freedom. This sort of uncontrolled polysemy is characteristic of equivocation.

14. Fallacy of composition

This fallacy occurs when an argument attributes some property to a whole or a group, solely upon the Grounds that the property attaches to the parts of that whole or group.

Example: (Background: a political strategy-planning session.) We should seek the support of the Millionaires Club. That club's treasury must be loaded, since every member is rich.

Analysis: Claim: The Millionaires Club treasury must be loaded.
Ground: Every member of the club is rich.
Warrant (implied): If the individual members of a club are rich, then the club must be rich.

The problem here is in the implied Warrant. Just because the individual members of a group are rich, it does not follow that the group, as a group, is also rich. Perhaps the members of the Millionaries Club are all rich skinflints who do not pay their dues.

15. Fallacy of division

This fallacy occurs when an argument attributes some property to the parts of a whole or a group, solely on the Grounds that that property attaches to the whole or to the group as a whole.

Example: John Smith must be rich, for he is a member of the Club Ritz, and that club has a million dollars in its treasury.

Analysis: This example parallels the one used above to explain the fallacy of composition. Just because a group or club, as a group, is well-to-do, it does not follow that every member of the group is rich.

16. Questionable classification

This fallacy occurs when an argument uses a word or phrase to describe or characterize something or someone in a "loaded" or arguable fashion.

Example: (Background: an argument against the acceptability of abortion.) Those doctors who perform abortions are nothing less than murderers.

Analysis: To characterize abortionists as murderers is false, at least in the legal sense. The arguer might be claiming that abortion should be illegal because, according to some "higher law," abortion is murder. Note that the Warrant here (the "higher law") is itself open to debate. But to make this statement as a Ground in such an argument begs the question involved in the debate over abortion. Adjectives, adverbs, and other descriptive qualifiers which indicate such a one-sided view of an issue, fact, or person often beg the question in this manner. Thus many questionable classifications are doubly fallacious.

A Fallacy Analysis of *Civil Disobedience,* First Four Paragraphs

We now apply our knowledge of fallacies to a text, the first four paragraphs of *Civil Disobedience,* to supplement the topological analysis we did in Chapter Five above. Our topological analysis found several analogies (relations of comparison) and many causal claims. Our knowledge of fallacies warns us that analogies and causal claims can be fallacious in texts read as argument. Therefore we should take a closer look at, and assess, these parts of the text. A couple of examples will suffice to illustrate.

At the end of Paragraph 2, Thoreau makes the following analogy between government agents and "mischievous persons":

. . . if one were to judge these [government] men wholly by the effects of their actions and not partly by their intentions, they would deserve to be classified and punished with those mischievous persons who put obstructions on railroads.

The point of this analogy is made clear by the beginning of the sentence (leading up to the beginning of the above quotation) and the sentence preceding it:

For government is an expedient by which men would fain succeed in letting one another alone; and, as has been said, when it is most expedient, the governed are most let alone by it. Trade and commerce, if they were not made of India-rubber, would never manage to bounce over the obstacles which legislators are continually putting in their way; and, if one were to judge the men wholly by the effects of their actions. . . .

Now the analogy is clear: government men, in their job of regulating trade and commerce, create obstacles to trade and commerce much like mischief-makers who throw up obstacles blocking passage on railroads.

Once we have clarified the analogy, we may begin to assess it. Is it fair to compare (setting aside intentions, as Thoreau suggests) the passing of tariff laws, to erecting barricades on a railroad? The point of the analogy seems clear enough: obstacles impede progress. But are the two forms of progress sufficiently comparable to permit this argument by analogy? Trains which run from town to town on time certainly represent progress. But what about totally unrestricted trade

Exerpts from *Civil Disobedience* from *Major Writers of America* by Henry David Thoreau. Harcourt, Brace & World, Inc.

and commerce? Many Americans might not view the complete de-regulation of trade and commerce as progress. Indeed, many of the admittedly troublesome and complex laws governing trade and commerce were passed in order to protect manufacturers, vendors and consumers from unfair business tactics. Therefore one might see Thoreau's Warrant here as based on an unconvincing *analogy.*

In Paragraph 4, Thoreau presents us with a causal claim:

> A common and natural result of an undue respect of law is, that you may see a file of soldiers, colonel, captain, corporal, privates, powder-monkeys, and all, marching in admirable order over hill and dale to the wars against their wills, ay, against their common sense and consciences, which makes it very steep marching indeed, and produces a palpitation of the heart.

Thoreau goes on to suggest that these soldiers, because they have "an undue respect of law," are no longer even human. Let us assess this causal claim. What causes a man to become a soldier? Is it solely "an undue respect of law?" Wartime posters often say, "If you respect the law, fight for your country." Love of life, liberty, homeland and family are all involved in a person's decision to go to war. To claim that all this stems merely from "an undue respect of law" is thus quite possibly a *false cause* fallacy.

A knowledge of fallacies can function, within the Toulmin Model, to provide insight into potentially problematic lines of reasoning based on counterfeit warrants. In the next chapter, we will deal with assessing arguments as wholes and with classifying them by type of claim.

Chapter 10
Closing the Circle: Assessment

Closing the Circle

We have been around this track before; we have dealt with the *parts* of argument as parts—Claim, Grounds, Warrant—and now we are in a position to consider the argument *as a whole*. From our investigation of the text using the general heuristic methodologies, we arrived at an understanding of the meaning of the text which we could then articulate as a thesis and, looking at the text as argument, we saw the thesis as a Claim. We then proceeded to consider the parts of the structure, Grounds and Warrant, in order to evaluate the Claim. Our understanding of the argument is ultimately our considered evaluation of the Claim. Whether the argument is one we have read or one we have constructed, its power resides in an understanding of the Claim as supported by Grounds and Warrant.

At this distance, as we consider whole arguments, it will be helpful to attend to a final set of classifications. Claims are not all alike; they differ according to their object or referent. On this basis we can divide them into four types: **fact, cause, value** and **policy.**

Factual Argument

A factual argument deals with a Claim which is a statement about an actuality, past or present. In this type the Claim proposes that such and such is so and attempts to demonstrate that equation. Note that the argument insists that its Claim is a fact; it does not presume it. If the Claim were universally accepted as fact, there would be no need to argue it. In the *Apology,* Socrates maintains that his accuser Meletus has not thought carefully about his allegations. In a murder trial, the question is whether Mr. X, the defendant, actually committed the murder. These Claims have to do with an actual present situation or an actual past event. Because the Claims deal with facts, it is highly unlikely that everyone will be absolutely convinced by any given argument; if the issue were plain, no argument would be possible. For instance, almost no one takes seriously an argument that the earth is flat or that the sun revolves around the earth. There was a time when both these propositions was controversial, but today they are dead issues. When, then, we argue about actualities, we attempt to muster the best evidence and the strongest Warrant for the facticity of our Claim, knowing full well that our argument will probably not finally settle the issue.

Causal Arguments

Causal Arguments might well be considered as a sub-class of factual arguments. We might, for instance, claim that it is a fact that smoking causes cancer. On the other hand, we can separate causal claims from factual claims in that causal claims are more complex and require a different treatment. The factual claim makes a statement about *what* exists or has existed. The causal claim makes a statement about *why* it exists or did exist. As a result there are at least two *factual* sub-claims to any *causal* claim. First, we may have to establish the cause as existent and describe its operation. Second, we might have to do the same for the effect. Then we must establish their relationship: that the first produces the second. This is complex because causality is not directly observable. What we observe is a sequence of events; we put a pot of water over the fire and the water boils or a moving billiard ball hits a stationary ball and both roll off in different directions. We do not see the fire causing the water to boil or the moving billiard ball transferring its energy to the stationary one. We remarked above, in Chapter Five, on the difficulty of establishing causal relationships in human behavior; establishing that Mr. X. committed a murder is much simpler than explaining why he did it. Causal claims are difficult to establish and often the best argument will result only in strong probability.

Value Arguments

A value argument involves a Claim that affirms or denies the worth of an entity or an action. The terms of the argument may be variants of "good" and "bad." For example, to state that an action or an institution or a physical object is beneficial or harmful, advantageous or disadvantageous, desirable or undesirable would be to make a value claim about it. The value of a thing is ordinarily determined by its effectiveness in achieving its purpose; a pistol is "good" if it shoots straight, a government is "good" if it promotes the welfare of its citizens, a voluntary action is "good" if it benefits both the doer and society. It is clear that there are different kinds of "goods" and that it is very important, in any value claim, to define its terms. Freedom is good, but my physical freedom to swing my fist ends morally at the point of your nose. Freedom of expression is good, but to exercise that freedom by shouting "fire" in a crowded theater is not. Ordinarily, we support value claims by factual and/or causal sub-arguments.

Policy Arguments

Policy arguments make a Claim that some action should be taken or avoided. Policy claims always concern future action. As such, they are the most complex of all argumentative claims and usually involve fact, value, and causal sub-claims in the development of the case. The complexity of the policy claim becomes clear when we consider that it is generally proposed to solve a problem. We need, then, to understand the problem we wish to solve—what it is and why it exists. So factual and causal claims become sub-arguments. Proposing an action to solve a problem also implies that current strategies for addressing the problem are inadequate and this requires a value argument. So, once the problem is defined and explained and the present situation evaluated, it remains to be demonstrated that a solution is possible, that the solution will actually reduce or eliminate the problem and that the means it proposes are good. In addressing an issue of policy, then, we will tend to draw on all the argument types we have considered here.

Let us look at an example of a text that contains both a value argument and a policy argument.

Pericles' Funeral Speech

Thucydides

1 In the same winter the Athenians, following their annual custom, gave a public funeral for those who had been the first to die in the war. These funerals are held in the following way: two days before the ceremony the bones of the fallen are brought and put in a tent which has been erected, and people make whatever offerings they wish to their own dead. Then there is a funeral procession in which coffins of cypress wood are carried on wagons. There is one coffin for each tribe, which contains the bones of members of that tribe. One empty bier is decorated and carried in the procession: this is for the missing, whose bodies could not be recovered. Everyone who wishes to, both citizens and foreigners, can join in the procession, and the women who are related to the dead are there to make their laments at the tomb. The bones are laid in the public burial-place, which is in the most beautiful quarter outside the city walls. Here the Athenians always bury those who have fallen in war. The only exception is those who died at Marathon, who, because their achievement was considered absolutely outstanding, were buried on the battlefield itself.

2 When the bones have been laid in the earth, a man chosen by the city for his intellectual gifts and for his general reputation makes an appropriate speech in praise of the dead, and after the speech all depart. This is the procedure at these burials, and all through the war, when the time came to do so, the Athenians followed this ancient custom. Now, at the burial of those who were the first to fall in the war Pericles, the son of Xanthippus, was chosen to make the speech. When the moment arrived, he came forward from the tomb and, standing on a high platform, so that he might be heard by as many people as possible in the crowd, he spoke as follows:

3 "Many of those who have spoken here in the past have praised the institution of this speech at the close of our ceremony. It seemed to them a mark of honour to our soldiers who have fallen in war that a speech should be made over them. I do not agree. These men have shown themselves valiant in action, and it would be enough, I think, for their glories to be proclaimed in action, as you have just seen it done at this funeral organized by the state. Our belief in the courage and manliness of so many should not be hazarded on the goodness or badness of one man's speech. Then it is not easy to speak with a proper sense of balance, when a man's listeners find it difficult to believe in the truth of what one is saying. The man who knows the facts and loves the dead may well think that an oration tells less than what he knows and what he would like to hear: others who do not know so much may feel envy for the dead, and think the orator over-praises them, when he speaks of exploits that are beyond their own capacities. Praise of other people is tolerable only up to a certain point, the point where one believes that one could do oneself some of the things one is hearing about. Once you get beyond this point, you will find people becoming jealous and incredulous. However, the fact is that this institution was set up and approved by our forefathers, and it is my duty to follow the tradition and do my best to meet the wishes and the expectations of every one of you.

4 "I shall begin by speaking about our ancestors, since it is only right and proper on such an occasion to pay them the honour of recalling what they did. In this land of ours there have always been the same people living from generation to generation up till now, and they, by their courage and their virtues, have handed it on to us, a free country. They certainly deserve our praise. Even more so do our fathers deserve it. For to the inheritance they had received they added all the empire we have now, and it was not without blood and toil that they handed it down to us of the present generation. And then we ourselves, assembled here today, who are mostly in the prime of life, have, in most directions, added to the power of our empire and have organized our State in such a way that it is perfectly well able to look after itself both in peace and in war.

Pericles' Funeral Oration from THUCYDIDES' HISTORY OF THE PELOPONNESIAN WAR, translated by Rex Warner (Penguin Classics, 1954, 1972), copyright (©) Rex Warner, 1954, pp. 143–151.

5 "I have no wish to make a long speech on subjects familiar to you all: so I shall say nothing about the warlike deeds by which we acquired our power or the battles in which we or our fathers gallantly resisted our enemies, Greek or foreign. What I want to do is, in the first place, to discuss the spirit in which we faced our trials and also our constitution and the way of life which has made us great. After that I shall speak in praise of the dead, believing that this kind of speech is not inappropriate to the present occasion, and that this whole assembly, of citizens and foreigners, may listen to it with advantage.

6 "Let me say that our system of government does not copy the institutions of our neighbours. It is more the case of our being a model to others, than of our imitating anyone else. Our constitution is called a democracy because power is in the hands not of a minority but of the whole people. When it is a question of settling private disputes, everyone is equal before the law; when it is a question of putting one person before another in positions of public responsibility, what counts is not membership of a particular class, but the actual ability which the man possesses. No one, so long as he has it in him to be of service to the state, is kept in political obscurity because of poverty. And, just as our political life is free and open, so is our day-to-day life in our relations with each other. We do not get into a state with our next-door neighbour if he enjoys himself in his own way, nor do we give him the kind of black looks which, though they do no real harm, still do hurt people's feelings. We are free and tolerant in our private lives; but in public affairs we keep to the law. This is because it commands our deep respect.

7 "We give our obedience to those whom we put in positions of authority, and we obey the laws themselves, especially those which are for the protection of the oppressed, and those unwritten laws which it is an acknowledged shame to break.

8 "And here is another point. When our work is over, we are in a position to enjoy all kinds of recreation for our spirits. There are various kinds of contests and sacrifices regularly throughout the year; in our own homes we find a beauty and a good taste which delight us every day and which drive away our cares. Then the greatness of our city brings it about that all the good things from all the world flow in to us, so that to us it seems just as natural to enjoy foreign goods as our own local products.

9 "Then there is a great difference between us and our opponents in our attitude towards military security. Here are some examples: Our city is open to the world, and we have no periodical deportations in order to prevent people observing and finding out secrets which might be of military advantage to the enemy. This is because we rely, not on secret weapons, but on our own real courage and loyalty. There is a difference, too, in our educational systems. The Spartans, from their earliest boyood, are submitted to the most laborious training in courage; we pass our lives without all these restrictions, and yet are just as ready to face the same dangers as they are. Here is proof of this: When the Spartans invade our land, they do not come by themselves, but bring all their allies with them; whereas we, when we launch an attack abroad, do the job ourselves, and, though fighting on foreign soil, do not often fail to defeat opponents who are fighting for their own hearths and homes. As a matter of fact, none of our enemies has ever yet been confronted with our total strength, because we have to divide our attention between our navy and the many missions on which our troops are sent on land. Yet, if our enemies engage a detachment of our forces and defeat it, they give themselves credit for having thrown back our entire army; or, if they lose, they claim that they were beaten by us in full strength. There are certain advantages, I think, in our way of meeting danger voluntarily, with an easy mind, instead of with a laborious training, with natural rather than with state-induced courage. We do not have to spend our time practising to meet sufferings which are still in the future; and when they are actually upon us show ourselves just as brave as these others who are always in strict training. This is one point in which, I think, our city deserves to be admired. There are also others:

10 "Our love of what is beautiful does not lead to extravagance; our love of the things of the mind does not make us soft. We regard wealth as something to be properly used, rather than as something to boast about. As for poverty, no one need be ashamed to admit it: the real shame is in not taking practical measures to escape from it. Here each individual is interested not only in his own affairs but in the affairs of the state as well: even those who are mostly occupied with their own business are extremely well-informed on general politics—this is a peculiarity of ours: we do not say that a man who takes no interest in politics is a man who minds his own business; we say that he has no business here at all. We Athenians, in our own persons, take our decisions on policy or submit them to proper discussions: for we do not think that there is an incompatibility between words and deeds; the worst thing is to rush into action before the consequences have been properly debated. And this is another point where we differ from other people. We are capable at the same time of taking risks and of estimating them beforehand. Others are brave out of ignorance; and, when they stop to think, they begin to fear. But the man who can most truly be accounted brave is he who knows the meaning of what is sweet in life and of what is terrible, and then goes out undeterred to meet what is to come.

11 "Again, in questions of general good feeling there is a great contrast between us and most other people. We make friends by doing good to others, not by receiving good from them. This makes our friendship all the more reliable, since we want to keep alive the gratitude of those who are in our debt by showing continued goodwill to them: whereas the feelings of one who owes us something lack the same enthusiasm, since he knows that, when he repays our kindness, it will be more like paying back a debt than giving something spontaneously. We are unique in this. When we do kindnesses to others, we do not do them out of any calculations of profit or loss: we do them without afterthought, relying on our free liberality. Taking everything together then, I declare that our city is an education to Greece, and I declare that in my opinion each single one of our citizens, in all the manifold aspects of life, is able to show himself the rightful lord and owner of his own person, and do this, moreover, with exceptional grace and exceptional versatility. And to show that this is no empty boasting for the present occasion, but real tangible fact, you have only to consider the power which our city possesses and which has been won by those very qualities which I have mentioned. Athens, alone of the states we know, comes to her testing time in a greatness that surpasses what was imagined of her. In her case, and in her case alone, no invading enemy is ashamed at being defeated, and no subject can complain of being governed by people unfit for their responsibilities. Mighty indeed are the marks and monuments of our empire which we have left. Future ages will wonder at us, as the present age wonders at us now. We do not need the praises of a Homer, or of anyone else whose words may delight us for the moment, but whose estimation of facts will fall short of what is really true. For our adventurous spirit has forced an entry into every sea and into every land; and everywhere we have left behind us everlasting memorials of good done to our friends or suffering inflicted on our enemies.

12 "This, then, is the kind of city for which these men, who could not bear the thought of losing her, nobly fought and nobly died. It is only natural that every one of us who survive them should be willing to undergo hardships in her service. And it was for this reason that I have spoken at such length about our city, because I wanted to make it clear that for us there is more at stake than there is for the others who lack our advantages; also I wanted my words of praise for the dead to be set in the bright light of evidence. And now the most important of these words has been spoken. I have sung the praises of our city; but it was the courage and gallantry of these men, and of people like them, which made her splendid. Nor would you find it true in the case of many of the Greeks, as it is true of them, that no words can do more than justice to their deeds.

13 "To me it seems that the consummation which has overtaken these men shows us the meaning of manliness in its first revelation and in its final proof. Some of them, no doubt, had their faults; but what we ought to remember first is their gallant conduct against the enemy in defence of their native land. They have blotted out evil with good, and done more service to the commonwealth than they ever did harm in their private lives. No one of these men weakened because he wanted to go on enjoying his wealth: no one put off the awful day in the hope that he might live to escape his poverty and grow rich. More to be desired than such things, they chose to check the enemy's pride. This, to them, was a risk most glorious, and they accepted it, willing to strike down the enemy and relinquish everything else. As for success or failure, they left that in the doubtful hands of Hope, and when the reality of battle was before their faces, they put their trust in their own selves. In the fighting, they thought it more honourable to stand their ground and suffer death than to give in and save their lives. So they fled from the reproaches of men, abiding with life and limb the brunt of battle; and, in a small moment of time, the climax of their lives, a culmination of glory, not of fear, were swept away from us.

14 "So and such they were, these men—worthy of their city. We who remain behind may hope to be spared their fate, but must resolve to keep the same daring spirit against the foe. It is not simply a question of estimating the advantages in theory. I could tell you a long story (and you know it as well as I do) about what is to be gained by beating the enemy back. What I would prefer is that you should fix your eyes every day on the greatness of Athens as she really is, and should fall in love with her. When you realize her greatness, then reflect that what made her great was men with a spirit of adventure, men who knew their duty, men who were ashamed to fall below a certain standard. If they ever failed in an enterprise, they made up their minds that at any rate the city should not find their courage lacking to her, and they gave to her the best contribution that they could. They gave her their lives, to her and to all of us, and for their own selves they won praises that never grow old, the most splendid of sepulchres—not the sepulchre in which their bodies are laid, but where their glory remains eternal in men's minds, always there on the right occasion to stir others to speech or to action. For famous men have the whole earth as their memorial: it is not only the inscriptions on their graves in their own country that mark them out; no, in foreign lands also, not in any visible form but in people's hearts, their memory abides and grows. It is for you to try to be like them. Make up your minds that happiness depends on being free, and freedom depends on being courageous. Let there be no relaxation in face of the perils of the war. The people who have most excuse for despising death are not the wretched and unfortunate, who have no hope of doing well for themselves, but those who run the risk of a complete reversal in their lives, and who would feel the difference most intensely, if things went wrong for them. Any intelligent man would find a humiliation caused by his own slackness more painful to bear than death, when death comes to him unperceived, in battle, and in the confidence of his patriotism.

15 "For these reasons I shall not commiserate with those parents of the dead, who are present here. Instead I shall try to comfort them. They are well aware that they have grown up in a world where there are many changes and chances. But this is good fortune—for men to end their lives with honour, as these have done, and for you honourably to lament them: their life was set to a measure where death and happiness went hand in hand. I know that it is difficult to convince you of this. When you see other people happy you will often be reminded of what used to make you happy too. One does not feel sad at not having some good thing which is outside one's experience: real grief is felt at the loss of something which one is used to. All the same, those of you who are of the right age must bear up and take comfort in the thought of having more children. In your own homes these new children will prevent you from brooding over those who are no more, and they will be a help to the city, too, both in filling the empty places, and in assuring her security. For it is impossible for a man to put forward fair and honest views about our affairs if he has not, like everyone else, children whose lives may be at stake. As for those of you who are now too old to have children, I would ask you to count as gain the greater part of your life, in which you have been happy, and remember that what remains is not long, and let your hearts be lifted up at the thought of the fair fame of the dead. One's sense of honour is the only thing that does not grow old, and the last pleasure, when one is worn out with age, is not, as the poet said, making money, but having the respect of one's fellow men.

16 "As for those of you here who are sons or brothers of the dead, I can see a hard struggle in front of you. Everyone always speaks well of the dead, and, even if you rise to the greatest heights of heroism, it will be a hard thing for you to get the reputation of having come near, let alone equalled, their standard. When one is alive, one is always liable to the jealousy of one's competitors, but when one is out of the way, the honour one receives is sincere and unchallenged.

17 "Perhaps I should say a word or two on the duties of women to those among you who are now widowed. I can say all I have to say in a short word of advice. Your great glory is not to be inferior to what God has made you, and the greatest glory of a woman is to be least talked about by men, whether they are praising you or criticizing you. I have now, as the law demanded, said what I had to say. For the time being our offerings to the dead have been made, and for the future their children will be supported at the public expense by the city, until they come of age. This is the crown and prize which she offers, both to the dead and to their children, for the ordeals they have faced. Where the rewards of valour are the greatest, there you will find also the best and bravest spirits among the people. And now, when you have mourned for your dear ones, you must depart."

Toulmin Analysis of Pericles' Funeral Oration

This piece is at one level not an argument at all, but a celebration of Athenian life (and death). It is a classic instance of **epideictic** or ceremonial rhetoric. Nonetheless, most any piece of literature which can be read as epideictic can also be read as argument—an argument for the *status quo*. In this case, the speech will be read as an argument for the Athenian way of life and government. It was delivered at a funeral for war dead, in the midst of a war which would obviously continue. Therefore, in celebrating the dead, Pericles was also stirring the Athenian spirit by reasoned dialectic, by giving **reasons** as well as citing values to convince the Athenians that they must continue the war, if necessary, to preserve the Athenian way of life.

Note how, for the most part, Pericles emphasizes the Grounds of his "arguments," leaving the audience to fill in the Warrants. He relies upon the audience to recognize their common values. In the same way that teachers sometimes help students to learn and remember by getting them to arrive at answers and meanings by themselves through the skilled use of leading questions, the skilled orator often reinforces social values by using them as unstated but implied Warrants. Only an audience with a knowledge of Athenian values could fully appreciate the strength of this argument.

The main line of argument breaks down into two separate lines:

(A) (Value argument)
Claim: Athens' form of government is admirable and worth maintaining.

(B) (Policy Argument)
Claim: You (the audience) must make whatever sacrifices necessary to maintain Athens' independence in the continuing war.

The overall structure of the oration breaks down this way:
  I. Introduction praise of ancestors, and of the audience. (This, too, can be read as argument.)
 II. Value argument (A)
III. Policy argument (B)

Here we will analyze the first two arguments (actually, sets of arguments), and only sketch the third.

I. Introduction

The introduction can be read as presenting three arguments, one in praise of the audience, one in praise of their fathers (the elders), and one in praise of their ancestors. The arguments are presented modestly (note the ethos and pathos in this—modesty is a value which plays a great role in the following arguments), in the opposite order.

Claim: Our ancestors deserve commendation.
Ground: By this valor our ancestors won the freedom Athenians currently enjoy.
[Unstated but implied Warrant: Liberty is to be valued.]

Claim: Our fathers deserve great commendation.
Ground: Our fathers maintained the liberty they inherited.
Ground: Our fathers maintained this liberty through great labor of their own (through war with barbarians and other Greeks).

[Implied Warrant: Anyone who maintains a free government through great labor, and passes that government on to their descendents in freedom, deserves high commendation.]
[Implied Claim: We ourselves deserve commendation.]
Ground: We ourselves have added to the strength of Athens [through war with barbarians and other Greeks—recall the occasion].
[Implied warrant: Anyone increasing the strength of a great nation deserves commendation.]

Note that the information about the epideictic purpose of the speech, honoring the war dead, is provided in the introduction by Thucydides and in Pericles' own introduction: thus we need not go "beyond the text" to figure out how to interpret this text as argument.

II. The Value Argument

This argument takes up most of the speech. The following interpretation of the value argument in the oration identifies fifteen major Grounds, with seven of these supported by sub-arguments. All of the major statements of the argument are Grounds, with the Warrants left to be supplied by the audience. We will list the stated Claim and Grounds of the argument, and will merely "sketch" in the missing Warrants.

Claim: Athens' form of government is admirable and worth maintaining.

G1:   The government of Athens is a democracy.
[UW: Democracy is an admirable form of government.]

G2:   Athenians confer dignities upon men not because of their house [class or inherited status] but because of their virtue or ability.
[UW: Virtue/ability is more valuable than wealth or a famous family name.]

G3:   Athenians are not kept from service to the state because of poverty.
[UW: [Good] men are more valuable than rich ones.]

G4:   Athenians are tolerant of others who differ from them.
[UW: Tolerance is good/valued.]

G5:   Athenians are obedient to the laws and to those that govern.
[UW: Obedience to [good] laws and governors is good.]

G6:   Athenians are obedient to the unwritten laws, the breaking of which brings shame to the transgressors.
[UW: Shame is bad/to be avoided.]

G7:   Athenians enjoy many forms of recreation to keep them happy.
[UW: "All work and no play makes Jack a dull boy."]

G8:   Athens imports goods from all over the world for our enjoyment.
[UW: Cosmopolitanism is good. (Compare this with the last Warrant, above.)]

G9:   Athenians' studies of war ["military security" in another translation] are superior to those of our enemies.

[UW: Superior understanding of matters of war is good.]

G10:   Athenians love bravery ["beauty" in another translation!], but are not extravagant.

[UW: Bravery/beauty is good.]

[UW: Extravagance is bad.]

G11:   Athenians love things of the mind, but without mollification["softness" in other translation] of the mind.

[UW: Intelligence is good/valued.]

[UW: Mollification/softness is bad.]

G12:   Athenians admire wealth as something to be used [action, utility] rather than for boasting about[words, *hubris*].

[UW: Action, usefulness are good.]

[UW: "Mere words" (*hubris*) are bad.]

G13:   Athenians are interested not only in their own affairs, but also in those of the state.

[UW: In a democratic state, citizens should be interested in the state's afffairs.]

G14:   Athenians submit their policy decisions to *proper* discussion. [Note: this may be a stated Warrant ('proper').]

[UW: Proper discussion of policy decisions is good.]

G15:   Athens differs [for the better] from other states "in matter of bounty" [other translation: "in questions of general good feeling"].

[UW: Bounty/good feeling is good.]

III. The Policy Argument

For (B), what is needed is simply to show:

Claim: You (the audience) must make whatever sacrifices necessary to maintain Athens' independence in the continuing war.

Warrant: (Result of value argument): Athens' form of government is admirable and worth maintaining.

Ground: If you struggle bravely, you can maintain Athens' form of government.

Note the form of the shift from the value argument to the policy argument: (1) You can (G); (2) you must (W); therefore (3) you should (C). This is common to policy arguments: it is only fair to ask people to do what they *can* do, as well as what they *should* do.

In examining the Pericles text, we discovered that the policy argument is supported by the value argument as the two are supported by factual and causal sub-arguments. To see the policy argument as the large issue is to understand the text as whole; Pericles is arguing for maintaining Athen's form of government through sacrifice and struggle.

Argumentative Structures

In discussing types of argument in the Pericles text, we noted that their treatment can be complex. We need to consider the different structures, more or less complex, that shape the arguments we will encounter in our reading and construct in our writing.

The Single Argument Structure

In a text structured by a single argument, there is only one Claim being made and only one supporting argument for it. For example, if a text argues that the United States should take early military action against the Soviet Union now to prevent World War III, the evidence might include a series of historical situations such as those surrounding World War I and World War II. Such a text could be lengthy, but would develop only one major argument. The single argument structure lends itself essentially to one Toulmin Model diagram.

THE SINGLE ARGUMENT STRUCTURE

Backing

Grounds—Warrant—(Qualifier)   Claim

Rebuttal

The Series Argument Structure

Much more common than the single argument is the series structure in which each argument in the series supports the same claim. However, the Grounds and Warrant of each argument in the series are different. Thus, a diagram of a series would include several different Toulmin Model elements sharing a common claim. For example, if in addition to the inductive argument made for military intervention in the example above, the same Claim were also supported by a series of comparisons showing how the historical instances were similar to the present situation, then a second argument from analogy would emerge. If a third argument were to be added based on treaty commitments with the involved nations, the Claim would be further supported by an argument from principle. In such a series, it often happens that each argument taken alone has weaknesses, but their convergence in support of the same claim renders it more convincing.

THE SERIES OF ARGUMENTS STRUCTURE

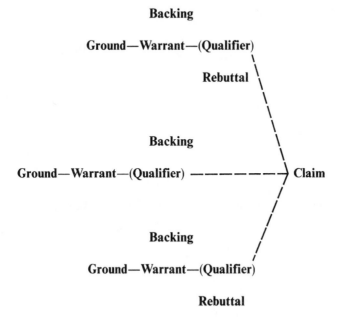

Backing

Ground—Warrant—(Qualifier)

Rebuttal

Backing

Ground—Warrant—(Qualifier) — — — — — → Claim

Backing

Ground—Warrant—(Qualifier)

Rebuttal

The Chain Argument Structure

As the name indicates in this arrangement each argument hangs on the one before it. So the Claim of an initial argument becomes the Ground for the Claim of the next argument, and the final Claim of the chain is the overall thesis of the text—the point of the whole argument. Chain arguments are necessary when an audience does not accept the Grounds for a Claim. In order to move to a Claim which the audience is not inclined to accept, the chain moves back to a more easily substantiated Claim which the audience is more likely to accept. It then uses this Claim to support the next. How many links the Chain requires depends on the nature of the Claim and the makeup of the audience. Another use of the chain structure is to take a Claim which seems bold, extreme, or too encompassing and break it into smaller and more easily arguable Claims. Pericles' argument in the Funeral Oration uses the chain structure. Thoreau's thesis in *Civil Disobedience,* too, is such a Claim: there are times when a citizen is obligated to disobey legitimate authority. The traditional position that the citizen's responsibility is to obey makes it necessary to argue the case for the opposite step-by-step. In causal argumentation, chains of argument are very common.

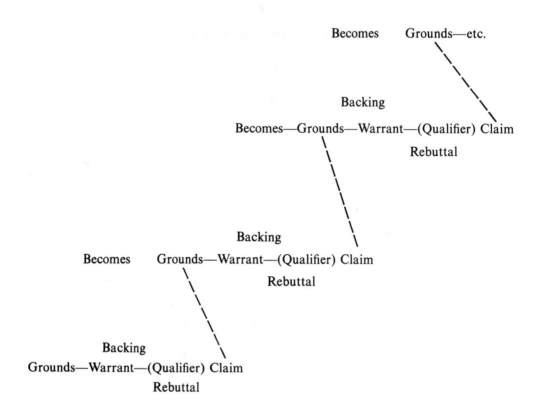

Series and Chains

It is always possible that a text will combine two of the above structures. If a Warrant of an argument is critical to it and highly controversial, the backing for that Warrant might take either the series or the chain form. A series structure could be a series of chains (each chain has a common Claim, but the chains do not link to each other). Noting the way in which a complex argument is structured is a valuable help to understanding the argument as a whole and a help to any explanation of the whole argument we might be attempting to make.

Evaluating the Argument

After we have a basic understanding of the arguments a text makes, and have identified the type of Claim and the structure supporting the Claim, we are in a position to evaluate the whole argument. Ultimately we are interested in whether or not an intelligent reader or audience should accept the Claim. Evaluating an argument is not the same as agreeing or disagreeing with a Claim.

In evaluating an argument we are simply saying that—given these Grounds, Warrants, Backing and Rebuttals—this particular Claim is, to some degree, worthy of belief or not. We may agree with the Claim, but find the argument for it unsound. For instance, we might agree with the Claim in *Civil Disobedience* that citizens sometimes have an obligation to disobey the law, but find Thoreau's Grounds and Warrant for this Claim unconvincing. We might, on the other hand, disagree with the Claim that military action now against the Soviet Union would prevent greater damage in the future, while admitting that an argument based on earlier historical situations makes a good case for the Claim. In short, we want to appraise the argument on its own terms according to appropriate standards of evaluation.

Some general standards for evaluation are:

1. The argument should be complete with Claim, Grounds and Warrant and any sub-arguments necessary to substantiate the Claim.
2. The argument should be clear with appropriate definitions and divisions of all the main terms.
3. The Grounds, Warrant, Backing and Rebuttal should be verified and sufficient to establish the Claim; if authoritative sources are used as Grounds, those sources should be identified and documented.

Making these appraisals depends in part on 1) classifying the argument in terms of the kind of Claim—fact, cause, value, policy—it makes and the sort of Warrant—GASCAP—it uses and also on 2) checking the structure of the argument. An argument which meets these internal criteria is a strong argument. Another approach to the evaluation of argument uses an external criterion.

This approach considers consequences, logical or practical, to which the Claim of the argument would lead. If, for instance, early military action in a preemptive war would lead to nuclear destruction for the planet, we might be unwilling to accept the Claim, even though the argument for preemptive military action were strong. Thoreau's claim that every citizen should be morally responsible for the actions of government might lead to a prison system full of political offenders; if every citizen were to decide what laws were fair, chaos might result. So if the consequences of accepting a Claim lead to inconsistencies or contradictions with other systems or to absurdity, then considering the consequences might lead us to reject the Claim.

When we turn from appraising arguments to writing our own evaluation of those arguments we ought to note that, if we are using internal criteria to evaluate the Claim, our own Claim will be factual. It is a question of fact whether or not the given Claim meets the standards of completeness, clarity, truth and connectedness. If we are using the argument from consequences, our own Claim will be a causal claim. That is, we will be arguing that the Claim in question leads to good or bad consequences.

Writing an Argument about an Argument

When we are dealing with an argument in a written text, it is our responsibility, in the first place, to understand the argument being proposed. In this section we have spent a good deal of time on how to analyze a text as argument. Once we are able to identify Claim, Ground and

Warrant and to evaluate the argument with the help of this analysis, we are prepared to write an argument in response to the argument of the text.

There are three basic approaches to responding to an argument of the text.

1. We may attempt to refute the Claim or argument of the text.
2. We might support the Claim of the text by additional arguments or by providing additional Grounds, Warrants or Backing to the argument.
3. We might use the Claim of the text as a Ground, Warrant or Backing for a Claim of our own.

It is probably necessary to repeat that all these approaches require an understanding of the argument of the text; we can not refute or support what we fail to understand.

If we attempt to refute the Claim, we can use either internal or external criteria. We can expose fallacies in the text or discover inadequacies in the Grounds or the Warrant in support of a Claim that is not adequately qualified. We can introduce rebuttals to the original argument by introducing arguments which support a contrary or contradictory Claim to the one made in the text. In refuting a Claim we should be careful to give the argument in the text the benefit of the doubt so that we are not arguing against a straw man.

If we are supporting the Claim in the text, we can supply more precise Grounds or more Backing for the Warrant or we can add a new series of arguments by providing additional Grounds and additional Warrants. In arguing a case for *Civil Disobedience,* for instance, we might review the civil rights movement, the protests against the Viet Nam war, the nuclear disarmament movement as additional Grounds supporting the Claim that citizens have a moral responsibility to disobey particular laws. The Warrant might be the principle that the government does not have the authority to enact or enforce unjust laws. It may be that we support the Claim of a text for different reasons than those articulated in the text. So we might discard Thoreau's argument for civil disobedience and build our own.

Finally, when we believe that a text has strongly established a particular Claim, we may use that Claim as Ground or Warrant or Backing in an argument of our own with a new Claim. When we are writing a paper in a particular course, history or political science or chemistry, we are entitled to build our argument on the Claims made by previous scholars. Our research on a given topic in one of those areas involves analyzing other texts written on the topic and evaluating the arguments in them. We can then use the results of previous research to support our own Claim. This is the way a "research paper" relates to argumentation. By gathering and analyzing data from experiments or from primary texts or from secondary sources, we come to understandings of our own relative to the topic. These understandings we articulate in a thesis which then becomes the Claim of our argument. The reading and analysis we have done can then be used as Grounds in support of our Claim. The new Claim that we propose in our own text depends on our own insight into the material we have gathered and analyzed. In this way all argumentation focused on a new Claim moves us into a realm of self-expression as the argument we develop represents our own insight and understanding.

In the following section we will attend in detail to this self-expressive aspect of texts. Just as we can view a text as expository or as argumentative, so we can view the same text as self-expressive. This aspect of the text views its world as artifact, that is, as a creation of a mind and of an imagination. With this consideration we round out the perspectives that texts offer, that engage the attention of the literate mind.

Book Three

The Literate Mind and the World as Artifact: Reading and Writing from the Perspective of Self-Expression

Chapter 11
Text as Artifact

Introduction

Any text which we encounter is an artifact. It is a collection of words, phrases, sentences arranged in a unique way. It is a system of signs that conveys meaning. There are no texts in nature; there are only objects. So a text is a made thing the purpose of which is to communicate. We have looked at texts as they are expository, that is, as they inform and explain; we have considered texts as argumentative, that is, as they attempt to persuade. We now wish to consider them as they are works of art or craft, that is, as they are a construct of the human imagination and language.

When we say that a text is a construct, we acknowledge that it is built of words put together in a selective order. If there were, as the beer commercial insists, one word that really said it all, we would have only a single text comprised of a single word. But, in fact, our experience is too complex and too extensive to be captured in a single word, a single sentence, or a single work. Texts as artifact construct our experience of a complex world.

We could, if we wished, go back to the texts we studied in the first semester. The description of the Roman Legion, for example, tells us how the Legion was constituted, what its parts were, and how it functioned. Looking at this text as artifact, we see that it contains a judgment, that it implies that the Legion was a superior fighting force, better adapted to the job than other military organizations. So the text not only gives details about the Roman Legion; it also delivers an opinion on the Legion's effectiveness. When we consider Turner's text on the frontier, we discover that it is so arranged that the qualities induced in the American character by the frontier experience are the qualities we most prize: individualism, a spirit of independence, a love of freedom, practicality and resourcefulness. Joan Didion's "On Keeping a Notebook" is even more to the point here; this text is clearly an artifact. It tells us that we keep a notebook to keep in touch with ourselves. It gives us a series of examples of how reading over our past entries enable us to recall the people we were. The entries that the text presents include, not only what was, but what might have been, and, for purposes of getting in touch with the self, there is no appreciable difference between the two. So, in this text we are offered the opinion that our memories are artifacts, constructed from details—actual or imaginary. The Didion text itself exemplifies the opinion which it expresses. It contains selections from here and there among the notebook entries and orders them in a way that creates for us an impression of the "I" of the work. We understand, then, that what is *given* in the text is also *created* by the text.

When we consider a text as artifact, our inspectional reading will allow us to view what the text says as an opinion or judgment. Our preunderstanding will include the notion that the text is saying "I think that . . . ," or "We believe that . . . ," or "In my judgment it is the case that. . . ." Built into the text is an evaluation of the world the text proposes. Often this evaluation is presented in terms of the experience of the "I" of the text. For instance, in *Civil Disobedience* there is a section relating the experience of a night in prison and the effects of that experience.

The unique and individual nature of this description can be viewed as evidence for the thesis of the work; it is also clearly a basis for a judgment about the relationship between the individual and the commonwealth. A night in prison, as anyone will attest who has been there, can create a myriad of different impressions. In *Civil Disobedience* the text offers specific impressions about that experience which fit the judgment the text is leveling at the community.

So when the text engages an object, idea, or situation from the actual world of experience, as artifact it includes an opinion or a judgment about the object, idea, or situation. One way of articulating this view of the text is to say that it is self-expressive. The "self" is recognizable in the text precisely in the opinion or judgment expressed. Looking at this feature of self-expression from the point of view of the writing enterprise, the "self" expressed in our own composition appears in exactly the same way; it is an opinion or a judgment which we attempt to express through our compositional strategies. It may help to consider an example of a text from the point of view of self-expressive artifact.

Oxford as I See It

. . . Yet in spite of its dilapidated buildings and its lack of fire-escapes, ventilation, sanitation, and up-to-date kitchen facilities, I persist in my assertion that I believe that Oxford, in its way, is the greatest university in the world. I am aware that this is an extreme statement and needs explanation. Oxford is much smaller in numbers, for example, than the State University of Minnesota, and is much poorer. It has, or had till yesterday, fewer students than the University of Toronto. To mention Oxford beside the 26,000 students of Columbia University sounds ridiculous. In point of money, the $39,000,000 dollar endowment of the University of Chicago, and the $35,000,000 one of Columbia, and the $43,000,000 of Harvard seem to leave Oxford nowhere. Yet the peculiar thing is that it is not nowhere. By some queer process of its own it seems to get there every time. It was therefore of the greatest interest to me, as a profound scholar, to try to investigate just how this peculiar excellence of Oxford arises.

It can hardly be due to anything in the curriculum or programme of studies. Indeed, to any one accustomed to the best models of a university curriculum as it flourishes in the United States and Canada, the programme of studies is frankly quite laughable. There is less Applied Science in the place than would be found with us in a theological college. Hardly a single professor at Oxford would recognise a dynamo if he met it in broad daylight. The Oxford student learns nothing of chemistry, physics, heat, plumbing, electric wiring, gas-fitting or the use of a blow-torch. Any American college student can run a motor car, take a gasoline engine to pieces, fix a washer on a kitchen tap, mend a broken electric bell, and give an expert opinion on what has gone wrong with the furnace. It is these things indeed which stamp him as a college man, and occasion a very pardonable pride in the minds of his parents. But in all these things the Oxford student is the merest amateur.

This is bad enough. But after all one might say this is only the mechanical side of education. True: but one searches in vain in the Oxford curriculum for any adequate recognition of the higher and more cultured studies. Strange though it seems to us on this side of the Atlantic, there are no courses at Oxford in housekeeping, or in Salesmanship, or in Advertising, or on Comparative Religion, or on the influence of the Press. There are no lectures whatever on Human Behaviour, on Altruism, on Egotism, or on the Play of Wild Animals. Apparently, the Oxford student does not learn these things. This cuts him off from a great deal of the larger culture of our side of the Atlantic. "What are you studying this year?" I once asked a fourth year student at one of our great colleges. "I am electing Salesmanship and Religion," he answered. Here was a young man whose training was destined inevitably to turn him into a moral business man: either that or nothing. At Oxford Salesmanship is not taught and Religion takes the feeble form of the New Testament. The more one looks at these things the more amazing it becomes that Oxford can produce any results at all.

The effect of the comparison is heightened by the peculiar position occupied at Oxford by the professors' lectures. In the colleges of Canada and the United States the lectures are supposed to be a really necessary and useful part of the student's training. Again and again I have heard the graduates of my own college assert that they had got as much, or nearly as much, out of the lectures at college as out of the athletics or the Greek letter society or the Banjo and Mandolin club. In short, with us the lectures form a real part of the college life. At Oxford it is not so. The lectures, I understand, are given and may even be taken. But they are quite worthless and are not supposed to have anything much to do with the development of the student's mind. "The lectures here," said a Canadian student to me, "are punk." I appealed to another student to know if this was so. "I don't know whether I'd call them exactly punk," he answered, "but they're certainly rotten." Other judgments were that the lectures were of no importance: that nobody took them: that they don't matter: that you can take them if you like: that they do you no harm.

An inspectional reading of this text yields some obvious data. The topic is colleges and education. In the "world" of higher education the text asserts that Oxford approaches an ideal. The "self" is an observer who presents experience as the basis for his judgment. The text is studded with descriptions that are blatantly comic. The remark about an Oxford professor not recognizing a dynamo in the street makes its point by absurd overstatement. Knowledge of plumbing, wiring, and the interior of a combustion engine are marks of the American college graduate which cause his parents "pardonable pride." This comic perspective and *reductio ad absurdum* are selective slants on the data intended to reinforce the judgment which the text makes about education. Through these palpable devices, the text tells us what education should and should not be. Note that we can also view the text as exposition, as data about universities here and abroad, or as argument, the case for a liberal as against a technical education. But we can also, and in this case quite clearly, treat the text as self-expressive, the expression of an opinion or a judgment about the topic addressed.

To this point we have been speaking of verbal constructs that present an opinion or a judgment. It would be more accurate to say that the text as self-expressive presents *an opinion that is a judgment*. "On Keeping a Notebook" offers us an effective way of "keeping in touch with ourselves" on the grounds that self-knowledge is a good thing. The piece on Oxford judges that education should go beyond the practical. In short, the textual artifact moves beyond the world as given or the world as problematic to present the vision of a world that, in the opinion of the self of the text, *ought to be.*

The Self in the Text

The preliminary understanding that we bring to text as artifact, then, includes an awareness that the text envisions a world of which the self is a part. The "self" appears in the text as "I" or as the subject of the personal experiences the text presents or both. The self is then defined or described in the text and represents, if you like, an authority qualified to express an opinion or make a judgment. When we spoke earlier about the rhetorical situation, one of the four elements, you will remember, was "the self." From the perspective of the writing enterprise this had to do with the way you wished to define the "I" that might appear in your composition. The self, "I," is part of the construct which is the text. In explaining the text as artifact, we wish to include this "self" in our explanation.

We already have at our disposal methodologies which allow us to deal with this component. The topos of definition provides a way of describing the self in a given text. For instance, the self of "On Keeping a Notebook" is a writer of fiction. The entries in her notebook are not only re-membered events from her life, but also materials for her stories. The self of "Oxford as I See It" is an observer and a humorist. The topos of relationship in both these pieces is registered in terms of effect on the self in the text. The Oxford piece sees a comparison of the curricula at Oxford over against American and Canadian universities "frankly, quite laughable." The comparison here is not straightforward but in relation to the self who is expressing an opinion about education. If we as readers miss the understatement the text perpetrates here, the joke will be on us.

In applying the other general heuristic to the text as artifact, we can see the self in terms of the unit to be explored. Part of the systematic construct that is the text, the self can be viewed as a unit-as-system and a unit-in-system. In *Civil Disobedience* "Thoreau" is a citizen who takes a position towards his relationship with the state. An analysis of this unit shows us that Thoreau has his own principles which are based on his own experience and which insist on his freedom of choice, his moral responsibility, and his sense of community with those he sees as oppressed. As a unit-in-system, he goes to jail for refusing to pay his taxes. The place of "Thoreau" with relation to the state in *Civil Disobedience* finally describes what a citizen ought to be in a democracy. Whatever we may think about the argument of this text, examining it in the light of the self leaves no doubt about the judgment the text renders.

The Self and Judgment

We have noted that any text can be read three ways. The *Apology* of Plato is a notable il-lustration; it can, as we have seen, be read as expository and argumentative. Now we wish to consider it as self-expressive. The self of the *Apology* is, obviously, Socrates, and he tells us not a little about himself and his situation. We do well to note, as part of our preliminary investigation of the text, that the author's name is Plato, a disciple of Socrates. The self of the text is not identifiable with its author. So Socrates is also a construct, a collection of qualities that make up a constituitive part of the text. When we set out to define or describe the self in this text, when we consider Socrates as a tagmemic unit, we are working with an identity established only in the text. Nonetheless, the Socrates of the text takes on a personality through the ordered language of the text. The analysis of the text as artifact can easily focus on the Socrates which it presents. The text does not tell us all the things we may want to know about this Athenian philosopher. We do not know—from the *Apology,* at any rate—what Socrates customarily had for breakfast; we don't know how he got on with his wife; we have no notion of his annual income (although the inference is that he was not rich); we do not know what kind of parent he was. The Socrates who got up in the morning, put on his *chiton* and sandals, and worked as a stone-cutter is not available in the *Apology*. We do know, however, what he thought about being a good citizen and a good philosopher. We can come to understand why he takes the positions he does. We can also come to appreciate what the state ought to be and do and what the citizen of the state ought to be. Again, whatever we think of the arguments Socrates uses against his accusers, the *Apology* tells us what his position is with relation to the community. The *Apology* includes this vision of the *polis* and of its citizenry artfully presented in the context of Socrates' defense.

Two other texts included among the readings may not, at first glance, appear to be appropriate instances of self-expressive texts. *The Declaration of Independence* and the *Communist Manifesto* are monuments designed to engender allegiance in their audiences. We search in vain for expres-sions like "I believe" or instances of personal experiences. In both pieces, however, there is an obvious "we" present in the texts. The text speaks on behalf of this "we"; and the "we" of the text is constituted by a collection of characteristics that, like the Socrates of the *Apology,* present a personality. This personality is part of the text and stands in relation to the subject matter that makes up the other parts. The *Declaration of Independence* and the *Communist Manifesto* present a judgment about the way, in the opinion of the "we" in the text, society will be organized. Like any self-expressive judgments about what ought to be, both documents look to a future situation which is proclaimed to be better than the present or the past. The texts are prophetic in both senses: (1) they speak for the community represented by the "we" (a prophet is literally a "speaker-for"); (2) they look to a future for that community. Whenever time-future is a consideration, it is clear that we are dealing with a construct, an artifact and a vision. The future only exists in the vision of the text. So it is perfectly appropriate that we consider these texts from this self-expressive viewpoint.

Summary

Because it is made of words, every text is a construct, every text is self-expressive. A text is a made thing. Whether the "I" or the "we" is explicit or implicit, the text includes an opinion or a judgment. The data which a text presents, then, is always conditioned by that collection of qualities (characteristics and values) that make up the "I" or "we." The judgments that the text levels at the data include an *ought* or a *will;* they look to an ideal present or future. When we bring our methodologies to bear in explaining text as artifact, we define and describe the relationship of the individual or community making the judgment to the data in the text. When we understand the text, we understand this relationship and finally are able to make our own judgment about it. If we like or admire or identify with the individual or the community speaking in the text, clearly that influences our judgment. When we try to produce our own text in the writing enterprise, when we become the "I" in our own writing, we want to exemplify those qualities with which our audience will identify. Both the text as artifact and our writing as self-expressive draw on the potential of words for presenting an ideal, a vision, a prophetic statement. It is in this aim that we may see language as most powerful and most personal.

Chapter 12
Narrative

Storytelling

"Let me tell you about the one that got away." "A funny thing happened to me on the way to the bank." "Daddy, tell me a story." Wherever fishermen gather, there are always stories about "the one that got away." Our conversations inevitably include stories about the funny or painful or exciting events of the day. Before bedtime, the child wants a story. In the fourth century, B.C., Aristotle pointed out that we are all natural storytellers. Our word "history" contains the word "story." "Narrative" is another word for "story," the presentation of a series of events in time and space generally with a beginning, a middle, and an end.

Though it may not be obvious at first blush, any narrative is a construct and any text that is a narrative is an artifact. In considering text as artifact, we can appropriately examine the notion of narrative and explore the kinds of narrative that we encounter. Consider for a moment the following text.

Jane: What's the matter? You look terrible.

Dick: When I got up this morning, it was raining. On the way to work, there was a major accident on Central Expressway and the traffic was jammed for miles. I was late to work, the boss saw me come in and then the computer was down. The mid-morning meeting ran late and I had to skip lunch. My stomach was growling all afternoon; when I got out to the parking lot, my car wouldn't start. May I have a Martini?

Any text can and often does include events, but when we consider a text as expository, the event is described or explained; when we view a text as argumentative, the event constitutes evidence. Only the text as narrative is a self-contained story with beginning, middle and end.

The text about Dick's day describes a series of events in the course of the day in a number of different places. The events are ordered not only chronologically, in terms of time sequence from morning to afternoon, but also intrinsically, in terms of the kind of event included. This narrative is not, and it does not claim to be, a complete report of the day's events; it is a selective report. Some fortunate or enjoyable events may have happened in the course of the day, but they are not included here. Presumably, with the consumption of the Martini, the troubles of the day are at an end so that the narrative has moved from A to B to C in a conclusive manner. When we present a personal experience in narrative form, we tend to follow this pattern, selecting those incidents and those details that make our narrative coherent and which give it some point. There is a name for the individual who habitually offers unselective and pointless narratives; the name is "boor." Even if we could relate our personal experience in every detail, we would find we soon lacked an audience. This is why, as the adage has it, there is an art to storytelling.

Narrative and History

Narratives that deal with our personal experience treat of events in our past in an ordered sequence relative to time and place. Narratives that deal with more general treatments of the past are either historical or biographical as they treat either events relative to a nation, a race, or a culture or events relative to a life of a person or persons other than the writer. The stuff of history books is narrative, that is, the selection and arrangement of significant events from the past. It is to be noted that this selection and arrangement, just as in our own personal histories, involves an interpretation. The historian decides what is important and why and proceeds to report on events in a way that reveals the narrator's opinion about their causes. The following is an excerpt from Thomas Babington Macaulay's life of Robert Lord Clive, the conqueror of India. Macaulay describes the battle by which the English were able to establish control of the Indian Empire.

The Battle of Plassey

The day broke, the day which was to decide the fate of India. At sunrise the army of the Nabob, pouring through many openings of the camp, began to move towards the grove where the English lay. Forty thousand infantry, armed with firelocks, pikes, swords, bows and arrows, covered the plain. They were accompanied by fifty pieces of ordnance of the largest size, each tugged by a long team of white oxen, and each pushed on from behind by an elephant. Some smaller guns, under the directions of a few French auxiliaries, were perhaps more formidable. The cavalry were fifteen thousand, drawn, not from the effeminate population of Bengal, but from the bolder race which inhabits the northern provinces, and the practised eye of Clive could perceive that both the men and the horses were more powerful than those of the Carnatic. The force which he had to oppose to this great multitude consisted of only three thousand men. But of these nearly a thousand were English; and all were led by English officers, and trained in the English discipline. Conspicuous in the ranks of the little army were the men of the Thirty-Ninth Regiment, which still bears on its colours, amidst many honourable additions won under Wellington in Spain and Gascony, the name of Plassey, and the proud motto, *Primus in Indis*.

The battle commenced with a cannonade in which the artillery of the Nabob did scarcely any execution, while the new field-pieces of the English produced great effect. Several of the most distinguished officers in Surajah Dowlah's service fell. Disorder began to spread through his ranks. His own terror increased every moment. One of the conspirators urged on him the expediency of retreating. The insidious advice, agreeing as it did with what his own terrors suggested, was readily received. He ordered his army to fall back, and this order decided his fate. Clive snatched the moment, and ordered his troops to advance. The confused and dispirited multitude gave way before the onset of disciplined valour. No mob attacked by regular soldiers was ever more completely routed. The little band of Frenchmen, who alone ventured to confront the English, were swept down the stream of fugitives. In an hour the forces of Surajah Dowlah were dispersed, never to reassemble. Only five hundred of the vanquished were slain. But their camp, their guns, their baggage, innumerable waggons, innumerable cattle, remained in the power of the conquerors. With the loss of twenty-two soldiers killed and fifty wounded, Clive had scattered an army of nearly sixty thousand men, and subdued an empire larger and more populous than Great Britain.

Macaulay does not go into a great deal of detail in describing the battle; the outline of events is clear. The British army of three thousand men, including a thousand British soldiers of the Thirty-Ninth Regiment, was trained under British discipline, and so was able to rout the mob assembled by the Rajah. Their general, Clive, was a man of daring and enterprise who risked his three thousand troops against sixty thousand of the natives. In a single stroke he dismantled the

Thomas Babington Macaulay, "Lord Clive," in Harrold and Templeton, *English Prose of the Victorian Era* (New York: Oxford University Press, n.d.), 401.

power of the Indian emperor. Clearly Macaulay is telling this story with a positive view of British imperialism; his emphasis falls on the courage, enterprise and discipline of the British army. An Indian historian might present a very different narrative in describing the same battle.

Embedded in the narrative are relationships which allow us to draw some conclusions about cause and effect. If we apply this topos to the narrative of the battle, we discover that the principal reason given by Macaulay for the superiority of the British is discipline under fire. This discipline is grounded in tradition; the Thirty-Ninth Regiment fought under the Duke of Wellington in the Napoleonic Wars and distinguished itself at Waterloo. By virtue of their engagement in India and their part in this battle, their banner bears the inscription *Primus in Indis,* that is, "First in India"; in our present parlance, "We're Number One." The British army brings tradition and discipline to bear against the forces of chaos and disorder. The Rajah listens to cowardly and conspiratorial advice. The effect is the complete rout of the Rajah's army and the beginning of the conquest of India.

Any historical narrative will order the past events of which it treats by using specific definitions, divisions, and cause and effect relationships that highlight the significance of the events. The result is obviously an interpretation of the past and an interpretation which looks back on the events from the vantage point of the present. A history of the major political and social events that occurred between 1861 and 1865 in this country has been described in various ways: "the Southern Rebellion," "the War Between the States," or "the Civil War." It is clear from these definitions what sorts of narratives we might expect under these different titles. In a scenario about "the Southern Rebellion," Southern politicians are likely to play the role of villains whereas the Northerners appear as the defenders of human rights, free soil, and the Constitution. Where the "War Between the States" definition prevails, the perspective will be Southern and the narrative will dramatize the nobility of the "lost cause," and lament the passing of a unique and aristocratic way of life. The causes of the war embedded in the narratives are likely to be, on the one hand, Southern perfidy, and on the other, Northern meddling. Some five wars later, over a 125-year perspective, the narratives might well present a less partisan view of the events of the Civil War. So history can change, and the narratives through which the past is recreated reflect those changes.

Historical narratives deal with actual events, personages, and places of the past. These narratives purport to tell us, not only what happened, but in some fashion why it happened. Insofar as they are narratives, that is, insofar as they tell us what happened, they recreate the events of the past by selecting and ordering them. Insofar as they tell us why the events occurred, they employ the topos of relationship, of antecedent and consequent, of cause and effect. The result is, as we have said, an interpretation of actual past events in the light of the present.

At this point, it should be clear why there is an aspect of narratives which can be called "self-expressive." From all the actual events in a given historical period, from all the actual detail of all the actual events, the text presents a selection which makes the significance of the events clear. In presenting these events the text orders them so that there is a beginning, a middle, and an end. This is the principal device for establishing their significance. The actual events, of course, do not wear signs "the beginning," or "the end." Lee's surrender to Grant at Appomattox is the end of one story, the beginning of another, and the middle of a third. It is the end of the actual fighting of the Civil War, the beginning of Reconstruction, and a mid-point in our development as a nation. Where this event stands in the narrative, then, depends on which story the text is narrating. So the first question we should put to any narrative is: *What happens in the text?*

Narrative Structure

When we set out to summarize the narrative, we are forced to be selective just as the text is selective. If we were to summarize by including every event and every detail of every event, we would end up by retelling the story. Earlier we remarked that the kiss of death in storytelling is attempting to include everything; the same is true of narrative summaries. We need a method which allows us to select principal events from the narrative. A simple and straightforward method of selection is to apply to the narrative the structure we noted above: beginning, middle, and end.

If we apply this three-point structure to the description of the battle of Plassey quoted above, the summary might look like this. (1) At daybreak, the English forces confront the much larger army of the Rajah. (2) After an artillery barrage, the Rajah's army begins to retreat and the English seize that moment to attack. (3) The English put the Rajah's army to flight and win a complete victory. These three statements explain what happens on the field at Plassey in terms of the beginning, the middle, and the end of the narrative. As an explanation of the narrative, these statements describe the parts without encompassing the whole. They do not offer an understanding of what happened at the battle; neither do they get into the reasons why. But this summary of the events provides the ground for all the other details and for an understanding of their causes.

This method of analyzing a narrative, which seems simple enough, implies that, not only are there parts in the narrative, but the parts are connected to one another. The connection may simply be, on the face of it, temporal sequence; one event follows another. In the battle of Plassey, the artillery barrage comes before the retreat of the Rajah's army and the advance of the English. But we can also consider the structure of events as we noted above as having a causal relationship. The effectiveness of the artillery barrage produced consternation in the ranks of the Indians, and so they began to withdraw. From this point of view, the beginning produces the middle, the crisis event that determines the end. So, if we consider the events of the Civil War, a narrative can begin with the Confederate firing on Fort Sumter in Charleston Harbor and end with Lee's surrender to Grant at Appomattox and the event that joins these two—the middle—the defeat of Lee's army by the Union forces at Gettyburg. In short, the middle event *explains* the beginning and the end by forging a connection between them.

From what we have said this far about the methodology for analyzing narrative, it ought to be clear that it is a heuristic for dividing the text into parts; it is, in a sense, a specific application of the topos of division to a text as narrative. The longer and more complex the narrative, the more room there is for differing opinions about the structure of the text. Deciding on the battle of Gettysburg and its outcome as the central event in a narrative on the Civil War requires explanation in terms of chronology and of cause and effect in a given narrative. Another reading may see Grant's victory at Vicksburg and his assumption of command of the Union forces as the critical event. The methodology provides a way of examining what happens in the narrative; it also provides structural principles for examining what happens. The method does not, however, offer an algorithmic approach that determines *which* specific event or events are crucial.

Summary

The narratives which we have been examining in this chapter all deal with actual events, persons and places of the past. The "past" can be our own personal experiences; if we organize these in an inscribed text and deal with our past life experience as a whole, we will have written an *autobiography*. We will have selected and arranged those experiences in a way that reveals how we have changed and grown through our life experiences. John Bunyan, in his *Grace Abounding,* tells how he changed from sinner to saint; Charles Darwin, in *"The Voyage of the Beagle,"* from his *Autobiography,* tells how his interest in science led to *The Origin of the Species.* The autobiography presents the life of the narrator, his or her experiences of the past in the light of the present. We can also, in a narrative, tell the story of another's life experience, selecting and arranging the events of that life so that its significance for the person and for the reader appears. We will then have written a *biography.* The biographical narrative offers the past of a person in the light of the present. Macaulay's "Lord Clive" presents Clive's rise from clerk to ruler of India. Biography is equivalently the history of a life. If we narrate the past events of a community—a tribe, a sect, a race, a nation—as those events affect the life of the community again in the light of the present, we will have written a *history.* Gibbon's *The Decline and Fall of the Roman Empire* describes the central events of that epoch. The selection and arrangement of events constitutes an interpretation of the past; it elaborates not only what happened but also why it happened.

The methodology for examining and explaining the narrative is also a selective process which determines the structure of the narrative in terms of beginning, middle, and end. Once we establish this three-point division, we can easily relate all the events of the narrative to one or another of these three points. The methodology is heuristic in that it specifies a structure. The basic principle for determining a specific structure is causal; the beginning contains those elements of change that move to the middle, the crisis, which forecasts the end. This structure allows us to see what happens in any narrative text and how its parts are related to one another.

We have considered autobiographical, biographical, and historical narratives. These deal with actual events, persons, and places. We are ready now to look at a different kind of narrative, the fictional narrative. This kind of narrative does not deal with the actual worlds of the past which exist in memory, but with possible worlds which exist in the imagination. In the next chapter, we will investigate texts as fictional narrative, what they are and how they work.

Chapter 13
The Fictional Narrative

"The day broke, the day which was to decide the fate of India." "Once upon a time there was a dear little girl who was loved by everyone who looked at her." Each of these sentences begins a narrative, the presentation of a series of events. Both texts select and arrange the events they present. The first is the opening sentence of Macaulay's text narrating the events of the Battle of Plassey, India, which we discussed in Chapter Twelve. The other sentence begins the story of "Little Red-Cap," which we discussed briefly in the first section of this book. The battle of Plassey is an historical narrative; it deals with actual places, persons and events from the past interpreted in the light of an early nineteenth-century present. "Little Red-Cap" is a fictional narrative which presents places, personae and a series of events which have no such reference. The "Little Red-Cap" text is fictional, in the first instance because it creates a world which does not refer to any *actual* place, or persons or events in the past or the present. Rather, the fictional narrative presents us with a world of possibilities in which the events reveal the way human beings *might* act in a variety of circumstances. The world of the fictional narrative is an artifact which presents human actions, thoughts, choices, and emotions and their consequences.

To refresh our memory, we might take a look at the text of "Little Red-Cap," and give it another inspectional reading.

Little Red-Cap

Once upon a time there was a dear little girl who was loved by every one who looked at her, but most of all by her grandmother, and there was nothing that she would not have given to the child. Once she gave her a little cap of red velvet, which suited her so well that she would never wear anything else; so she was always called "Little Red-Cap."

Once day her mother said to her, "Come, Little Red-Cap, here is a piece of cake and a bottle of wine; take them to your grandmother, she is ill and weak, and they will do her good. Set out before it gets hot, and when you are going walk nicely and quietly and do not run off the path, or you may fall and break the bottle, and then your grandmother will get nothing; and when you go into her room, don't forget to say, 'Good-morning,' and don't peep into every corner before you do it."

"I will take great care," said Little Red-Cap to her mother, and gave her hand on it.

The grandmother lived out in the wood, half a league from the village, and just as Little Red-Cap entered the wood, a wolf met her. Red-Cap did not know what a wicked creature he was, and was not at all afraid of him.

"Good-day, Little Red-Cap," said he.

"Thank you kindly, wolf."

"Whither away so early, Little Red-Cap?"

"To my grandmother's."

"What have you got in your apron?"

"Cake and wine; yesterday was baking day, so poor sick grandmother is to have something good, to make her stronger."

"Where does your grandmother live, Little Red-Cap?"

"A good quarter of a league farther on in the wood; her house stands under the three large oak-trees, the nut-trees are just below; you surely must know it," replied Little Red-Cap.

The wolf thought to himself, "What a tender young creature! what a nice plump mouthful— she will be better to eat than the old woman. I must act craftily, so as to catch both." So he walked for a short time by the side of Little Red-Cap, and then he said, "See, Little Red-Cap, how pretty the flowers are about here—why do you not look round? I believe, too, that you do not hear how sweetly the little birds are singing; you walk gravely along as if you were going to school, while everything else out here in the wood is merry."

Little Red-Cap raised her eyes, and when she saw the sunbeams dancing here and there through the trees, and pretty flowers growing everywhere, she thought, "Suppose I take grandmother a fresh nosegay; that would please her too. It is so early in the day that I shall still get there in good time"; and so she ran from the path into the wood to look for flowers. And whenever she had picked one, she fancied that she saw a still prettier one farther on, and ran after it, and so got deeper and deeper into the wood.

Meanwhile the wolf ran straight to the grandmother's house and knocked at the door.

"Who is there?"

"Little Red-Cap," replied the wolf. "She is bringing cake and wine; open the door."

"Lift the latch," called out the grandmother, "I am too weak, and cannot get up."

The wolf lifted the latch, the door flew open, and without saying a word he went straight to the grandmother's bed, and devoured her. Then he put on her clothes, dressed himself in her cap, laid himself in bed and drew the curtains.

Little Red-Cap, however, had been running about picking flowers, and when she had gathered so many that she could carry no more, she remembered her grandmother, and set out on the way to her.

She was surprised to find the cottage-door standing open, and when she went into the room, she had such a strange feeling that she said to herself, "Oh dear! how uneasy I feel to-day, and at other times I like being with grandmother so much." She called out, "Good morning," but received no answer; so she went to the bed and drew back the curtains. There lay her grandmother with her cap pulled far over her face and looking very strange.

"Oh! grandmother," she said, "what big ears you have!"

"The better to hear you with, my child," was the reply.

"But, grandmother, what big eyes you have!" she said.

"The better to see you with," my dear.

"But, grandmother, what large hands you have!"

"The better to hug you with."

"Oh!, but grandmother, what a terrible big mouth you have!"

"The better to eat you with!"

And scarcely had the wolf said this, than with one bound he was out of bed and swallowed up Red-Cap.

When the wolf had appeased his appetite, he lay down again in the bed, fell asleep and began to snore very loud. The huntsman was just passing the house, and thought to himself, "How the old woman is snoring! I must just see if she wants anything." So he went into the room, and when he came to the bed, he saw that the wolf was lying in it. "Do I find thee here, thou old sinner!" said he. "I have long sought thee!" Then just as he was going to fire at him, it occurred to him that the wolf might have devoured the grandmother, and that she might still be saved, so he did not fire, but took a pair of scissors, and began to cut open the stomach of the sleeping wolf. When he had made two snips, he saw the little Red-Cap shining, and then he made two snips more, and the little girl sprang out, crying, "Ah, how frightened I have been! How dark it was inside the wolf"; and after that the aged grandmother came out alive also, but scarcely able to breathe. Red-Cap, however, quickly fetched great stones with which they filled the wolf's body, and when he awoke, he wanted to run away, but the stones were so heavy that he fell down at once, and fell dead.

Then all three were delighted. The huntsman drew off the wolf's skin and went home with it; the grandmother ate the cake and drank the wine which Red-Cap had brought, and revived, but Red-Cap thought to herself, "As long as I live, I will never by myself leave the path, to run into the wood, when my mother has forbidden me to do so."

An inspectional reading tells us in a number of ways that "Little Red-Cap" presents a possible, not an actual, world. The places in the story are identifiable enough: the village, the forest, Grandmother's house. Notice, however, that these places are "unmoored," that is, neither the village or the forest are identified with *this village* or *this forest*. The forest and the village are not "moored" to, for instance, Germany or France or Texas or the moon. They are simply "the forest" and "the village." We can say the same thing, in spades, for the personae of the story. It might be that there was, at some time in history, a "dear little girl" who wore a red cap, went to her grandmother's house and was eaten by a wolf. But this narrative is not telling *her* story. The case of the wolf makes it perfectly clear that we are dealing with a possible world. If we visit the zoo and confront the animal called *canis lupus,* it is not likely to engage us in conversation. Talking wolves are not part of our experience; on the other hand, the imagination can construct the possibility of a wolf talking, just as it can construct the possibility of a flying horse or, for that matter, a flying man. To appeal to our topos of relation, there is no contradiction between "talking" and "wolf." The text of "Little Red-Cap" puts these two images together in the world that it creates. Other clear indications that we are dealing with a world of possibility rather than a world of actuality have to do with the wolf's devouring Little Red-Cap and her grandmother. There are no instances, at least in recent medical history, of a person emerging unscathed after being eaten by an animal. We need not go deeply into the effects of mastication and the operation of digestive juices on ordinary organic matter. When the woodman freed Little Red-Cap and her grandmother from the wolf's belly, they appear alive and undamaged. Again, it is clear that the world created in this narrative is not our ordinary everyday one.

The places in a fictional narrative are not moored to any actual places, though they may have on occasion the names of actual places; the personae do not represent actual people, although they may have the names of actual historical personages; the events are not a depiction of actual incidents, even though they may resemble actual occurrences. So another feature of these possible worlds in fictional narratives is that they do not deal with the actual past, like historical narratives, or the actual present or even a projected actual future. The "time" in "once upon a time" is really outside any and every actual chronology. When a fictional narrative text offers us this imaginative world, it takes us out of our own space-time situation into the time dimension of the imagination. Sometimes people will remark, when they are reading a novel, that they are "killing time." There is a sense in which this is substantially true in that the text takes them out of their own temporal situation and introduces them to a different time dimension through the text. The fictional narrative makes the events of the text present to us on its own terms; its events are always happening "now." If we ask when Little Red-Cap is eaten by the wolf, the answer is "now" and "always"; if we ask where, the answer is "here" and "everywhere."

Not all fictional narratives present a world that is so far from the actual as does "Little Red-Cap." Many narratives, as we noted above, use the names of actual places and actual personages and present us with a series of events which closely resemble events in our own experience. In Hemingway's story "The Killers" the town is called Summit and the scene is Henry's Diner; somewhere in the Midwest there may well be a town of that name and an actual diner called Henry's. Two gangsters may have come to execute a Swede there. On the other hand, discovering an actual town and diner and evidence of an attempt on a Swede's life does not contribute significantly to the events described in the text. The street names in *A Clockwork Orange* and the sections of town described may correspond to street names and locations in the city of London, but again that does not significantly affect the events presented. Moreover, the time frame in the text *A Clockwork Orange* is a "now" which involves a hypothetical future. We would look vainly in present-day London for the milk-bar at which the droogs gather. This is what we mean when we say that the places in a fictional narrative are "unmoored." They are, as it were, lifted out of actuality to serve the world of the possible. The same can be said of actual personages whose names appear in a fictional narrative. They do not appear as part of an actual past, even though they are part of such a past, but rather as figures in a possible world. They too are "unmoored" from their place in history to serve the world of the fictional text.

Lies, Lies, Lies

In the latter part of the sixteenth century, the Puritan party gained control of Parliament and one of their first actions was to close down the playhouses in the city of London. They did so because, according to their ideology, plays told lies; the actor playing Julius Caesar was not Julius Caesar, but only pretending to be. His assassination in the capitol was not actually happening, but only a pretense. They recognized that these "lies" were very seductive and entertaining and that they drew people away from the serious business of serving God and making a living. So they shut down play productions within the walls of the city.

We often hear a similar objection today. What is the use of fiction? What do possible worlds have to do with anything? All of these stories are not "real"; they are not "true." When we speak of possible worlds and actual worlds, we are *not* saying that either of these worlds is more *real* than the other. Our dreams, for instance, are very real *as dreams;* we know also that they can tell us something about ourselves and our situation in the world, even if we do not accept all the implications of Carl Jung's collective unconscious. Our aspirations, what we wish to become as individuals and as a society, are real, though they may have no actuality as yet. Love, loyalty and honor are real even though when we look through our closets, we cannot find them. In fact, we spend a great deal of time and energy dealing with possibilities and we never question their reality. We accept the understandings they offer about ourselves and our world.

The kind of understanding that we can discover in a possible world is different from the kind of understanding we might discover in an exposition, an argument, or an historical narrative. Nonetheless, it can be an understanding that does relate to ourselves in the same way that understanding our dreams or our potential relates to ourselves. An American poet, Marianne Moore, says that poetry presents "real toads in imaginary gardens." The fictional narrative, like the poem, present real actions (not actual ones) in unmoored situations. Like any real actions, we can learn from them.

As a test case, let us look again at "Little Red-Cap." Even a brief inspectional reading of the text offers us a number of obvious understandings of the tale. The last sentence says: "As long as I live, I will never by myself leave the path to run into the wood, when my mother has forbidden me to do so." It is obvious that at least one factor contributing to Little Red-Cap's difficulty with the wolf was her disobedience to her mother's mandate. One understanding that we might easily gather then is "Obey your mother." Little Red-Cap's statement at the end tells us that the events of the story apply to her own case; we might apply them to ours. Another understanding or "truth" which an inspectional reading might yield is "things are not always what they appear to be." Little Red-Cap, acute observer as she is, notices that, though the figure in the bed is wearing Grandma's clothes and Grandma's cap, there are some noticeable differences in the old lady's appearance.

Eyes, ears and teeth do not square with Little Red-Cap's image of Grandma. Again, this kind of general understanding is one we might wish to note; "all that glisters is not gold," "gild the farthing as you will/Yet it is a farthing still," "things are not always what they appear." There are, as we will note, other understandings of the tale, but these are adequate to illustrate the point. The realities or truths these understandings represent are discoverable in the possible world of the fictional narrative. They only become lies when we take as actual what are instances of the possible.

Events and Human Actions

The consideration of realities and truths offered in the possible world of the fictional narrative bring us back to the basic notion of narrative. Any narrative—autobiographical, biographical, historical—is a series of events selected and arranged in a given order. Ordinarily, these events involve human actions, things people do or say or think. The events, then, involve the actions of human beings or human surrogates. In "Little Red-Cap" the wolf has a personality; he speaks and acts like a human being. *The Little Engine That Could* is another case in point. The engine shows emotion, makes decisions, and overcomes obstacles. The real toads in the possible world's imaginary garden are *human actions*. Little girls do go wandering off in the woods against their parents' orders; desperate teenagers like Alex in *A Clockwork Orange* do attempt suicide. When we read a text as a fictional narrative, then, the realities and truths we encounter have to do with the way human beings think, feel, and act. "Obey your mother" or "you can be deceived by appearances" or "it is difficult to fight City Hall (the Minister of the Interior)" are understandings that we might gather from "Little Red-Cap" or *A Clockwork Orange*. These understandings relate to human action and to the human action that is presented in the possible worlds of these texts.

The Storyteller

When we approach a text as artifact, and specifically as a fictional narrative, our preunderstanding includes: (1) narrative as a series of selected and ordered events; (2) in the possible, not an actual world; (3) with unmoored places and out-of-chronological time; (4) consisting of human actions by human (or human-surrogate) agents. We must now add there must be a storyteller. This need is clear enough. It is also obvious that storytellers can be of different kinds and can work in different ways. For instance, the narrator of *A Clockwork Orange* appears prominently in the text. He not only tells the story, but he is also the principal persona. In "The Killers," on the other hand, though Nick Adams is a principal persona, he is not the storyteller. There is, in fact, no storyteller identified in "The Killers." Yet clearly the story is being told and there are occasional comments on the personae or the events. When the two gangsters arrive at Henry's Diner, they are compared in the text to a "vaudeville team." This is an impression that the two create, but this impression is not attributed to anyone in the text. Alex, as it were, speaks for himself in *A Clockwork Orange;* the narrator in "The Killers" is anonymous. The point here is: (1) every narrative is a narration, that is, every story has a storyteller; (2) there are different kinds of storytellers.

We have already noted two kinds of storytellers. There is the anonymous storyteller of "Little Red-Cap" or "The Killers" who is absent from the narrative; the narrator does not figure as a persona in the events of the story. Another kind of narrator relates the events in *A Clockwork Orange*. Alex is not only the narrator, but also the principal persona or actor in the events. A third sort of narrator is a persona in the story who is not a principal or central actor. The position of the narrator with regard to the events of the story—whether he or she is inside or outside of the narrative and whether he or she is a principal or a subordinate actor in them—makes a difference in our understanding of them. Alex tells the story from his own perspective; we as readers may grasp more of the implications of a situation than he does. For instance, when he disciplines George and Dim, he alienates them so that he cannot depend on their support. To his surprise (but not necessarily ours) they betray him at the Catwoman's house. When a persona in the text tells the story, we can anticipate a certain bias which reflects the qualities of that persona. When the narrator is outside the story, we might expect a more distanced and "objective" view of the events.

What about the author of the narrative? Should we not consider the narrator of "The Killers" the person whose name appears as author, in this case Ernest Hemingway? Should we not view Anthony Burgess as the narrator of *A Clockwork Orange?* Sometimes knowing something about the author of a text sets up certain expectations about the narrator of the text and the kind of events which will be presented. When this is the case, it is because we have read other works by the same author and because we have found that these works usually contain a certain kind of narrator and tell a certain kind of story. But all we really need to know about the narrator is always in the text itself. It is obvious in *A Clockwork Orange* that the narrator is not "Anthony Burgess." Even if we agree that Burgess is responsible for this text, that he is the author, Alex as narrator has his own identifiable qualities and way of speaking that are not those of Anthony Burgess. Our investigational reading should include a consideration of the kind of narrator who is telling the story.

Summary

When we read a text as narrative, we view it first as a series of events. It can relate to an actual past in chronological time with actual settings and actual personages. The events are selected and ordered by a narrator who is either within the text or outside it. Such narratives we identify as autobiographical if the narrator is an actual personage within the text, biographical if the narrative is a personal history with the narrator outside the text, or historical if the narrative presents events relative to a community—a nation, society, or societal group. A fictional narrative text presents a selected and ordered series of events with an unmoored setting out of actual time which constitute a possible world. It is told by a narrator who is either within the text or outside it. Our inspectional reading of the text as narrative allows us to identify the kind of narrative and the kind of narrator which the text presents and allows us to determine (tentatively) whether the world of the text is possible or actual.

In the next chapter we wish to investigate ways of explaining the fictional narrative. To arrive at insights about the meaning of the fictional text we need to understand how the events are arranged in a given narrative and the ways in which they are interconnected. Like the autobiographical, biographical, and historical narratives, the fictional narrative has a beginning, a middle and an end. Our explanation of the text attempts to show how these three divisions relate to one another. Understanding fiction means understanding human action, understanding real life through events presented in a possible world.

Chapter 14
Agents and Events in the Fictive World

In explaining any text—telling what the text says—we have come to expect that our first job of work is dealing with its parts. If a narrative is made up of events, then the parts with which we are principally concerned are individual events and the way in which they are ordered. As we have seen in the foregoing chapters, we can begin with a simple set of categories and divide the text on the principle that every narrative has a beginning, a middle, and an end. This division seems uncomplicated enough and it makes an assumption that all of us recognize, namely, that a story should have a conclusion. If we are telling our friends about a ball game or a battle, they will inevitably (if we have not bored them to death in the telling) want to know how it came out. We also generally assume that the end has some relationship to the middle and the middle to the beginning. In short, a narrative is complete when it does have, in some sense or other, a beginning, middle, and an end.

The tale about Little Red-Cap, for instance, begins with the little girl's mission to deliver the cakes and wine to Grandmother and her meeting with the wolf. These two events make the beginning of the story because they indicate what Little Red-Cap is doing in the woods and the danger she encounters there. It seems appropriate to divide the beginning into two phases: 1) the point of entrance for the story and 2) the inciting moment. The point of entrance most often provides us with a description of some of the principal personae and their situation. In this case, Little Red-Cap is described as "a dear little girl" and her mother gives her directions to Grandmother's house and an errand to run. The inciting moment is an event which defines the issue or conflict with which the rest of the story deals. Meeting the wolf, "a wicked creature," puts Little Red-Cap and her mission in jeopardy. The middle of the story focuses on a crisis, that is, a turning point or change of fortune. It follows on the inciting moment and is an event that balances the issues that the story joins. In the middle of "Little Red-Cap" the wolf devours the little girl. There is no question but that this is the critical event for Little Red-Cap and a turning point in the tale. The narrative might well end here, and in some versions it does. But the narrative we are considering goes on to a happy ending.

The end of the narrative again includes two elements: the climax or resolution of the issue or conflict and a wrap-up or dénouement. In "Little Red-Cap" the climax is the rescue of Little Red-Cap and her grandmother by the woodsman. He frees the duo from the wolf's belly and destroys the wolf once and for all. This event resolves the conflict and settles the issue between Little Red-Cap and the wolf definitively. In the dénouement, the little girl, her grandmother, and the woodsman-savior celebrate the rescue and Little Red-Cap determines never to disobey her mother again.

We have, then, elaborated our initial division of beginning, middle, and end by dividing both beginning and end into two parts. This gives us a five-point structure for dealing with a fictional narrative:

1. point of entrance   ⎫
2. inciting moment   ⎬ Beginning
3. crisis   Middle
4. climax   ⎫
5. dénouement   ⎬ End

Obviously, selecting five events out of any narrative means that there will be some omissions. In our discussion of "Little Red-Cap" we have not mentioned a number of events: Little Red-Cap's detour to pick flowers, the wolf's devouring of Grandmother and his disguising himself in her clothes, the woodsman's taking notice of the wolf's snoring. Once we have arrived at a division of the story into five parts, it is fairly simple to see how these events mentioned above fit into the ordered arrangement of the narrative. The wolf disguises himself as Grandmother in order to devour Little Red-Cap. The wolf's snoring alerts the woodsman to his presence in the cottage and so provides the occasion for the rescue. Eventually, of course, all the events of the narrative can be included within the five-point structure. A topological analysis using categories like similarity and contrast or cause-and-effect will reveal the relations among the events. Choosing an event as our unit, we can also explore these relations by the tagmemic method. We will consider how the topoi and tagmemics may be applied at greater length further in this chapter.

Let us try applying this five-point structure to a longer work. *A Clockwork Orange* is a fictional narrative of greater scope than "Little Red-Cap." It is, therefore, harder to keep the entire work in mind when considering the structure of its events. Nonetheless, the same principles apply in determining beginning, middle and end for this work as for "Little Red-Cap."

1. **Point of Entrance.** Alex and his droogs engage in their violent activities.
2. **Inciting Moment.** Alex is caught by the police at the house of the Cat-Woman.
3. **Crisis.** Alex is rendered non-violent by Dr. Brodsky's treatment.
4. **Climax.** The non-violent Alex attempts suicide.
5. **Dénouement.** Alex is "cured" of his non-violent behavior.

This selection of events divides up the narrative and so provides an outline of what happens in *A Clockwork Orange*. All the other events of the plot, as we noted, can be related to these five points. For instance, in the introductory section, Alex's activities include: harassing an old man and destroying his books, robbing a drugstore, fighting with a rival gang, invading a home and participating in a gang-rape, fighting with the members of his own gang. All of these incidents illustrate the kind of violent activity in which Alex and his companions engage. They are at war with society and even with one another.

These incidents all make roughly the same point. They illustrate, in a crescendo, the violent character of Alex and his gang. Each incident has successively more serious consequences for the victims of their attacks. In the final incident of this sequence, the ground is prepared for Alex's capture by the police. There is no honor among these thieves and gang members; the leader must rule with a whiphand and always risks alienating his confederates. When the Cat-Woman resists Alex's single-handed attempt at robbery, Dim, whom Alex holds in contempt, blinds him with a chain and leaves him to the tender mercies of the cops. All of these incidents, then, constitute the point of entrance into the narrative. They also lay the groundwork for Alex's capture.

The incidents in prison and at the treatment center may be divided up in the same way, leading to the crisis: Alex's total aversion to any kind of violence. He tries to ingratiate himself with the prison authorities, particularly the chaplain, but when he fights off a homosexual and he and his cell-mates assault the newcomer, his cell-mates betray him by putting all the blame for the man's death on Alex. He submits to the treatment which involves a process of drugging and exposure to a series of violent films. The films show an old man being beaten, a gang-rape, a man slashed with a razor (Alex's favorite weapon), an assault on an old woman and Nazi atrocities in the camps of World War II. At the end of the treatment, Alex, although he still has the impulses to violence, cannot even contemplate aggressive action without becoming physically sick. Each of these incidents display the progressive conditioning by which Alex becomes physiologically non-violent. In the final episode of this sequence the authorities view the results of Dr. Brodsky's treatment, and Alex rendered incapable of violent aggression.

The incidents which lead up to the climax, Alex's suicide attempt, illustrate the defenselessness that the conditioning has effected. He is knocked about by an old man; though his instincts when he meets a girl in distress are to assault her, he acts the white knight and tries to protect her; he is beaten by the old man whose books he destroyed earlier; the rival gang leader and Dim, his former droog, now policemen, beat him up. In the final episode the writer whose wife he raped in Part One rescues him in order to use him for political purposes. Fearful that the writer will recognize him and trapped in "the prison" of his new conditioning, Alex attempts to kill himself.

The dénouement, Alex's recovery of his old aggressive self, is prepared for by a series of incidents in the hospital. He has a transfusion of "new blood" which allows him to contemplate violence without nausea. The Minister of the Interior visits him, and it is clear that Alex is being used as a political pawn for the second time. Finally, Alex asserts that he is completely "cured."

On the basis of this five-point structural division in the narrative, we can relate all the incidents of the novel to one another in the structure. It is important, at this point, to recall that this division into a five-point structure is a heuristic; we could have, had we chosen, stayed with a three-point division or added more principal events to our structure. We might, for example, consider Alex's imprisonment by the writer and his political associates as a *catastasis,* a false climax. Then we would have a six-part structure. Other readers might wish to assign different incidents as the inciting moment or the climax or the dénouement. There can, and will, be differences of opinion about pivotal incidents in any given narrative. Nonetheless, this five-point division provides one set of grounds for an explanation of the narrative from which understandings of the text may emerge.

The Personae: Representative Types

Our explanation of any narrative begins with the division of events; in our description of the events we must perforce include the personae, or actors, who perform them. It is Little Red-Cap, not Little Boy Blue or Jack the Giant-Killer, who is eaten by the wolf. Nick Adams, not George or Sam, goes off to warn the Swede of his danger. Dim and Billy-Boy become policemen and beat up the nonviolent Alex. If Little Red-Cap were described in the story as forty-two years old, our understanding of the meaning "Obey your mother" would be modified considerably. It is with a shock that we discover, at the end of Part One of *A Clockwork Orange,* that Alex is fifteen years old. In short, our explanation of the text must include a *description* of the various personae who are its actors.

The word *persona* is itself a broad hint about describing the actors in a fictional narrative. Literally, *persona* means "mask." In Greek and Roman drama the actors wore masks to represent their gender and their status in society. So the king would wear a mask with male features and a crown, his counselor would wear the mask of an old man wreathed with laurel, the queen a female mask with a coronet. The mask, then, would *represent* to the audience essential characteristics of the actors. Our English term "character" echoes the notion of "characteristic" qualities of the actors. We said earlier in our discussion that, as the happenings in a fictional narrative occur in a possible world, so the personae do not refer to actual people. We are now in a position to explain what that statement means. They do not refer to actual individuals, but rather represent types— they are a collection of characteristics, of qualities of a generic sort. Little Red-Cap may be described as "an innocent, amiable little girl who lives in a village." She is inexperienced and playful. There are a good many features of Little Red-Cap that the narrative does not bother to give us. We know next to nothing about her physical appearance, what her favorite foods are, where she goes to school, exactly how old, in fact, she is. The text presents us with just those qualities which are relevant to the happenings of the story. If we have any doubt about the representative nature of the personae, we have only to consider the wolf. This persona is a theriomorph, that is, a collection of human qualities in the form of an animal. The wolf is crafty, persuasive, destructive, and lives in the woods. He is, as the tale informs us, "an evil creature." There are also a number of things about the wolf which the story does not tell us: what he looks like, whether he goes on four paws or stands erect, what his age and size are. Again, we know about him only those features which are necessary for the narrative.

It is important to our explanation of "Little Red-Cap" to specify that Little Red-Cap is an innocent, little girl of the town and that the wolf is a wicked and persuasive inhabitant of the woods. The girl is out of her element and does not know what to expect; the wolf is in his element and is able to control the situation. Thus when we say that Little Red-Cap is devoured by the wolf, we are equivalently saying that the innocent girl of the village is devoured by a crafty inhabitant of the forest. The "little girl" and "the wolf" are typical of their age, condition, and so to speak, social status.

We can obviously put together typical descriptions of the personae in "The Killers" and *A Clockwork Orange*. The two men who come into Henry's lunchroom are dressed like twins, wear tight overcoats, eat with their gloves on, carry sawed-off shotguns, and exude an air of menace. We are not long into the narrative when we recognize them as gangsters, hitmen. They display a typical braggadocio and a professional disdain for the people in the diner. These details fill out the mobster type they represent. Again, there are a number of facets of their characters about which the narrative tells us nothing. Whatever pictures of them we may form in our imagination, we do not really know what they look like individually. We do not know how many members are in their families, if indeed they have families. They appear in the story as executioners of a particular stripe and this is all we need know about them. The persona of Nick Adams, on the other hand, is more fully developed. But we begin to explain him and his function in the narrative by seeing him as, first, a young man living in a small town. Like Little Red-Cap, he too is something of a naïf; he has not before encountered the impersonal violence of the world outside Summit from which the team of hitmen comes. Unlike George and Sam, he feels a certain obligation to get involved, to inform the Swede of his present danger. He cannot hide his fear in the face of the gangsters' threat, but his idealism leads him to take a risk. These are the qualities of youth, spent in a relatively secure environment, of an inexperienced idealism. Nick, then, represents these qualities which contrast sharply with the attitudes of the gangsters and, in a different way, with the attitudes of George and the cook.

Even though *A Clockwork Orange* presents a possible world in time and space which has little resemblance to any actual world we know, that is, it is "futuristic," the personae are easily recognizable as types. Alex is a teenage gang leader, with a penchant for destructive activity. The chaplain represents the religious bureaucrat who tries to reconcile vague religious values with his status in the establishment. Dr. Brodsky and his assistant embody an impersonal science at the service of the state. The writer and his friends are "liberal" opponents of the party in power. The Minister of the Interior is a representative of that political power which finally controls the activities of all the other personae. As agents of the action, these types allow us to classify and qualify the events of the narrative.

Agents and Events

We can now proceed to a further stage of our explanation of the narrative. We have defined the personae or agents in the narrative by type; for the names of the personae in our five-point division we can substitute our description of the type. For "Little Red-Cap" we can insert "an innocent young girl from the village" and for "the wolf" "a wicked creature from the woods." We can define the name "Nick" in "The Killers" as "an inexperienced, idealistic young Midwesterner." Alex and his droogs are representative of the teenage gang. Identifying the types which the personae represent clarifies the nature of the event itself. In any given fictional narrative the name or description of the persona is shorthand for a type.

Having divided the events of the narrative into our five-point structure and defined the agents or personae by type, we can now begin to apply other topoi.

Similitude

Similarities and contrasts can help us group personae and events together. For instance, in "Little Red-Cap" the little girl and her mother are alike in that both are associated with the village and both are concerned about Grandmother. Grandmother and the woodsman are alike in that, though they are inhabitants of the woods, they have connections with the village. The wolf is associated with Grandmother because he disguises himself as the old lady and appropriates her place. Since the wolf devoured Little Red-Cap and Grandmother, the narrative binds them together through this event. By contrast, the wolf is the only persona completely identified with the wood.

These alignments allow us grounds for a further explanation of the events. The girl, in all innocence, encounters the dangers of the woods in the figure of the wolf. Grandmother, because she lives in the woods and is weak, old and sick, is similarly in danger. She is not only devoured by the "evil creature," but she is also transformed into the wolf. The woodsman, on the other hand, is aware of the dangers which the wolf represents and has the knowledge and the tools to avert them. At this point in our analysis we can see that the events of "Little Red-Cap" represent a struggle between the village and the woods, between those qualities which the inhabitants of the village represent over against the qualities manifested by the inhabitant of the woods. Little Red-Cap, and her mother and the woodsman are concerned with helping and saving; the wolf is concerned only with his own interests.

In "The Killers" there is a sharp contrast between the townspeople in the diner and the two gangsters. The hitmen come in from out of town, intent on their mission to kill the Swede. They bring destruction and violence into the placid routine of Summit. George, Sam, and Nick are at their mercy. Like the gangsters, the Swede is an outsider but he has assimilated to the routine of the town. Nick stands out from the rest of townsfolk in that he is willing to get involved, to risk warning the Swede. The outcome makes it clear that his warning is to no avail. Finally, Nick is different than Sam and George in that he is going "to get out of this town."

There are other interesting minor contrasts in the story. For instance, George runs (and presumably owns) Henry's Diner. Hirsch's boarding house is run by Mrs. Bell. The clock on the wall is twenty minutes fast and it is never clear exactly what time it is. These contrasts add to the uncertainty Nick must face in dealing with the gangsters.

A Clockwork Orange offers a number of interesting similarities in the events. In the opening section Alex and the gang beat an old man and destroy his books, engage in a gang-rape, fight with razors and chains, and attempt to rob an old woman. The films which Alex is shown in the prison hospital include an old man being beaten, a gang-rape, a throat-slashing with a razor, and an assault on an old woman. After Alex's release, and in his nonviolent phase, he is beaten by an old man, defends the honor of a young girl threatened with rape, is beaten by cops who are ex-gang members. The last set of incidents also offer a contrast in that Alex is no longer the victimizer; he has become the victim. In prison he is in the custody of the state, after his release he falls into the hands of the writer and his activist associates; he finds himself again "in prison."

The most striking contrast in the novel, of course, is the violent Alex and the nonviolent Alex. His situation is reversed in that he becomes a victim, the classical music which incited to violence now makes him nauseous, the society which he threatened now threatens him. At the dénouement, the old, violent Alex reappears, making a sharp contrast with the nonviolent Alex. At the end of the narrative Alex has the same aggressive qualities which he had at the beginning.

These topoi, similarity and contrast, help us examine the events and the personae of the narrative in ways that illuminate the conflict and the changes which it embodies. They also provide clues to the value systems which are operative in the possible world of the text. As these topoi order personae and events, they lay the groundwork for insight about their meaning.

Cause and Effect

Another useful topos which we can apply to the narrative structure deals with the relationship between and among events. If I tell you that this morning I discovered a huge pit in my backyard which had not been there the night before, you are probably going to inquire as to what caused it. I might reply that (1) it was dug by a band of pirates seeking hidden treasure, or (2) a huge asteroid crashed there, or (3) it was the footprint of a gigantic monster who passed that way. Each one of these explanations is an adequate cause for the pit; each one of them carries a different degree of probability. If this incident of the pit were part of a fictional narrative, the probability of each one of these causes would depend on the events that went before in the story. Our preunderstandings about fiction generally include the expectation that there is some connection between and among the events and that, given the kind of possible world the text establishes, that these connections be fairly probable. For instance, if in the middle of "The Killers" Superman were to appear and annihilate the gangsters, we might have some problem with the probability of this happening in that text. On the other hand, in the possible world of "Little Red-Cap" where we find talking animals, the probability of "Little Red-Cap" emerging unscathed from the wolf's belly is high enough. So the cause and effect which we are examining in the narrative text is not a scientific principle, but rather a relationship established in terms of the world the story presents.

When we consider the relationships among the events in "Little Red-Cap," we may notice a number of oddities. For instance, there seems on the face of it no reason why the wolf, since he has both the capability and the opportunity, does not devour Little Red-Cap when they first meet. If the wolf were only a wild animal, we would expect that to happen. In fact, the narrative tells us that the wolf must first devour Grandmother and then disguise himself before he can finish off Little Red-Cap. The story does not explain *why* this is so. It is also not terribly clear why the woodsman is passing by Grandmother's cottage at the opportune moment. It is indeed a happy accident for Grandmother and Little Red-Cap that he does so. Finally, it is interesting that snipping open the wolf's stomach does not guarantee that this evil creature is permanently out of action. The woodsman must skin the beast and fill the carcass with rocks to ensure his demise. In any explanation of the tale, these anomalies must be accounted for. The causalities involved invite further explanation.

Examining cause-and-effect relationships in "The Killers" reveal the dimensions of the possible world the narrative constructs. The gangsters arrive from "elsewhere" to kill Ole Andreson. They have nothing personally against the Swede; in fact, they never met him. Somebody sent them. Because they are hitmen, they come to do a job. The Swede's life hangs on an anonymous decision made elsewhere. There is some speculation by Nick and George about the reasons for the killers' mission, but the Swede sums it up simply by saying, "I got in wrong." Though the people in the diner have nothing to do with the case, their lives too are in jeopardy. The qualities that Nick displays—his youth and his idealism—make it altogether probable that he go to the rooming house to warn the Swede. His inability to save Ole Andreson is a major factor in his later resolve to "get out of this town."

We have already noted some of the cause-and-effect issues in *A Clockwork Orange*. Alex is taken by the police because (1) he determines to act on his own in robbing the Cat-Woman, (2) he has alienated his droogs by forcing them to accept his leadership, (3) he underestimated the shrewdness of the old woman. These observations might lead us to the insight that Alex is not as clever as he thinks he is. This same overestimation of his ability to control situations leads him to volunteer for the hospital program. He wants desperately to get out of prison and so he tries to play model prisoner. When his cellmates turn on him and charge him with killing the loud-mouthed homosexual, Alex has, as he sees it, no other recourse but to accept reformation. Again, he is overconfident about his ability to handle the system. When the nonviolent Alex recognizes that one of his rescuers is the writer whose wife he assaulted, and that the writer and his associates have him in their power, his attempted suicide makes sense as the only way out. Thus, when we consider the causal patterns in the narrative, we discover that, in spite of appearances, Alex has much less control over his destiny than the sociopolitical system has over it.

Obviously, as we look at causes for the events of a narrative, we are not likely to find a single, clear, demonstrable causal chain. As we noted in the section on argument, the events depict human action and, human actions are seldom simple, clear and uncomplicated. There may be a number of different probable causes for any one event. Nonetheless, applying this topos to a narrative provides us with some explanation of the way in which events develop and how they are related one to the other. As we explain these relationships, the chances are good that we will have an insight or two that point us toward the meaning of the narrative.

The Cultural Perspective

Once we have divided the narrative into a five-point structure and defined the personae types in it by qualities and characteristics, once we have examined the similarities and oppositions among the personae and the relationships among the events, it ought to dawn on us that we have described qualities and characteristics of the possible world which the narrative presents. The personae typify not only age, gender and race, but also positions in a social order—doctor, lawyer, merchant chief, tinker, tailor, soldier, sailor. They may be associated with a certain section of the country— Southerner or Yankee or Californian—or with a certain class of society—rich, middle-class, poor. The similarities and differences among personae associate them in ways that constitute a social or political or economic order. Taken together, these associations reflect what we might call "the cultural aspect of the possible world presented by the narrative."

Here again we may detect a connection between the actual world of our experience and the possible world of the narrative text. We are part of a social, political and economic order as we are members of our family, university students, citizens of our state and of the United States. We have certain attitudes and values and we rely on certain institutions. Whatever we do, we do in the context of this culture which surrounds us. This is the *actual* world of our experience. The possible world of the fictional text encompasses the same kinds of cultural relationships as does our actual world. However strange and different the cultural characteristics of the possible world might seem at first glance, it will have many of these same elements: a social, political and economic order; different classes of people; certain attitudes, values and institutions.

It might seem somewhat farfetched to talk about a social or economic order in a folktale like "Little Red-Cap." In fact, we have already done just that; we remarked that Little Red-Cap and her mother are associated with the village, that Little Red-Cap's mission is to go to the assistance of her sick grandmother, that the woodsman is aligned with Little Red-Cap and the values of the village in hunting down the wolf. The wolf is outside the social order of the village; he has his own objectives and values. He is "an evil creature" because he does represent a different set of values, those of the woods. If the story were to end with the wolf devouring Little Red-Cap, not only the events but also the social order would be rearranged. We also noted that the woodsman is an appropriate savior in that, though he knows the dangers of the woods, his values are those of the village. Unlike Little Red-Cap, he "knows the territory." The contrast between the village and the woods represents an opposition of cultural values, ideas and institutions.

The personae in "The Killers" represent a similar kind of opposition; on one hand, there are the townsfolk of Summit and on the other, the gangsters who come from elsewhere. The townsfolk follow a routine and observe certain rules. The management of the diner does not serve dinner before six, the Swede generally comes in to eat at the same time every day, the casual customers who come to the diner expect to be served promptly. The killers disrupt this routine; they introduce a major note of uncertainty into the proceedings. The possible world of the narrative contrasts the settled normalities of the small town with the destructive unpredictability of belonging to a wider world. Nothing much out of the ordinary happens in Summit; one of the gangsters asks: "What do you do here nights?" His accomplice replies, "They eat the dinner . . . they all come here and eat the big dinner." Of the people in the diner, as we have noted, only Nick feels responsible for warning the Swede. The others passively accept the notion that there is nothing they can do. The manace from outside renders them helpless. The possible world that the narrative presents, by virtue of the advent of the killers, is a world wider than just the small town of Summit. And the town offers no protection against the uncertainties and the potential destruction that invasion from without affords. The institutions, values and strategies of Summit are all challenged by the unfamiliar forces that the gangsters represent. If Nick is actually going "to get out of this town," in order to escape the killers, we wonder where he might go.

In considering the cultural aspect of *A Clockwork Orange,* it might be helpful to use a tagmemic approach. If we were to take the teenage gang of which Alex is leader as our unit, our analysis might go this way.

	Unit	Unit as System	Unit in System
	Nadsat [teenage] Gang	Nadsat Gang	World of the Gang
S	Young	Alex—leader	Minister of Interior
T	Uneducated	Dim—the enforcer	Hospital Doctor Brody
A	Brutal	George—assistant	Police—Prison
T	Obscene	Pete—assistant	
I	Crude		prison inmates writer/revolutionaries
C			rival gang — Gang
			Alex's Mother and father citizens
D	Take drugs	Alex—leader	Minister of Interior
Y	Kill	↓	|
N	Rape	Nonviolent victim	police
A	Rob	↓	
M	Terrorize	aggressor	Citizens writer
I	Destroy		revolutionaries
C	Disperse	Dim→Cop	
		George→killed	Nonviolent Alex—hospital
		Pete→disappeared	↓
			Violent Alex

When we look at the unit-in-system, it is clear that we have represented the sociopolitical order of the possible world in *A Clockwork Orange.* The gang, as appears when we consider the unit-as-system, is a self-contained, hierarchical organization with a specific function. The gang members meet at the milk bar and set out to harass and assault the citizenry. They operate over against a social order which seems, at the outset, unable to control them. There are, however, controlling agencies, as Alex discovers, the police, the prison guards and the chaplain, the doctors at the hospital reformation center and, finally, the Minister of the Interior. The gang also encounters other members of the society, the citizens they harass, a rival gang. Alex also deals with his mother and father who do not know, or want to know, what their son is up to. When Alex is rendered incapable of violent action, he slides to the bottom of the social scale. One of the gang members becomes a cop and the citizens who were Alex's victims become themselves aggressors. When Alex is cured, it is not by virtue of any major change in the sociopolitical system. The Minister of the Interior is still the power who controls the society. In *A Clockwork Orange,* the more things change, the more they are the same.

The cultural characteristics of *A Clockwork Orange* include the institution of a police state whose citizenry, from the old man whose books the gang destroys to Alex, are all inclined to violence. The Nadsat language that Alex and his droogs speak includes a good many words that are Russian derivatives; from a cultural perspective this suggests a communist state run by police power. In this context the personae and the events reflect the values and attitudes of this type of society. The police are not constrained by democratic principles or citizens' rights; the doctors are not principally healers; the chaplain, though ostensibly a representative of religion, is a "Charlie" who works for the state. So these personae are not only types, but they are types in *this particular cultural configuration.* The institutions and values that they represent are specified by what they do in this configuration.

Our explanation of the cultural aspect in the possible world of the text provides us with considerable potential for insight about meaning in the text. As we move through the division of events, the identification of types, the exploration of similarities and contrasts in the events and the personae, the relationships of cause and effect among the events, the cultural aspect which the above analyses include, we have gone a considerable distance toward describing and evaluating the elements in the narrative. It remains for us, then, to consider the larger perspective that is afforded by different types of narration. As we noted above, every story involves a storyteller and there are different ways of telling the story. How it is told has considerable bearing on what the story means. In the next chapter we will look at narrative and narration, the relation between story and storyteller, and consider how that relation affects our explanation of, and insights about, the text.

Chapter 15
Narrative and Narration

When a friend wants to tell us a story and does not know where to start, our advice is frequently "Begin at the beginning." If our friend is an experienced storyteller or a cagey critic, he might reply, "Yes, but where is the beginning?" The storyteller is free to determine where he might begin and he does not necessarily have to begin at the beginning, if by that expression we mean the first incident in a chronological series. The title of our chapter indicates that there can be a difference between narrative-time and narration-time, between the chronological order of events in a possible world and the order in which those events are narrated.

We are accustomed to the fact that certain narratives give us the outcome and then fill in the details; they tell us the ending and then flash back to earlier incidents. For instance, stories in the sports section of the newspaper that report games generally give the score at the outset, along with the decisive incidents. "The Waxahachie Eagles defeated the Lewisville Cowboys 23–20 when Timmy Hardtoe, with 1:57 remaining, kicked a 27-yard field goal." The rest of the story consists of significant incidents in the game which led up to the decisive kick. Among fictive narratives the detective-mystery story works much the same way; it presents a corpse in the first few chapters; the rest of the text is devoted to reconstructing the events that led up to the murder and so identifying the murderer. Were all the events preceding the murder to be narrated at the beginning of the narrative, there would be no mystery. The detective's function is to fill in the gap between the situation preceding the murder and the murder itself. The chronological order of events, "narrative-time," and the order in which the events are narrated, "narration-time," are considerably different in the cases cited above.

In the fictional narratives we have been using to illustrate our methods of explanation, "Little Red-Cap," "The Killers," *A Clockwork Orange,* narrative-time and narration-time are identical. The chronology of the events follows in strict order. "Little Red-Cap" begins with Little Red-Cap's mission and the events follow in the order of antecedent/consequent in time to the end of the story. "The Killers" opens with the arrival of the two gangsters and each event follows chronologically until the discussion among Nick, Sam and George closes the story. The events in *A Clockwork Orange* follow the same kind of chronological pattern. The cause-and-effect connection between and among the events can also be seen as antecedent/consequent; our explanation of the events of the story proceeds along a linear time sequence that the narrative establishes. We want to look now at a fictional narrative in which chronological order and narrational order are quite different to see what effect this different kind of arrangement has on our explanation of the text.

A Rose for Emily

I

When Miss Emily Grierson died, our whole town went to her funeral: the men through a sort of respectful affection for a fallen monument, the women mostly out of curiosity to see the inside of her house, which no one save an old manservant—a combined gardener and cook—had seen in at least ten years.

It was a big, squarish frame house that had once been white, decorated with cupolas and spires and scrolled balconies in the heavily lightsome style of the seventies, set on what had once been our most select street. But garages and cotton gins had encroached and obliterated even the august names of that neighborhood; only Miss Emily's house was left, lifting its stubborn and coquettish decay above the cotton wagons and the gasoline pumps—an eyesore among eyesores. And now Miss Emily had gone to join the representatives of those august names where they lay in the cedar-bemused cemetery among the ranked and anonymous graves of Union and Confederate soldiers who fell at the battle of Jefferson.

Alive, Miss Emily had been a tradition, a duty, and a care; a sort of hereditary obligation upon the town, dating from that day in 1894 when Colonel Sartoris, the mayor—he who fathered the edict that no Negro woman should appear on the streets without an apron—remitted her taxes, the dispensation dating from the death of her father on into perpetuity. Not that Miss Emily would have accepted charity. Colonel Sartoris invented an involved tale to the effect that Miss Emily's father had loaned money to the town, which the town, as a matter of business, preferred this way of repaying. Only a man of Colonel Sartoris' generation and thought could have invented it, and only a woman could have believed it.

When the next generation, with its more modern ideas, became mayors and aldermen, this arrangement created some little dissatisfaction. On the first of the year they mailed her a tax notice. February came, and there was no reply. They wrote her a formal letter, asking her to call at the sheriff's office at her convenience. A week later the mayor wrote her himself, offering to call or to send his car for her, and received in reply a note on paper of an archaic shape, in a thin, flowing calligraphy in faded ink, to the effect that she no longer went out at all. The tax notice was also enclosed, without comment.

They called a special meeting of the Board of Aldermen. A deputation waited upon her, knocked at the door through which no visitor had passed since she ceased giving china-painting lessons eight or ten years earlier. They were admitted by the old Negro into a dim hall from which a stairway mounted into still more shadow. It smelled of dust and disuse—a close, dank smell. The Negro led them into the parlor. It was furnished in heavy, leather-covered furniture. When the Negro opened the blinds of one window, a faint dust rose sliggishly about their thighs, spinning with slow motes in the single sunray. On a tarnished gilt easel before the fireplace stood a crayon portrait of Miss Emily's father.

They rose when she entered—a small, fat woman in black, with a thick gold chain descending to her waist and vanishing into her belt, leaning on an ebony cane with a tarnished gold head. Her skeleton was small and spare; perhaps that was why what would have been merely plumpness in another was obesity in her. She looked bloated, like a body long submerged in motionless water, and of that pallid hue. Her eyes, lost in the fatty ridges of her face, looked like two small pieces of coal pressed into a lump of dough as they moved from one face to another while the visitors stated their errand.

She did not ask them to sit. She just stood in the door and listened quietly until the spokesman came to a stumbling halt. Then they could hear the invisible watch ticking at the end of the gold chain.

Her voice was dry and cold. "I have no taxes in Jefferson. Colonel Sartoris explained it to me. Perhaps one of you can gain access to the city records and satisfy yourselves."

"But we have. We are the city authorities, Miss Emily. Didn't you get a notice from the sheriff, signed by him?"

"I received a paper, yes," Miss Emily said. "Perhaps he considers himself the sheriff . . . I have no taxes in Jefferson."

"But there is nothing on the books to show that, you see. We must go by the—"

"See Colonel Sartoris. I have no taxes in Jefferson."

"But, Miss Emily—"

"See Colonel Sartoris." (Colonel Sartoris had been dead almost ten years.) "I have no taxes in Jefferson. Tobe!" The Negro appeared. "Show these gentlemen out."

II

So she vanquished them, horse and foot, just as she had vanquished their fathers thirty years before about the smell. That was two years after her father's death and a short time after her sweetheart—the one we believed would marry her—had deserted her. After her father's death she went out very little; after her sweetheart went away, people hardly saw her at all. A few of the ladies had the temerity to call, but were not received, and the only sign on life about the place was the Negro man—a young man then—going in and out with a market basket.

"Just as if a man—any man—could keep a kitchen properly," the ladies said; so they were not surprised when the smell developed. It was another link between the gross, teeming world and the high and mighty Griersons.

A neighbor, a woman, complained to the mayor, Judge Stevens, eighty years old.

"But what will you have me do about it, madam?" he said.

"Why, send her word to stop it," the woman said. "Isn't there a law?"

"I'm sure that won't be necessary," Judge Stevens said. "It's probably just a snake or a rat that nigger of hers killed in the yard. I'll speak to him about it."

The next day he received two more complaints, one from a man who came in diffident deprecation. "We really must do something about it, Judge. I'd be the last one in the world to bother Miss Emily, but we've got to do something." That night the Board of Aldermen met—three gray-beards and one younger man, a member of the rising generation.

"It's simple enough," he said. "Send her word to have her place cleaned up. Give her a certain time to do it in, and if she don't. . . ."

"Dammit, sir," Judge Stevens said, "will you accuse a lady to her face of smelling bad?"

So the next night, after midnight, four men crossed Miss Emily's lawn and slunk about the house like burglars, sniffing along the base of the brickwork and at the cellar openings while one of them performed a regular sowing motion with his hand out of a sack slung from his shoulder. They broke open the cellar door and sprinkled lime there, and in all the outbuildings. As they re-crossed the lawn, a window that had been dark was lighted and Miss Emily sat in it, the light behind her, and her upright torso motionless as that of an idol. They crept quietly across the lawn and into the shadow of the locusts that lined the street. After a week or two the smell went away.

That was when people had begun to feel really sorry for her. People in our town, remembering how old lady Wyatt, her great-aunt, had gone completely crazy at last, believed that the Griersons held themselves a little too high for what they really were. None of the young men were quite good enough for Miss Emily and such. We had long thought of them as a tableau; Miss Emily a slender figure in white in the background, her father a spraddled silhouette in the foreground, his back to her and clutching a horsewhip, the two of them framed by the back-flung front door. So when she got to be thirty and was still single, we were not pleased exactly, but vindicated; even with insanity in the family she wouldn't have turned down all of her chances if they had really materialized.

When her father died, it got about that the house was all that was left to her; and in a way, people were glad. At last they could pity Miss Emily. Being left alone, and a pauper, she had become humanized. Now she too would know the old thrill and the old despair of a penny more or less.

The day after his death all the ladies prepared to call at the house and offer condolence and aid, as is our custom. Miss Emily met them at the door, dressed as usual and with no trace of grief on her face. She told them that her father was not dead. She did that for three days, with the ministers calling on her, and the doctors, trying to persuade her to let them dispose of the body. Just as they were about to resort to law and force, she broke down, and they buried her father quickly.

We did not say she was crazy then. We believed she had to do that. We remembered all the young men her father had driven away, and we knew that with nothing left, she would have to cling to that which had robbed her, as people will.

III

She was sick for a long time. When we saw her again, her hair was cut short, making her look like a girl, with a vague resemblance to those angels in colored church windows—sort of tragic and serene.

The town had just let the contracts for paving the sidewalks, and in the summer after her father's death they began to work. The construction company came with niggers and mules and machinery, and a foreman named Homer Barron, a Yankee—a big, dark, ready man, with a big voice and eyes lighter than his face. The little boys would follow in groups to hear him cuss the niggers, and the niggers singing in time to the rise and fall of picks. Pretty soon he knew everybody in town. Whenever you heard a lot of laughing anywhere about the square, Homer Barron would be in the center of the group. Presently we began to see him and Miss Emily on Sunday afternoons driving in the yellow-wheeled buggy and the matched team of bays from the livery stable.

At first we were glad that Miss Emily would have an interest, because the ladies all said, "Of course a Grierson would not think seriously of a Northerner, a day laborer." But there were still others, older people, who said that even grief could not cause a real lady to forget *noblesse oblige*—without calling it *noblesse oblige*. They just said, "Poor Emily. Her kinsfold should come to her." She had some kin in Alabama; but years ago her father had fallen out with them over the estate of old lady Wyatt, the crazy woman, and there was no communication between the two families. They had not even been represented at the funeral.

And as soon as the old people said, "Poor Emily," the whispering began. "Do you suppose it's really so?" they said to one another. "Of course it is. What else could. . . ." This behind their hands; rustling of craned silk and satin behind jalousies closed upon the sun of Sunday afternoon as the think, swift clop-clop-clop of the matched team passed: "Poor Emily."

She carried her head high enough—even when we believed that she was fallen. It was as if she demanded more than ever the recognition of her dignity as the last grierson; as if it had wanted that touch of earthiness to reaffirm her imperviousness. Like when she bought the rat poison, the arsenic. That was over a year after they had begun to say "Poor Emily," and while the two female cousins were visiting her.

"I want some poison," she said to the druggist. She was over thirty then, still a slight woman, though thinner than usual, with cold, haughty black eyes in a face the flesh of which was strained across the temples and about the eyesockets as you imagine a lighthouse-keeper's face ought to look. "I want some poison," she said.

"Yes, Miss Emily. What kind? For rats and such? I'd recom—"

"I want the best you have. I don't care what kind."

The druggist named several. "They'll kill anything up to an elephant. But what you want is—"

"Arsenic," Miss Emily sid. "Is that a good one?"

"Is . . . arsenic? Yes ma'am. But what you want—"

"I want arsenic."

The druggist looked down at her. She looked back at him, erect, her face like a strained flag. "Why, of course," the druggist said. "If that's what you want. But the law requires you tell what you are going to use it for."

Miss Emily just stared at him, her head tilted back in order to look him eye for eye, until he looked away and went and got the arsenic and wrapped it up. The Negros delivery boy brought her the package; the druggist didn't come back. When she opened the package at home there was written on the box, under the skull and bones: "For rats."

IV

So the next day we all said, "She will kill herself"; and we said it would be the best thing. When she had first begun to be seen with Homer Barron, we had said, "She will marry him." Then we said, "She will persuade him yet," because Homer himself had remarked—he like men, and it was known that he drank with the younger men in the Elk's Club—that he was not a marrying man. Later we said, "Poor Emily," behind the jalousies as they passed on Sunday afternoon in the glittering buggy, Miss Emily with her head high and Homer Barron with his hat cocked and a cigar in his teeth, reins and whip in a yellow glove.

Then some of the ladies began to say that it was a disgrace to the town and a bad example to the young people. The men did not want to interfere, but at last the ladies forced the Baptist minister—Miss Emily's people were Episcopal—to call upon her. He would never divulge what happened during that interview, but he refused to go back again. The next Sunday they again drove about the streets, and the following day the minister's wife wrote to Miss Emily's relations in Alabama.

So she had blood-kin under her roof again and we sat back to watch developments. At first nothing happened. Then we were sure that they were to be married. We learned that Miss Emily had been to the jeweler's and ordered a man's toilet set in silver, with the letters H. B. on each piece. Two days later we learned that she had bought a complete outfit of men's clothing, including a nightshirt, and we said, "They are married." We were really glad. We were glad because the two female cousins were even more Grierson than Miss Emily had ever been.

So we were not surprised when Homer Barron—the streets had been finished some time since— was gone. We were a little disappointed that there was a not a public blowing-off, but we believed that he had gone on to prepare to Miss Emily's coming, or to give her a chance to get rid of the cousins. (By that time it was a cabal, and we were all Miss Emily's allies to help circumvent the cousins.) Sure enough, after another week they departed. And, as we had expected all along, within three days Homer Barron was back in town. A neighbor saw the Negro man admit him at the kitchen door at dusk one evening.

And that was the last we saw of Homer Barron. And of Miss Emily for some time. The Negro man went in and out with the market basket, but the front door remained closed. Now and then we would see her at a window for a moment, as the men did that night when they sprinkled the lime, but for almost six months she did not appear on the streets. Then we knew that this was to be expected too; as if that quality of her father which had thwarted her woman's life so many times had been too virulent and too furious to die.

When we next saw Miss Emily, she had grown fat and her hair was turning gray. During the next few years it grew grayer and grayer until it attained an even pepper-and-salt iron-gray, when it ceased turning. Up to the day of her death at seventy-four it was still that vigorous iron-gray, like the hair of an active man.

From that time on her front door remained closed, save for a period of six or seven years, when she was about forty, during which she gave lessons in china-painting. She fitted up a studio in one of the downstairs rooms, where the daughters and granddaughters of Colonel Sartoris' contemporaries were sent to her with the same regularity and in the same spirit that they were sent on Sundays with a twenty-five cent piece for the collection plate. Meanwhile her taxes had been remitted.

Then the newer generation became the backbone and the spirit of the town, and the painting pupils grew up and fell away and did not send their children to her with boxes of color and tedious brushes and pictures cut from the ladies' magazines. The front door closed upon the last one and remained closed for good. When the town got free postal delivery Miss Emily alone refused to let them fasten the metal numbers above her door and attach a mailbox to it. She would not listen to them.

Daily, monthly, yearly we watched the Negro grow grayer and more stooped, going in and out with the market basket. Each December we sent her a tax notice, which would be returned by the post office a week later, unclaimed. Now and then we would see her in one of the downstairs windows—she had evidently shut up the top floor of the house—like the carven torso of an idol in a niche, looking or not looking at us, we could never tell which. Thus she passed from generation to generation—dear, inescapable, impervious, tranquil, and perverse.

And so she died. Fell ill in the house filled with dust and shadows, with only a doddering Negro man to wait on her. We did not even know she was sick; we had long since given up trying to get any information from the Negro. He talked to no one, probably not even to her, for his voice had grown harsh and rusty, as if from disuse.

She died in one of the downstairs rooms, in a heavy walnut bed with a curtain, her gray head propped on a pillow yellow and moldy with age and lack of sunlight.

V

The Negro met the first of the ladies at the front door and let them in, with their hushed, sibilant voices and their quick, curious glances, and then he disappeared. He walked right through the house and out the back and was not seen again.

The two female cousins came at once. They held the funeral on the second day, with the town coming to look at Miss Emily beneath a mass of bought flowers, with the crayon face of her father musing profoundly above the bier and the ladies sibilant and macabre; and the very old men—some in their brushed Confederate uniforms—on the porch and the lawn, talking of Miss Emily as if she had been a contemporary of theirs, believing that they had danced with her and courted her perhaps, confusing time with its mathematical progression, as the old do, to whom all the past is not a diminishing road, but, instead, a huge meadow which no winter ever quite touches, divided from them now by the narrow bottleneck of the most recent decade of years.

Already we knew that there was one room in that region above stairs which no one had seen in forty years, and which would have to be forced. They waited until Miss Emily was decently in the ground before they opened it.

The violence of breaking down the door seemed to fill this room with pervading dust. A thin, acrid pall as of the tomb seemed to lie everywhere upon this room decked and furnished as for a bridal: upon the valance curtains of faded rose color, upon the rose-shaded lights, upon the dressing table, upon the delicate array of crystal and the man's toilet things backed with tarnished silver, silver so tarnished that the monogram was obscured. Among them lay a collar and tie, as if they had just been removed, which, lifted, left upon the surface a pale crescent in the dust. Upon a chair hung the suit, carefully folded; beneath it the two mute shoes and the discarded socks.

The man himself lay in the bed.

For a long while we just stood there, looking down at the profound and fleshless grin. The body had apparently once lain in the attitude of an embrace, but now the long sleep that outlasts love, that conquers even the grimace of love, had cuckolded him. What was left of him, rotted beneath what was left of the nightshirt, had become inextricable from the bed in which he lay; and upon him and upon the pillow beside him lay that even coating of the patient and biding dust.

Then we noticed that in the second pillow was the indentation of a head. One of us lifted something from it, and leaning forward, that faint and invisible dust dry and acrid in the nostrils, we saw a long strand of iron-gray hair.

In considering William Faulkner's "A Rose for Emily," we might note, at the outset, the kind of narrator who tells the story. We have already discussed types of narrators (see p. 127); like Alex, the narrator in *A Clockwork Orange,* the narrator of "A Rose for Emily" is inside the story, but, unlike Alex, is not the principal persona. In fact, the narrator here is a "we," a spokesperson for the townsfolk who observe Miss Emily throughout her lifetime. The storyteller, then, unlike the narrator of "The Killers," is involved in the story as an interested and engaged observer of the events reported.

"A Rose for Emily" begins with the announcement of the principal persona's death and a statement that "the whole town" attended her funeral. The narrator goes on to distinguish between "the men's" and "the women's" reaction to Miss Emily. The whole town was, to different degrees and in different ways, involved in her life, and so reacts to her death. The point of entrance for this narrative is clearly the end of a chronological sequence and so the story, as we read on, consists of flashbacks.

The second incident in the story explains Miss Emily's relationship to the town. Since her father's death, she has paid no taxes. A new generation of town fathers decides to revoke her exemption; she turns them preemptorily away, insisting that she "has no taxes in Jefferson. See Colonel Sartoris." In this episode Miss Emily is an older, small, fat woman in black.

In the next reported episode—the problem with "the smell"—she is thirty years younger. Again the townsfolk complain, this time about a particularly noxious odor coming from Miss Emily's house. The mayor cannot "accuse a lady of smelling bad"; a delegation furtively spreads quicklime around the house and the smell goes away. This is when, the narrator reports, people really began to feel sorry for Miss Emily. The narrator goes on to explain the circumstances surrounding the episode of the "smell." The summer after her father's death, Homer Barron, a Yankee construction foreman, arrives in town, a large, ebullient man who becomes a center of activity and laughter in the town square. Soon the townsfolk see Homer Barron and Miss Emily driving out on Sunday afternoons. This relationship becomes the subject of general gossip in the town. It is during the visit of her female cousins, which is explained further on in the narrative, that Miss Emily buys arsenic and the druggist inscribes the package "For rats." The narrative then continues with the Homer Barron episode; the townsfolk try to put an end to the scandal by summoning the female relatives from Alabama to influence Miss Emily. While they are on the scene, Homer Barron disappears, but Miss Emily buys a nightshirt and hairbrushes with "H. B." engraved upon them. The townsfolk are sure that Miss Emily and Homer Barron are married or to be married. When the female cousins depart in a few weeks, Homer Barron is seen sneaking back into the Grierson house. He is never seen again.

After the disappearance of Homer Barron the town sees little of Miss Emily. For a "six or eight year period" Miss Emily gives lessons in china-painting to the children of well-to-do citizens; eventually the pupils stop coming and the house is closed permanently to the town. Except for the annual tax notice and her manservant growing grayer, the town has no contact with Miss Emily.

At this point the narrative returns to the time of the point of entrance—Miss Emily's death. The house is opened and, in a locked room on the second floor, the townsfolk discover the decomposed body of Homer Barron mingled with the bed and the bedclothes and an iron-gray hair on the indented pillow beside the corpse.

The townsman-narrator tells the story of Miss Emily *as the town observed it,* piecing together the significant incidents of her life as the town discovered them. The order of events in Miss Emily's life in this possible world is related, not in the order of their happening, but in the order of their discovery by the town. They had access only to what they observed from the outside and their image of her was constructed from what they saw, heard, and overheard. The women of the town level different judgments than the men; it is the women who decide to put a stop to Miss Emily's relationship with Homer Barron by insisting that the female cousins be notified. As the incidents of the tax notice, the smell and the rat poison indicate, the men are incapable of dealing effectively with Miss Emily's imperiousness. The story in narration-time elaborates the relationship between the townsfolk and Miss Emily.

The structure of the story in the order of narration, then, may be divided as follows:

Point of entrance: Miss Emily's death and funeral—the whole town's involvement with Miss Emily

Inciting moment: the tax notice—the attempt to treat Miss Emily like an "ordinary citizen"; the incident of the smell—an earlier incident involving the same kind of attempt

Crisis: the courtship of Miss Emily and Homer Barron—the scandal of their relationship and the report of the purchase of the arsenic

Climax: the discovery of Homer Barron's body

Dénouement: the discovery of the "iron-gray hair" on the indented pillow. The order of narration begins with Miss Emily's death and continues through the reconstruction of Miss Emily's life through a series of observations by the townsman-narrator. The end of the narrative is the townsfolk's discovery of the central and critical incident in Miss Emily's life.

It is possible, using the details presented in the order of narration, for us to construct the chronology implied in the text. It looks like this:

1854—Miss Emily Grierson is born
1884—Miss Emily's father dies
1885—Homer Barron comes to town and courts Miss Emily
1886—the female cousins come to visit; Miss Emily buys arsenic; the female cousins leave; Miss Emily poisons Homer Barron and installs him in the upper bedroom; the neighbors complain about "the smell"; the smell disappears
1904–1910—Miss Emily gives china-painting lessons to selected daughters of the town
1916—the deputation from the town council visits to collect the Grierson taxes
1928—Miss Emily dies and is buried in the town cemetery; Homer Barron's body is discovered in the upper bedroom

It is not hard to imagine how different this story would be if its events were told in chronological order. Imagine its being narrated like "The Killers"; it might include only those incidents from 1894 through 1896. In short, it would be a completely different story involving a different possible world. In the order of chronology the focus of the incidents is Miss Emily and her actions; in the order of narration the focus is the relationship between Miss Emily's actions and the observations of the townsfolk.

Our explanation of narrational order in "A Rose for Emily" leads us inevitably to consider the cultural aspect of this possible world. Regardless of her eccentricities, her independence, and her imperiousness, Miss Emily is considered an integral member of the town's community. She is buried in the town graveyard; she "had gone to join the representatives of those august names where they lay in the cedar-bemused cemetery among the ranked and anonymous graves of Union and Confederate soldiers who fell in the battle of Jefferson." The town considers her "a tradition, a duty, and a care." Whatever she does, and however she does it, she belongs, as a Southern lady, to this community. (Note how, at this point, we see Miss Emily as representing a *type*.) Her father may consider the suitors of the town unsuitable for his high-born daughter; Miss Emily may keep company with a Yankee during Reconstruction; she might even consider a declassé marriage to him; the ladies of the town may feel it incumbent upon them to prevent such a marriage, but the town never seriously considers excommunicating her. The way the story is told makes it clear that this is the case. If Homer Barron is "a rat" to be poisoned, the town will not question (though its citizens may not condone) Miss Emily's right to take such an action. Because Homer Barron does not belong to the town, no one investigates his disappearance. That she becomes a recluse is her business; the townsfolk simply accept her decision. Our explanation of the events of the story, in narrational order, make it clear what kind of community the town of Jefferson is and what kind of values it embraces.

This analysis of "A Rose for Emily" illustrates the point that *the way the story is told* is as significant to its meaning as *what happens in the story*. We could, as we noted above, construct a very different kind of story around the events of Miss Emily's life. The possible world which this text presents includes a point of view, a particular slant which the narrator provides. Some years ago a popular television series, "Dragnet," had a main character who was constantly inquiring after "just the facts." Even those narratives that create the impression of giving "just the facts" are always giving *somebody's* "facts." The relatively straightforward voice of the narrator in "The Killers" still, as we have seen, includes some commentary. The possible world of the narrative, unlike the actual world of our experience, is so constructed that attitudes and values are built in. When we consider narration, we are considering precisely the way in which the events acquire their significance. If I tell you a story about a man who slips on a banana peel, the way I tell it will determine whether you find it funny or sad or something in between.

Summary

There are a number of ways a storyteller may tell a story; we have considered only a few of the possible combinations. Each narrative has its own special combination of narrator, narrative-time, and narration-time. There are, however, certain general categories of narrator types and narration types that can help us in examining any given narrative.

Narrators

The narrator may be, first, *absent from his own narrative.* The narrator of "The Killers" is a good instance of the absent narrator. Secondly, the narrator may be *the principal persona in the story.* The narrator, then, tells the story in the first person; he or she is the "I" of the narrative. *A Clockwork Orange* presents us with this kind of narrator in the person of Alex. Thirdly, the narrator can be a *persona involved in the story, but not the principal actor.* He or she can be more or less involved in the events of the narrative; at one extreme, a simple observer, at the other extreme, a persona intimately involved in the major events of the story. The "we" who narrates "A Rose for Emily" is an observer whose involvement in the events is minimal.

So the narrator can be outside the events of the story, or inside the events of the story or inside the events of the story and also the principal persona. In longer fictional narratives we may find combinations of all three types of narrators.

We can also judge the narrator in terms of quality: how much does the narrator know and how open is the narrator likely to be? Some narrators will know more about the events they narrate than the personae in the story do; the narrator of "The Killers" is outside the events of the narrative and not only reports the events, but also comments on them. Some narrators know less than the personae; the narrator of "A Rose for Emily" can only guess at the nature of the relationship between Miss Emily and Homer Barron. There are instances of narrators who know spectacularly less than other personae in the text. In another work by William Faulkner, *The Sound and the Fury,* the first section is "narrated" by a thirty-three-year old who has the mind of a child. Finally, sometimes the narrator moves on the same level as the rest of the personae; this is true, for instance, of the narrator of *The Great Gatsby.*

A way of testing the relationship of the narrator to the rest of the personae is to do a tagmemic analysis using the narrator as the unit. The qualities of a given narrator appear when the narrator is considered as unit-as-system; the situation of the narrator with regard to the other personae appears when the narrator is considered as unit-in-system. The changes in narrative focus will appear when the dynamic aspects of the narrator are considered.

Narration

The basic division which we have made relative to narration, the way a story is told, is *chronological order* as distinguished from *narrational order*. The text establishes the former when it follows a chronological sequence of events, beginning with the earliest event in the sequence and following through to the end. It establishes the latter when it does not follow chronological sequence, beginning at the end of the chronological sequence or somewhere in the middle of it.

We have noted that "Little Red-Cap," "The Killers" and *A Clockwork Orange* establish chronological order. These stories begin with the first event of the sequence and continue without interruption to the end. "A Rose for Emily" establishes narrational order by beginning almost at the end of the chronological segment covered in the story and filling in significant events through flashback.

In narrational order, devices like the flashback or flashforward are standard techniques. The flashback recounts events antecedent to the event just narrated and the flashforward anticipates events which are to come. All the incidents antecedent to Miss Emily's funeral in "A Rose for Emily" are flashbacks; in the incident of the rat-poison purchase, the reference to the visit of the two cousins from Alabama is a flashforward, that is, it anticipates an event which will be described further on in the story.

In explaining the relationship between and among the events of the story the distinction between these two orders is crucial. This becomes clear when we apply the cause/effect topos to a narrative. Often the flashback is required to explain the causes for certain effects already narrated. Why, for instance, in "A Rose for Emily" did the whole population turn out for the funeral of a reclusive spinster who had no living relatives in the town? The effect—large attendance at the funeral—is explained in the events narrated in the flashbacks. In the rat-poison incident, the reference to the visit of the two cousins serves to place that purchase shortly before the disappearance of Homer Barron, thus establishing an interesting connection between arsenic and the Yankee overseer. The order of events in the possible world of the text may be as meaningful as the events themselves.

We are now in the position to say something more specific about the possible world which the fictional narrative presents. It is made up of human action presented in a selected and ordered sequence of events in unmoored time and place by a narrator. The personae engaged in these events represent a collection of qualities that constitute types. The actions they perform in this possible world are *real actions:* they deliver baskets to grandmother, they disobey their mother's commands, they try to warn an acquaintance who is in danger, they are tied up with towels in their mouths, they hang around at the local milk bar, they participate in a gang rape, they attempt to commit suicide, they refuse to pay taxes, they commit murder. All these real actions garner their significance from the types of personae who perform them in given circumstances within the possible world.

Our explanation of any given fictional narrative is a description of these elements in the possible world of the text. As we have attempted to explain the selection and the ordering of events, the relationships among the types of personae, the relationship between the narrator and the world he or she presents, we have undoubtedly come upon certain insights about the meaning of these stories. In examining the parts, we have come to further understandings of the whole. In the next chapter we want to consider the kinds of understandings that might emerge from our explanation of the fictional narrative.

Chapter 16
Symbol, Action-Type and Meaning

The human being can be described as "a symbol-making animal." The use of symbols sets us off from the rest of the animals; the monkey, the horse and the kangaroo do not post signs. The word "symbol" means a mark or a sign; our use of the term refers to a reality in one order that points to a reality in another order. For instance, the stop sign at an intersection is a physical reality, an hexagonal piece of wood or metal painted red with white lettering and mounted on a pole. Granted that it could be used for firewood or scrap metal, its purpose as a physical reality is to point at a legal reality. The meaning of the stop sign is, then, that the authority in the community declares that all law-abiding citizens should come to halt at this intersection before proceeding on their way. Notice that we are dealing here with a different order of reality than the physical. If a tree falls across the road, we have to stop because there is a physical obstacle; the stop sign does not physically block anybody's way, but it does invoke the order of law based on legitimate authority. From this point of view, the stop sign is a symbol, that is, it is a reality in the physical order of things that points to a reality in the legal order of things, a specific exercise of the power of legitimate authority.

Not all signs are *ipso facto* symbols. When we considered the topos of antecedent/consequent under "relation," we indicated that this relationship often has a sign function. If we see smoke, we ordinarily judge that there is a fire; if we detect the odor of food cooking, we may conclude that it is close to mealtime. Smoke and the odor of barbecue are natural signs indicating respectively the presence of fire and a strong probability of dinner. These signs are not symbols because they operate in the same order or reality, the physical order. Even road signs, which are not natural signs, need not be symbols. For instance, a diamond-shaped road sign which has a snake-like configuration on it indicates a series of sharp curves ahead. It is antecedent to the consequence of the road winding, and it does not point to a different order of reality. We might indeed argue that all road signs are established by state authority, but the difference between the stop sign and the winding road sign clearly refer to two different orders of reality. The sign as symbol establishes a relation between two orders which goes beyond a simple antecedent/consequent function.

One of the earliest uses of the term "symbol" was ecclesiastical; church texts like the Apostles' Creed or the Nicene Creed were called "symbols." These texts begin with the words "I (or we) believe." The rest of the text contains a series of statements relative to the Christian religion: one God; the incarnation of Jesus Christ, the son of God; his passion, death, resurrection and exaltation; the Holy Spirit; the Church; the forgiveness of sins and eternal life. It is not immediately clear how this kind of text can be called a symbol. It can be read as a series of statements about what a Christian believes and so it can be viewed simply as an expository text. But in fact, for church members, the recitation of this text was also a sign; it pointed to something more than a statement of what a Christian believes; it also signified a commitment, a profession of faith, on the part of the reciter. So the external action of reciting the Creed was a sign pointing to an internal act of commitment by the believer. Reciting the text with comprehension of its meaning is one order of reality which points to another order of reality distinct from the first, an internal faith commitment in the context of a community.

We have considered two symbols, a stop sign and a credal text. They are quite different in themselves, one a physical object with one word painted on it and the other a fairly sophisticated text. They have in common: (1) they are signs that point to something outside themselves and (2) they are symbols in that what they point to is in a different order of reality than they are. We can detail a whole list of symbols that surround us daily: the eagle clutching a sheaf of arrows in one talon and an olive branch in the other symbolizing the United States, the cross on our churches symbolizing Christianity, a set of scales symbolizing our judicial system, a crowned woman with uplifted torch symbolizing "the land of opportunity." All these symbols are objects in one order of reality which point to a reality in a different order.

The "different order" to which the symbol points has certain characteristics: (1) it is more general and less particular and/or (2) it is more abstract and less concrete and/or (3) it is more mental and less physical. In symbolizing the United States, the eagle points to an idea and an ideal rather than to a topographical map of the country. The symbol tells us that we are a far-sighted nation, strong in war and ready for peace; our aspirations are not earthbound and we can surmount any obstacles to our progress. The "scales of justice" do not weigh in the balance gold or silver but rather the rights and duties of the individual over against the rights and duties of the community. "Justice" is a general, abstract idea, not a physical object. The religious creed, as discussed above, is not simply a collection of black marks on a page, nor is it even, as a symbol, a series of significant statements, but it points to the faith commitment of a religious community. So the different order which is being symbolized deals with an order of understanding and/or an order of values.

Just as objects and personae in the actual world of our experience can symbolize realities in a higher order, so objects and personae in the possible world can have this same function. We want to look, then, at the literary symbol as it works in the fictional narrative. Our objective, as always, is to explain the parts of the text in the light of the whole in order to come to an understanding of the meaning of the whole text.

We have already come to some understandings about the fictional narratives we have been considering. After looking at what the text says by dividing the events, and by looking at what the personae represent, we have drawn some conclusions about the meaning of "Little Red-Cap," "The Killers," *A Clockwork Orange,* "A Rose for Emily." We have seen, for instance that a fairly simplistic understanding of the meaning of "Little Red-Cap" is "obey your mother." We have also noted that a meaning on the cultural level deals with the relationship of the personae of the village and the personae of the woods. The innocent young girl from the village who represents help for others is devoured by the destructive forces of the forest in the person of the wolf and is saved by the canny woodsman who knows the ways of the forest and embraces the values of the village. But we were not on this level able to explain very well why the wolf did not eat up Little Red-Cap on their first meeting. Given what we now understand on the cultural level, we might try an explanation of this seeming anomaly by looking at the symbolism of the story.

We pointed out in our discussion above that the wolf is clearly not just an animal, but is a theriomorph, that is, a human in animal form. He is a wood-dweller, and so represents an earlier cultural stage of human development than the personae who inhabit the village. We can, then, see him as a symbol of this earlier stage, that is, a symbol of the primitive urges in all human beings.

The idea of the "primitive" includes these characteristics: protection of one's tribe and one's turf, concern for survival in a hostile environment, use of violence and physical force as the principal means of obtaining necessities and ensuring survival. Little Red-Cap and her mother, as symbols, balance this primitivism by pointing to those civilized and civilizing tendencies in human beings that foster cooperation, the acceptance and development of an ordered lifestyle, an equitable distribution of the necessities of life for all the members of society. This civilizing tendency comes into conflict with primitive urges in all of us; in the possible world of "Little Red-Cap" the little girl and the wolf might well symbolize these conflicting aspects of the human psyche.

In the wolf's first encounter with Little Red-Cap, he uses a civilized stratagem, persuasion, to divert her from her task. The sunlight and the flowers in the woods draw her off the path and into the freedom that the woods offers. Because she is innocent and ignorant, she does not recognize the dangers lurking in the woods. The civilizing tendency, not tempered by experience, may not recognize the presence of the primitive urge. Were it to recognize that tendency, there would be an accompanying awareness of its destructive power. So the primitive urge cannot devour the civilizing tendency unless the primitive urge is appropriately disguised. In terms of the tale, the wolf cannot devour Little Red-Cap unless he wears a familiar disguise. Grandmother, who in some sense belongs to civilization, still lives in the woods, is old and sick and so, in symbolic terms, is not able to resist the primitive. (Her latch string is out.) The civilizing tendency without the support of a civilized environment can fall prey to the primitive. So Grandmother can be transformed into the wolf. The woodsman is an important figure in that he symbolizes the need that the civilizing tendency has to recognize its enemy and to deal with the enemy in his own habitat. The woodsman uses primitive means—violence—to subdue the primitive urge; it is interesting, however, that he also uses an instrument of civilization to accomplish his purpose. He cuts open the wolf's belly with scissors to free Little Red-Cap and her grandmother and then skins the beast and fills the carcass with stones. It is necessary to weigh the primitive urges down or, presumably, they will revive.

Explaining the story in these symbolic terms sees the personae not only as types, but also as elements of the human psyche. The cultural aspect of the story deals with the possible world of social relationships; as the personae symbolize different interacting impulses and tendencies of the human spirit, the events of the story also operate in a different order of reality, the psychic order.

It might occur to you at this point that we are making a great deal of fuss about a folktale that is generally considered a children's story. Children have no trouble either following or enjoying the story without elaborate explanation. The events hold their interest and the story comes to the kind of conclusion that children (of all ages) appreciate. The possible world of "Little Red-Cap" or, in its various versions "Little Red Riding Hood," is one that children can accept without question. Our explanation of the symbolism in the story, as a way of dealing with problems the story raises, does not change one bit the text of the narrative; it merely explores further significances that the possible world of the tale contains. Even in a "children's story" like "Little Red-Cap," nothing is quite as simple as it looks.

To take this complication one step further, we must note that the same persona, image, or object can work in different symbolic ways. Because symbolism establishes relations between two orders of reality, and there are a number of orders of reality (the physical, the social, the intellectual, the volitive, the cosmic), the persona or image or object can point to a number of different relationships. We have seen that the wolf and the little girl can symbolize tendencies in our psychological make-up, forces in the psychic order. We showed how considering them as symbols could help us explain a problem with probability or causality in the tale. These same personae can also symbolize a relationship between two other orders of reality that serves the same explanatory function.

Our task, you recall, is to discover some plausible rationale for the wolf's delay in devouring Little Red-Cap. Explaining that delay in terms of symbols relating to the psychic order worked well enough, seeing the wolf as a symbol of primitivism and Little Red-Cap as a symbol of civilization. We can also see the wolf and the girl as symbols of a cosmic order. When the woodsman snips open the wolf's stomach, the first thing he sees is "the red cap shining." On exiting from the wolf's belly, Little Red-Cap exclaims: "How dark it was inside the wolf." The girl, when she strays off the path, is attracted by "the sunbeams dancing here and there through the trees." The color red, the red cape shining, the connection of the little girl with sunbeams suggest that Little Red-Cap is associated with the sun. The wolf, on the other hand, is explicitly associated with darkness. If we put these two symbolic images together, the tale may also be about the sun being swallowed up by darkness, that is, about a solar eclipse.

This symbolic relationship between the personae and the planetary system may seem incredibly farfetched. Our simple folktale about "obey your mother" can also be about interplanetary events. What kind of evidence can we mount for a claim as apparently preposterous as this one?

The text of the folktale "Little Red-Cap" exists in the midst of a whole constellation of other texts relating to the "wisdom" of the folk. The topos of similarity helps us to explore how things relate to one another in terms of their likenesses; what we know about other texts that are similar to the one we are investigating can shed light (no pun intended) on our investigation. In a book called *Grimm's Teutonic Mythology,* there is a narrative about "The Moon-dog." (We might also recall that "Little Red-Cap" appears in a collection of tales by the Brothers Grimm.) In this myth the moon is pursued across the sky by a pack of wolves. Periodically one of the wolves devours the moon; the moon is then itself turned into a wolf which pursues the sun. Periodically the sun is devoured by the moon-dog or wolf. Once we place this moon-dog text alongside "Little Red-Cap," it is not hard to see the similarity between that myth and the story of Little Red-Cap. We need only substitute "sun" for "Little Red-Cap" and "moon" for "Grandmother," (the moon goes through phases, waxes and wanes, is more strong or less strong in giving off light) and "moon-dog" for "wolf." The folktale becomes, in this reading, a primitive and imaginative explanation of the solar eclipse.

When we consider Little Red-Cap and the wolf as symbolizing planets, two different orders of reality are related—the social and cosmic. It might be helpful here to summarize our argument about this planetary symbolism on the basis of the Toulmin Model.

Claim: Little Red-Cap, the wolf, and Grandmother symbolize the sun, "the moon-dog," and the moon respectively.

Grounds:
1. Internal evidence: the little girl is associated with sunlight; the wolf is associated with darkness; the grandmother is "sick and weak."
2. External evidence: a text in *Grimm's Teutonic Mythology* tells the story of the moon-dog which shows considerable similarity to personae and events in "Little Red-Cap."

Warrant: There is a principal of intertextuality which states that texts with similar characteristics present possible worlds which can intersect and interact.

We will have occasion to comment further on this "principle of intertextuality." Given this cosmic symbolism, we have found another way of explaining probable causality in this folktale. As the moon-dog, the wolf cannot devour Little Red-Cap until he has been transformed into Grandmother (the moon) by devouring her. It would be neat indeed if we could find planetary symbolism in the woodsman. The fact is that, as we remarked above, the woodsman's appearance in this tale is largely based on happenstance. He happens by, for no reason that the story elaborates, and so is able to rescue the little girl and her grandmother. The planetary symbolism works well enough to get Little Red-Cap and the grandmother into the wolf's belly in the proper order, but it does not offer any suggestion about how they get out again. The Teutonic myth, to which we referred above, does not explain why the sun reappears. On the level of the cosmic symbolism, the reappearance of the sun can only be counted as a happy accident. In fact, the context of the myth gloomily predicts that finally the sun will not return and the world will come to an end. We can only hope that the cosmic woodsman will continue to happen by at the crucial moment.

Symbolism in "The Killers"

A narrative like "The Killers" seems to have little in it which could be called symbolic. Yet we noticed a number of ambiguities in the narrative: the problem with time, the difficulty identifying places and names, the mystery of who sent the gangsters and why the Swede "got in wrong." There is, however, one ineluctable certainty in the narrative. The Swede is sooner or later going to be killed. Nick does what he can to postpone that event and risks his own neck to do so. The Swede, however, accepts the inevitable. After a while he will "make up [his] mind to go out."

At the dénouement Nick and George discuss the situation of the Swede and the killers. Nick says that it is an awful thing and that he is going to get out of this town; George replies that he'd better not think about it. Sooner or later, in this town or some other, the awful thing will happen to Nick. "The killers" will come for him too.

We can, then, see the two gangsters of the story as symbolizing death, the one absolute certainty that all the personae face. Other texts acquaint us with a number of images that symbolize the inevitable end of every human being's life-course. In the medieval play *Everyman,* Death is a persona who arrives to summon Everyman to God's throne for judgment. In William Cullen Bryant's poem "Thanatopsis" Death is a sleep accompanied by pleasant dreams. Flannery O'Connor's novel *Wise Blood* images death as a candle-flame in the mind that grows weaker and finally goes out. In "The Killers" death is an anonymous and impersonal force from "elsewhere" that comes to take life away violently. The killers can be a speeding car in the night, a blood clot striking the heart, an invasion of cancerous cells or microbes, a fall in the shower. Symbolically the killers in whatever form will inevitably arrive no matter what town Nick settles in.

The two gangsters as a symbol of death take the meaning to a general truth embedded in the particular events of this story, from a cultural level to a philosophic one. It provides us with an insight about the meaning of the story that generalizes the specifics. All we need do, once we have grasped the symbolism, is substitute "death" for "the two gangsters" in our five-point summary of the narrative. This substitution tells us how death is defined in the possible world of "The Killers."

Symbolism in "A Rose for Emily"

The dénouement of "A Rose for Emily" concludes with a shocking detail: on the pillow next to the decomposed body of Homer Barron is an indentation of a head and "a long strand of iron-grey hair." These two images tell us that, not only did Miss Emily poison the Yankee foreman and keep his body in the house, but she also slept beside the corpse. The shock of this recognition fixes the image of the strand of grey hair in our imagination and raises a question about its significance. It completes the narrative's description of Miss Emily; she will go to any lengths to keep Homer Barron, who is not the marrying kind, at her side. He may not keep faith with her, but she will certainly be faithful—in her own indomitable way—to him. The "iron-grey hair," a physical object, tells us, in the first instance, about the relationship between Miss Emily and Homer Barron. It also tells us how this reclusive Southern lady responds to the threat of being abandoned by her lover. Is there possibly anything more to it?

On the cultural level, this narrative deals with the relationship of Miss Emily and the towns-folk and their discovery of the nature of Miss Emily's relationship with Homer Barron. Miss Emily is a Southern lady, the town of Jefferson is a Southern town, Homer Barron is a Yankee outsider. Applying our principle of intertextuality, we can compare "A Rose for Emily" with the stories in Thomas Nelson Page's *In Ole Virginny* for other instances of Southern ladies marrying Yankees. In Page's stories and in other fictional narratives set in the South after the Civil War, it frequently happens that the Southern lady marries a Yankee captain and saves the old plantation. The charm of the South overwhelms the practicality of the North and the breech between the two erstwhile enemies is healed. The story we are considering does not turn out quite like these romances. But Miss Emily does "marry" a Yankee; she is buried among Union and Confederate soldiers; some of the people at her funeral are wearing Confederate uniforms. The iron-grey color of Miss Emily's hair is also the color of the Confederate uniform. On this basis Miss Emily might well symbolize the South, not the geographical region but rather that collection of attitudes and values ascribable to a Southern mentality.

All of Miss Emily's characteristics reveal attitudes in the possible world of the South during the period of Reconstruction. Pride, indomitability, the attempt to effect an equitable and honorable rapprochement in her erst-while adversary, a sense of betrayal, and a final inability and unwillingness to forgive and forget. The significance of the gray hair grows from the physical object to a representative type to the idea of the South and this accumulation of insights shows how symbolization works in this story. "The South" is an abstraction—an integrated consciousness which constitutes an ideal. The iron-grey hair as symbol can trigger these insights.

Symbolism and Meaning

These illustrations from the stories we have examined show how symbolism can enlarge their meaning. It is very important to remember that, while these objects and personae can function symbolically, the symbolism does not wipe out their other functions in the stories. The symbol relates two orders of reality and *both* orders remain valid. The strand of hair remains a strand of hair even as it symbolizes the South. The two gangsters remain two gangsters even as they symbolize death. Little Red-Cap is an innocent and ignorant girl from the village even as she symbolizes the sun. If this seems all too complex and confused, consider that, if you run your car into the stantions supporting a stop sign, you will smash up your grill even as the stop sign represents an abstraction. In the possible world as in the actual world the same object can serve a number of different purposes and work on a number of different levels.

Events and Action Types

We have been considering the way in which *objects* and *personae* can encompass a number of levels of reality through symbolism; we now need to consider how *the events themselves* in the possible world of the fictional narrative can contain more universal meaning. We began our investigation of the narrative by postulating a general order of events involving a beginning, a middle and an end. Events in the actual world of our experience and in biographical or historical narratives that present an actual world do not, as we have seen, wear signs declaring that they are "a beginning," or "an end." The same event can be, from different perspectives, all three. For instance, a wedding can be the end of a courtship, the beginning of married life, the middle of a life-course. There are, however, *patterns of events* that define human action in the possible world. Identifying these patterns helps us come to fuller understanding of the fictional work.

To get at these patterns, which we might call *action-types,* we will consider, using the topos of similarity, the pattern of events in "Little Red-Cap" and "The Killers" to see what the pattern of events in these stories has in common. Little Red-Cap, following her mother's command, ventures out of the village into the woods, a new and unfamiliar situation. She does not recognize the wolf for what he is and so undergoes a fearful experience in the wolf's belly. She emerges from this ordeal as a member of a new community—Grandmother, the woodsman, and Little Red-Cap share cakes and wine together. This pattern of events produces a new consciousness in the girl; she is a changed person because of it. Nick Adams, in "The Killers," does not go out into a strange place; rather, the strange place comes to him. With the invasion of the hitmen the town of Summit, a secure and stable environment, is transformed into a "woods" full of danger and uncertainties. Nick, too, undergoes a trial, one that is imposed from without and another which he imposes on himself. The gangsters hold him under the gun and he takes the risk of going out to warn the Swede. At the end of this trial Nick is a changed person in that he recognizes that the security he took for granted is illusory. What Little Red-Cap learns and what Nick learns are quite different, but there is a noteworthy similarity in the pattern of events in each of the stories.

Action-Type: Initiation

We may describe this action-type pattern of events generically as follows: (1) the persona is separated from his accustomed community and environment; (2) the individual undergoes a trial or ordeal; (3) the individual is initiated into a new "community." The beginning of this action pattern is the separation, the middle is the test or ordeal, the end is incorporation into a new community with a new status.

When this action-type appears in the actual world of our experience, and it does, we call it a ritual. A ritual is a ceremony that a society enacts to achieve a specific purpose. The initiation ritual incorporates new members into the society. We can be initiated into the church by baptism, into the alumni by graduation, into citizenship by an oath of allegiance. These initiations deal with different orders of reality—religious, societal, political. Each of them follows the pattern of events that we have outlined above: separation, test or trial, incorporation. In the possible world of fiction we can recognize this initiation pattern in a wide range of variations.

159

The action-type as an element in the narrative heuristic is as much a heuristic as any of the categories of the topoi. It is a way of generally defining or categorizing the pattern of events in a given narrative or piece of fiction. So it is not enough simply to say that "Little Red-Cap" or "The Killers" is about initiation. The last statement, for instance, in the folktale has Little Red-Cap declaring that she will never again disobey her mother. This statement is at odds with a full-blown maturity. Nick Adams also does not come to a full realization of his predicament: unlike George and the Swede, he is going to try to escape the killers. In each case the incorporation into the new community is less than perfect.

Identifying the action-type can contribute substantially to a further understanding of the fictive narrative even when the incorporation is imperfect or unconsummated. It is possible to view *A Clockwork Orange* as initiation. Alex is separated from the gang and from his usual environment; he passes through the ordeal of reformation and his suicide attempt; he is restored to his community. This incorporation, however, is ironic because in fact nothing has changed, either for Alex or for the society. In the dénouement the old Alex reappears, and the society is still under the thumb of a repressive authority. This is an ironic instance of the action-type in that the change that should occur by virtue of this pattern of events does not occur. In the possible world of *A Clockwork Orange* the more things change, the more they are the same. If then we are depressed or disturbed by the impact of this fictive narrative, this failed expectation may explain why.

Action-Type: The Quest

Another action-type which is common in narratives and which resembles the initiation type is the quest. Think for a minute of the number of fictive narratives entitled "The Adventures of—." Tom Jones, Tristam Shandy, Huckleberry Finn, Augie March might come to mind. We can go back to classical literature, to the epics of Greece and Rome—the stories of the *Odyssey,* the adventures of Odysseus on his way home from the Trojan War, and the *Aeneid,* the search of Aeneas for a new home—and the medieval romances in which knights search for the Holy Grail. All of these narratives involve a quest, journeys and adventures, with a purpose. The action-type of the quest has the following elements: (1) the principal persona sets out on a journey; (2) he undergoes a series of trials or tests and overcomes a series of obstacles and/or opponents; (3) he achieves the object of his quest and enjoys its benefits and/or confers them upon his community.

The principal persona who undertakes the quest can be of high or low rank—a knight or a beggar—he can undertake the quest on his own initiative or find himself forced to journey forth, his mission can be as diverse as founding a city or discovering the Grail or making his fortune or escaping "sivilization." In this action-type the pattern provides us with a framework for understanding, but the meaning of a particular work depends on the details we described above: the kind of mission, the type of the persona, the outcome of the adventure.

Belonging

The action-types of initiation and the quest have a common causality or motivation. Both look to achieving a certain status in a community (the squire becomes a knight) or benefitting a community in specific ways (the knight marries the princess and harmony returns to the kingdom). The action pattern of initiation transforms the individual by incorporation into a different community; the quest results in the adventurer's founding a new community, joining a new community, changing status in the community or conferring some benefit upon the community. One of the basic human desires is to belong; we all want to have a sense of belonging—to our family, to our peer group, to our university, to our state and our nation. The motivation behind these action patterns is this desire to belong and the possible world of the fictive narrative, through the action-type, presents us with different ways of belonging to societal units. In the examples we have given it is clear that, in the possible world as in the actual world of our own experience, we do not always belong fully or in the way we might like or to an ideal society. But it is this aspiration to belong that drives the pattern, that supplies the causality and the continuity for the movement from event to event.

Purgation

Another major action-type which we can discover in the fictive work has to do with rooting out evil. When Miss Emily purchases the poison, the druggist writes on the package "For rats." In the possible world of "A Rose for Emily" Homer Barron is a rat—by Miss Emily's standards (and for different reasons, the town's) he represents an evil influence. So she gets rid of him. In a very literal way Miss Emily lives with the consequences of her action; it is often the case that the persona who must deal with the evil must also suffer its consequences. Coping with evil in oneself or in the community is the basis for the action-type of purgation.

A whole range of popular forms of fictive narrative manifest this action-type. We have already discussed, from the point of view of narrational order, the narrative of detection. The detective story begins with the discovery that a crime has been committed. The society of this possible world contains a criminal element, the murderer. The job of the detective is to ferret out the evil-doer and bring him or her to justice. The types of detectives vary from Miss Marple to Mike Hammer, the settings from an English country garden to the backstreets of San Francisco, the murderers from grandmothers to Mafia mobsters. But the action-type reveals a similar pattern: (1) the discovery of a crime; (2) the search for the criminal; (3) the discovery of the criminal and his or her elimination from society. The spy-thriller and the fiction of international intrigue (cf. the James Bond series) follow basically this same formula.

Our own specifically American contribution to this action-type is the Western. The conventional pattern of events involves the cowboy-hero riding into the little valley where the inhabitants are plagued by an outlaw gang or a greedy landgrabber. The hero fights corruption with his fists and his guns, and, occasionally, his wit. The outcome is the destruction of the forces for evil and peace comes to the valley. In this version of the purgation type, evil is easily identified and the hero needs only physical courage, quickness, strength and cunning to eliminate it. Again, heroes and their opponents vary in background and status, and the situation in the community may differ, but the action-type with its pattern of events remains constant.

Purgation and Guilt

In the examples of the detective story and the Western, the evil with which the principal persona is primarily concerned is external to the hero himself. The murderer and the bad guys have little in common with the detective or the good guy except that they both inhabit the same possible world. The case is somewhat different when the principal persona in some way participates in the evil. He or she does wrong or discovers a wrong which he or she has done. The result is guilt and the suffering that ensues from it. The persona struggles with the consequences of his or her deed and, if the pattern of events is complete, the struggle frees the personae from their sense of guilt and so restores order to the possible world.

161

This version of the purgation type has a simple enough structure: (1) the principal persona (knowingly or unknowingly) violates a law, commits a crime, breaks a taboo; (2) suffers the consequences of the deed; (3) is freed from the guilt associated with the deed by virtue of the suffering and is restored to the community. Because of the wide range of variation in the kinds of guilt, the varying degrees of responsibility individuals incur, and the range of orders—religious, social, legal—which impose burdens upon the individual, this action-type can seldom be applied straightforwardly to the events of a fictive narrative. *The Scarlet Letter,* for instance, is about Hester Prynne's affair with the Reverend Mr. Dimmesdale and the consequences of their deed. Hester certainly suffers dire consequences: she wears the scarlet letter, she is ostracized from the community, she must raise her child alone, she is persecuted by her husband, she must conceal the identity of her lover. But the community and the minister certainly share responsibility for her plight. In this instance, as in many others, there is quite enough guilt to go around. The minister is guilty, not only of adultery, but even more notably of hypocrisy when he fails to reveal his complicity. The community is stiff-necked in its application of the law and its unwillingness to forgive. Hester, then, not only redeems herself, but also provides the occasion for the minister's confession and the community's recognition of its fallibility. Again, the action pattern serves as a framework which is modified by the events and the personae.

Causality or motivation behind this action-type is the desire we all acknowledge to be free from the influences of evil from the past and in the present, in our own lives and in the lives of those around us. In the actual world of our experience, we deal with a world of sweets and sours, with good and evil intermixed in ways that seem inextricable. In the possible world of the narrative evil can be more easily identified, especially in popular versions like the detective story and the Western. Dealing with the evil recognizable in our own past and the guilt that stems from it is a more complex and difficult process. In the possible world of the narrative the problem of guilt, as we have seen, in our illustration from *The Scarlet Letter,* can be equally complex. The action-type of purgation, whether it deals with evil external to the individual or the evil of the past as it produces guilt in the present, involves this structure of events: (1) recognition of the presence of evil; (2) suffering and/or struggle resulting from the evil; (3) purgation of the evil and the reintegration of society and/or the individual.

Action-Type: Gnosis

"Gnosis" is a Greek word which means "coming to know." This action-pattern is one with which we are very familiar in using the methodologies for explanation and analysis. Preunderstanding, explanation, and understanding can be seen as an action-type. It is the process we use to discover meaning in the texts we read and the texts we write. We cannot understand the meaning of the text as a whole without the ability to explain the parts. Application of the methodologies, the process of analytic thinking, involves considerable expenditure of energy and effort—in short, it is a kind of ordeal. The result of this effort at explanation is often discovery, and insights about the meaning of the text. This pattern of events in our actual experience is also an action-type in the possible world of the fictive text.

The action-type of gnosis constitutes a more general category than the action-types of initiation and purgation and, as such, includes those other two action-types and their variations. We have seen that Little Red-Cap's encounter with the wolf and its consequences is a learning experience for the little girl, that Nick Adams comes to understand how uncertain life can be. We also noted that, after all his experience, it is ironic that Alex understands so little about himself and his own situation. Undergoing the experiences of dealing with the wolf and the gangsters,

Little Red-Cap and Nick Adams emerge with new awarenesses about themselves and their world. Alex emerges from his experiences essentially unchanged; he does not learn what he ought.

The action-type of gnosis is particularly relevant to "A Rose for Emily." The townsman-narrator pieces together the public events of Miss Emily's life in a way that leads to discovery. The narrational order of the story orders the events in terms of gnosis. We do not finally know the internal workings of Miss Emily's consciousness: what the psychological dimensions of her relationship with Homer Barron were, whether she felt any remorse about the murder, what her feelings were as she lay down nightly beside the corpse. We do know how the town responded to her and the results of their new awarenesses about her on the discovery of Homer Barron's body. Viewing the story in the light of this action-type provides a rationale for the order of events in the narrative.

In *The Scarlet Letter,* Hester Prynne learns about guilt and the consequences of her deed. In the crisis event of the novel, she meets Dimmesdale in the forest and they discuss escaping together. She would leave behind the community, her past, and the scarlet letter. Across a small brook their child is playing and has fashioned an "A" from greenery and placed it on her breast. Hester realizes, contemplating her child, that she cannot run away from her past without denying the new person she has become because of it. Through the suffering of ostracism and the burden of child-rearing and the weight of keeping the minister's secret, she has arrived at a new awareness of herself and her place in her world.

The pattern of events that lead to gnosis may be described as: (1) a preunderstanding of the problem endemic in the initial situation; (2) a series of experiences that clarify the situation; (3) a new understanding of the self and the world. This generic action-type corresponds to our desire to know, to know ourselves, to know the people around us, to understand the society and the cosmos which make up our universe. In the possible world, also, we expect that experience will lead the personae to new knowledge; where it does not, we cannot help but level a judgment against the personae and their society. If Alex turns out to have learned nothing, we can only conclude that there is something lacking in him or in his society.

Overlap and Interface

Sharp-eyed readers have assuredly noticed that there are significant similarities among the action-types we have described above. The central element in each of them involves what the Greeks call *pathos:* a test, a trial, a suffering. As Sophocles points out in the last chorus of *Oedipus Rex,* suffering leads to wisdom; and so, whether incorporation or purgation is the result of the pattern of events, the expectation would be that the personae would learn something from their experience. These action-types are not exclusive, but serve as heuristics which help us see a larger meaning in these events. We may not be able, in certain cases, to decide which action-type predominates and there may be differences of opinion on the matter, but these types provide us with still another way of arriving at meaning in a fictive narrative.

Summary

In this chapter we have taken another turn around the hermeneutic circle of preunderstanding, explanation, and understanding. We took our division of the events of the narrative into a five-point structure and our identification of the personae as types to another level of interpretation in which we saw objects and personae as symbolic and the pattern in these events as action-types. In employing these methods we saw that first a narrative can span a number of orders of reality—physical, social, cultural, cosmic, moral and religious. The symbol allows for the interaction of these different orders with one another. We have also seen how the pattern of events can establish meaning within and across those orders of reality in the possible world of the text. Because the possible world created by language can be as complex as the actual world of our experience, no interpretation of the text, however valid, will ultimately exhaust its meaning. Each time we read a piece of fiction, it will reveal new vistas, yield new understandings. Francis Bacon points out, in his essay "Of Books," that some books are to be re-read. Any fictive text offering us a complex possible world qualifies for re-reading. Each time we re-read such a book, we swing again around the interpretative circle, bringing new preunderstandings, additional explanations, and fresh insights.

There are other forms of fictive texts which create possible worlds in ways other than the narrative. In the next chapter we will consider the dramatic text to see how the play creates a possible world and how we get at the meaning of it.

Chapter 17
Drama

In fictive narratives we have considered to this point, there has always been a story and a storyteller. The narrator is free to tell us whatever is necessary about the events, the personae and the circumstances of the story. There are, however, fictive texts that have no storyteller. This kind of fictive text contains principally the words of the personae as they act out the events. We generally call this kind of fictive text "drama" and individual instances of this kind of text "plays."

A dramatic text, like any fictive narrative, presents a series of events with a beginning, a middle, and an end, in an unmoored place out of historical time, dealing with human action, but unlike other fictive narratives, there is no storyteller as such within the dramatic text itself. The words of the text, with the exception of stage directions, are all those of the dramatis personae, the agents acting out the events. We come to know what happens in a play by attending to the words of the dramatis personae.

There is another obvious difference between the drama and other types of fictive narratives. We can view the play on stage presented by actors with scenery and scenic effects; we can read a dramatic text on the page. In both instances we are experiencing the play: 1) in viewing what is on the stage, we observe actors playing out what is happening; 2) in reading what is on the page, we interpret the text in order to discover what is happening. Just as in reading other fictive texts our first concern is the events, so in grasping the dramatic text, our first concern is the events, what is happening in the play.

If we are reading a play rather than seeing one, in order to discover what the text says, we must supply, from the words of the personae, the physical movements and gestures which the actors would play out on stage. Our approach to a dramatic text must include what the personae are *doing* as well as what they are *saying*. Though the stage directions which the dramatic text contains describe physical movements and gestures, often enough these directions simply make explicit what is implicit in the dialogue. We might now look at some instances of dramatic texts to see how we might supply the spectacle that a stage production would present.

Here are two short episodes that serve to illustrate what we must do to supply the spectacle.

Enter Brabantio, Roderigo, *and* Officers
with torches and weapons

Iago.	It is Brabantio. General, be advis'd; he comes to bad intent.
Oth.	Holla! stand there!
Rod.	Signior, it is the Moor.
Bra.	Down with him, thief!
	[*They draw on both sides.*]
Iago.	You, Roderigo! come, sir, I am for you.
Oth.	Keep up your bright swords, for the dew will rust them.
	Good signior, you shall more command with years than with your weapons.

(*Othello*, 1.2. 55–61)

Othello from *The Complete Plays and Poems of William Shakespeare* (William Allan Neilson and Charles Jarvis Hill, ed.)

Othello encounters Brabantio's men; they come "with bad intent." Othello demands that they stop: "Holla! Stand there!" He then tells them, "Keep up your bright swords, for the dew will rust them." From this line we know that Brabantio's men have drawn their swords and are ready to attack. Othello gives them an order to put their swords away, and issues a mild threat: "the dew will rust them." We imagine the posse coming to a halt on Othello's command, drawing their swords, and then backing down as Othello warns them that he is ready to fight. He makes it clear that he has no doubt as to the outcome of the fight; the dew will rust their bright swords. As we read the lines, we can envision the gestures, Othello's tone of voice, the posse's bright swords. What the text says is that Brabantio's men meet Othello and Othello backs them down. Another instance: in Shakespeare's *Romeo and Juliet,* Romeo is in the Capulet orchard when he says "But soft! what light through yonder window breaks/It is the east and Juliet is the sun." This speech is a response to the fact that a casement window above has opened and Juliet has stepped out on the balcony. Othello's line would make no sense if the posse were not brandishing their swords; Romeo's line makes sense only if Juliet has already appeared. We visualize the physical action and gestures of the persona, by inferring them from the dialogue.

We now want to look at a slightly longer text to discover what it "says," that is, what gestures can be inferred from the dramatic dialogue. The following is the opening scene of *Romeo and Juliet.*

Act I, Scene 1

Enter two other serving-men [ABRAHAM *and* BALTHASAR]

Sam.	My naked weapon is out. Quarrel! I will back thee.	40
Gre.	How! turn thy back and run?	
Sam.	Fear me not.	
Gre.	No, marry; I fear thee!	
Sam.	Let us take the law of our sides; let them begin.	45
Gre.	I will frown as I pass by, and let them take it as they list.	
Sam.	Nay, as they dare. I will bite my thumb at them; which is disgrace to them, if they bear it.	50
Abr.	Do you bite your thumb at us, sir?	
Sam.	I do bite my thumb, sir.	
Abr.	Do you bite your thumb at us, sir?	
Sam.	[*Aside to Gre.*] Is the law of our side, if I say ay?	55
Gre.	No.	
Sam.	No, sir, I do not bite my thumb at you, sir; but I bite my thumb, sir.	
Gre.	Do you quarrel, sir?	
Abr.	Quarrel, sir? No, sir.	60
Sam.	But if you do, sir, I am for you. I serve as good a man as you.	
Abr.	No better.	
Sam.	Well, sir.	

Romeo and Juliet from *The Complete Plays and Poems of William Shakespeare* (William Allan Neilson and Charles Jarvis Hill, tr.)

Gre.	Say "better"; here comes one of my	
	master's kinsmen.	66
Sam.	Yes, better, sir.	
Abr.	You lie.	
Sam.	Draw, if you be men. Gregory, remember	
	thy [swashing] blow.	*[They fight* 70
Ben.	Part, fools!	
	Put up your swords; you know not what you do.	

[Beats down their swords.]

Enter TYBALT.

Tyb.	What, art thou drawn among these heartless hinds?	
	Turn thee, Benvolio, look upon thy death.	
Ben.	I do but keep the peace. Put up thy sword,	75
	Or manage it to part these men with me.	
Tyb.	What, drawn, and talk of peace! I hate the word	
	As I hate hell, all Montagues, and thee.	
	Have at thee, coward!	*[They fight*

Enter three or four CITIZENS [*and* OFFICERS], *with clubs or partisans.*

Off.	Clubs, bills, and partisans! Strike! Beat them down!	80
	Down with the Capulets! down with the Montagues!	

The scene is a city street; two sets of serving men meet: Samson and Gregory; Abraham and Balthasar. As we read into the scene, it is clear that there is trouble brewing. The first pair of serving men (Samson and Gregory) draw their swords when they see the other pair approaching. They debate about whether to pick a quarrel and Samson makes a disparaging gesture (bites his thumb) as the others pass. He is not, however, ready to risk a fight and neither is Abraham. When Benvolio comes on the scene, Samson and Gregory take heart, insisting that they have the better master. As the servants begin to slash at one another, Benvolio draws his sword and steps between them. Tybalt enters, draws his sword, and jumps in to confront Benvolio. Benvolio refuses to fight. Tybalt charges Benvolio and they fall to dueling. Citizens and officers rush in with clubs and spears and part the fighters. We can visualize the false bravado and the timidity of the serving men as they reluctantly square off with one another, Benvolio's attempt to keep the peace, and the more sophisticated swordplay of Benvolio and Tybalt when Tybalt forces the fight.

This is what it means to supply spectacle, to specify movement and gesture for the personae. We make sense of the scene by visualizing the relationships among the personae and their physical interactions from inferences in the dialogue. This imaginative exercise is essential to our preunderstanding of a dramatic text; with practice envisioning the physical movement and gestures of the personae will become automatic. As we *read* the lines of dialogue, we also *see* what the personae are doing.

Preunderstanding and Action-Types

Because the events of the play are compacted in time and space and presented directly to eye and ear, it is important, in our inspectional reading, to experience the play as a whole. Like other narratives, a play has a beginning, a middle, and an end. The structure of the events, that is, the way the beginning relates to the middle and the middle to the end is the plot of the play, what happens on the page or on stage. Because there is no storyteller to elaborate on the events, the plots in drama tend to be more conventional than in other fictive narratives. "Conventional" here means that the same kind of plot structures are found in a wide variety of plays. This is not remarkable when we consider that the play must be self-explanatory and that the audience or reader must be able to grasp it immediately. Thus, when we talk of action-types in dramatic texts, we are referring to certain conventional plot structures that offer us a general outline of the action.

Expectations

We have discussed other versions of these conventional plots above, e.g., the detective-mystery story (p. 157). After we have read a few stories of this type, we know what to expect in the events: (1) a crime is committed by a person or persons unknown; (2) a detective comes on the scene and examines the evidence and pursues certain clues; (3) the detective discovers the criminal and he or she is appropriately punished. We can be fairly certain that the detective will discover the criminal: our interest is maintained because we want to know "who dunnit." The general outline of the detective-mystery narrative is conventional; we know the mystery will be solved and we are interested in how it is solved. Again, after we have seen a few Western films, we can pretty well predict how they will come out: (1) the cowboy hero will ride into a community whose members are being harassed or terrorized by "bad buys"; (2) the cowboy hero overcomes threats of violence and violence against his person by dint of his courage and dexterity; (3) the cowboy hero defeats the villains and rides into the sunset, leaving a secure and peaceful community behind. We enjoy the suspense of the hero's brushes with death because we can be fairly certain that he will come out unscathed and that justice will triumph. Such understanding of plot structures, as they fulfill our expectations, provides us with a preunderstanding about the plot as a whole, and can serve to facilitate our reading of dramatic texts.

Conventional plot structures not only provide us with preunderstandings, but they can also be heuristic in that our expectations are not always fulfilled. Occasionally the detective-mystery or the cowboy film does not turn out as we expect. There is a famous mystery, *The Murder of Roger Ackroyd,* in which the narrator turns out to be the murderer. In the western *High Noon,* the "honest citizens" do not support the marshal in his effort to rid the town of bad men; on leaving town after dispatching the villains, the marshal drops his badge in the dust. So even when the plot turns out quite differently than we anticipate, the conventional formula still plays a part in making meaning. Conventional plot structures or action-types in plays work this same way. They specify our expectations and offer us a heuristic for investigating the meaning of the play.

Dramatic Action-Types: Comedy and Tragedy

Often on the title page of a dramatic text we find a statement like "A Comedy in Three Acts" or *The Tragedy of. . . ." Oedipus the King, Antigone, Hamlet, The Death of a Salesman* are called tragedies; Aristophanes' *The Birds,* Shakespeare's *A Midsummer Night's Dream,* Molière's *Tartuffe,* Shaw's *Arms and the Man,* Neil Simon's *Barefoot in the Park* are called comedies. These designations set up certain expectations in the reader or viewer. They indicate, in general, the kind of play the text contains. These terms have been applied to dramatic texts for some twenty-five hundred years; they represent very durable conventions.

The first feature we should note about these terms is that we are using them in a technical sense. Our ordinary everyday use of "comic" and "tragic" describes the *quality* of certain events or situations. The explosion of the shuttle last January was "tragic." Johnny Carson's monologue on *The Tonight Show* is, generally, "comic." What we mean when we call the explosion of the shuttle "tragic" is that we experienced it as a loss, that we were shocked, saddened, and dismayed by the event. What we mean when we call Carson's monologue "comic" is that we find it funny. We are, in these cases, talking about an effect produced in us that is triggered by our perception of a *quality*—pathos or humor—in the event. When these terms are applied to a dramatic text, we use them to describe not an effect in us or a quality of the event, but rather a plot pattern or structure of events in the play. A certain kind of beginning, middle, and end allows us to describe a play as comic or tragic. Thus no *single* event in the play qualifies as comic or tragic in this technical sense.

Another important point to remember, in considering comedy and tragedy, is that these action-types are simply ways of looking at dramatic texts. As the topoi and tagmemics are general heuristics, ways of examining any texts, so comic or tragic patterns provide us with ways of organizing our investigation of dramatic texts. They are useful insofar as they identify general features of a given play. They are not rules which the text must follow and often it will be difficult to decide how to apply the comic or tragic pattern to a specific play. Indeed, sometimes we may be able to discern, in a single play, both comic and tragic structures. So these conventional patterns or action-types simply offer a point of departure for an investigation that emphasizes the integrity of the plot.

Comedy as an Action-Type

A quick survey of those plays that have been called comedies reveals that many of them conclude with a wedding. The Roman comedies of Plautus and Terence, the comedies of Shakespeare, nineteenth-century English melodrama, and twentieth-century Broadway comedies frequently have the same conclusion: boy gets girl. Another significant class of comedies concludes with the exposure of an imposter or the defeat of a villain. In these comedies poetic justice is always done; the good are rewarded and the evil appropriately punished. These conclusions allow us to divide the action-types of comedy into three categories: romantic comedy, satiric comedy, and melodramatic comedy. Each of these categories requires a little more attention.

Romantic Comedy

In a nutshell, a romantic comedy is a love story. So, as we noted above, the end of the play will be a wedding or a wedding-surrogate. But, as Lysander remarks in Shakespeare's *Midsummer Night's Dream*, "The course of true love never does run smooth." If it did, there would be, in essence, no play. We can, then, count on there being obstacles to the wedding that concludes the play. Thus, the action-type of the romantic comedy might be summarized this way:

1. Beginning: boy meets girl
2. Middle: boy loses girl
3. End: boy gets girl

It does not take a great deal of imagination to think of ways in which boy might meet, lose, and get girl. The obstacles to true love may lie in external circumstances; the boy may be too poor and the girl too rich to allow for compatibility or the other way around; the boy may be of superior and the girl of inferior social status; the parents or society might object to the match. Or the obstacles can be internal and personal; the boy is dedicated to his career and the girl wants a family or vice versa; either partner thinks the other too proud or too aloof; one or another wants to dominate the relationship. The middle of the romantic comedy has the two lovers struggling to overcome whatever obstacles lie in their way. In the action-type of the romantic comedy all turns out happily when the obstacles are finally overcome. The possibility of variations on this pattern are infinite; each individual romantic comedy realizes the action-type in its own unique way.

Satiric Comedy

There is a song in a Gilbert and Sullivan operetta which goes: "Things are seldom what they seem," and the same is true of people. Some comedies conclude by showing personae who have appeared to be one thing to be, indeed, another. When, in *The Music Man,* Professor Harold Hill comes to town, he appears to be a bonafide music director with the good of the town at heart, when he is, in fact, a confidence man who intends to bilk the townsfolk and run with the money. In a comedy of Molière, the apparently pious Tartuffe turns out to be a hypocrite bent on seducing his host's wife; in *The Bourgeois Gentleman,* a *nouveau riche* makes a fool of himself trying to be an aristocrat. The conclusion of satiric comedy involves unmasking the imposter or exposing pretentiousness or foolishness for what it really is. The action-type of satiric comedy, then, concludes by exposing the foibles of members of society and either expelling the offenders or converting them. The middle segment of this action-type generally presents the imposters threatening the stability and harmony of the social order. There is the possibility that Harold Hill might disappoint all those nice folks, dash the hopes of his young musicians and make off with the money. In Molière's *The Miser* there exists the possibility that the miser's greed will spoil his daughter's budding romance and ruin her life. We might summarize the action-type of satiric comedy this way:

1. Beginning: an outsider (or outsiders) who deviates from the norms and values of the society of the play becomes actively engaged in the activities of that society
2. Middle: the outsider, by his activities, threatens the harmony and welfare of the society
3. End: the outsider is exposed as an outsider, is ridiculed and either expelled from the society or converted to accept its values

We should note that an interesting variation on this pattern has the outsider get away with his effrontery and succeed in disrupting the social order. In George Bernard Shaw's *The Devil's Disciple* the Devil's disciple himself turns out to be the only true Christian in the community. In this variation the norms and values represented by the outsider are the values which the plot endorses; it is the community that is hypocritical. So, like the action-type of the romantic comedy, there is a wide range of variations on this action-type.

Melodramatic Comedy

We might view the action-type of melodramatic comedy as a variation on satiric comedy. In melodramatic comedy, an outsider poses a threat to the social order and the well-being of its members, and in the end the outsider is defeated and appropriately punished. The difference is that the outsider is not a pretender or an imposter, but represents values in serious opposition to those of the community. So he or she constitutes a serious threat to the order of society and deserves the name "villain." Often the villain is a persona who possesses power by virtue of wealth or position or knowledge, and so can do serious damage to the well-being of other personae in the play. When, for example, a conniving man or woman attempts to break up a happy marriage by blackmailing one of the partners and the attempt fails, we might recognize the melodramatic action pattern. Plays involving a trial in which an innocent party is vindicated can also conform to this action-type. The threat to the good personae is more serious in this pattern than in satiric comedy, but the outcome is the same. The threat is averted, the good are rewarded, and the guilty are punished. So the action-pattern of melodramatic comedy may be summarized thusly:

1. Beginning: personae who represent the values of a given society are threatened by agents who do not share those values
2. Middle: the "good" personae struggle with the evil personae
3. End: the good personae overcome the forces of evil and restore harmony to the society

In variations on this pattern, we sometimes find it hard to identify "good guys" and "bad guys"; indeed, the plot may have to sort them out for us.

The Comedic Plot-Pattern

We have identified three kinds of comedic action-types: romantic comedy, satiric comedy and melodramatic comedy. All three of these plots conventionally conclude with the renewal of society; viz., the action-pattern resolves the problems presented in the beginning and the middle in a harmonious and ordered unity. The plot concludes with a wedding, the formation of a new society, or it deals with the reformation of society when it incorporates or exiles villains, imposters, or dissenters. Whereas comedy is not always "funny," in its conventional form it offers a happy ending.

Tragedy As An Action-Type

There is, as you might suspect, an entire class of plays whose ending is not happy. The concluding event in these plays is often a death or deaths. The protagonist or principal persona dies of a wound, commits suicide, is maimed or blinded. In some instances, the page or the stage is heaped with bodies. At the end of *Oedipus the King,* Oedipus blinds himself and goes into exile; toward the end of the play *Antigone* the heroine hangs herself; *Hamlet* concludes with the death of the prince and of almost the entire court; Othello commits suicide; Macbeth dies in a battle with MacDuff; King Lear expires of old age and a broken heart. The conventional action-pattern that structures these plays is tragedy, and, like comedy, it provides us with a specific heuristic for investigating drama.

Since the conclusion of a tragedy is dark and bloody, we might properly assume that the beginning and the middle of this action-pattern will involve disorder, conflict and struggle. In the possible world of tragedy, things are disordered and out of joint. In *Oedipus the King,* the play begins with a plague raging in the city and threatening the life of its inhabitants; in *Hamlet,* a usurper holds the throne, the other courtiers are either foolish or corrupt, even the ghost of Hamlet's father is not to be trusted; in *Death of a Salesman,* Willy Loman can no longer make his rounds. At the beginning of each of these plays, then, the principal persona is implicated in disorder and must somehow come to grips with it. The middle of the tragic action-type has the principal persona suffering through the consequences of this disorder, dealing with the anxiety and the disruption it causes. Oedipus must find the criminal who has caused the plague in the city; Hamlet must decide whether or not to revenge his father; Willy Loman must try to discover why he is a failure. At the end of the tragedy, order is restored and the possible world of the play is set right, but, as we have seen, at a great price to the principal persona and to the society of the play.

Whereas the possible world of comedy merrily concludes with the personae getting their just desserts, the possible world of tragedy does not include this kind of poetic justice. That world includes mistakes in judgments, sin, guilt, crime and their consequences. It is not always clear who is at fault, who is responsible for the disorder, but it is always clear that someone has to pay the price for it. If the world of the play is to be set right, if the guilt is to be expunged, then the principal persona or personae will have to bear the burden and suffer the consequences. And it may always seem to us that the outcome is unfair—that the price is too high and the punishment does not fit the crime. Even though the evil is purged and the society of the play redeemed, we are shaken and dismayed by the price exacted. The action-type of tragedy may be summarized this way:

1. The possible world of the principal persona or personae is contaminated or disrupted.
2. The principal persona or personae suffer because of this disruption.
3. The possible world is set right by virtue of the principal persona or personae paying a considerable price.

Not infrequently, as we have seen, that price is the persona's life—that is, his/her identity and function in the world of the play are changed or destroyed.

Summary: Action-Types in Drama

If we range the action-types of comedy and tragedy alongside one another, we are bound to notice a certain similarity among them. This comparison shows that the beginning of each action-type involves a confrontation or a conflict. In the pattern of romantic or satiric comedy the confrontation is hardly hostile, but it does involve individuals establishing a relationship that includes potential problems. In melodramatic comedy and tragedy the beginning generally includes an overt conflict. The middle of each of these action-types includes complications or struggles growing out of the initial confrontation or conflict. The struggle which ensues results from complications which are external or internal or both. The end of the play is a resolution of the struggle and so of the initial conflict. This resolution may be a wedding, the expulsion or conversion of the imposter or imposters, the defeat of the villain, the deaths of the principal persona and the restoration of order. Thus we can, by this comparison, arrive at a *general* action-type for drama:

1. Beginning: confrontation and/or conflict
2. Middle: complications and struggle
3. End: resolution of the conflict.

As we do our inspectional reading of a dramatic text, we can reasonably expect to find this structure in one or another of its comic or tragic variations. We should note that this structure does not present us with the meaning of the play, but simply a heuristic outline of the plot. As we deal with the various parts of the plot in our explanation of the play, we specify the detail by which we can arrive at the play's meaning. It is not enough, in short, to say that *Romeo and Juliet* is a tragedy; we may say the same of *Hamlet* or *Oedipus* or *Death of A Salesman*. These plays are very different, one from the other; classifying them as "tragedies" simply provides us with an outline of the plot. Our explanation of the events, then, fills in this outline with specifics about conflict, complications and resolution. We will now consider how our explanation of a dramatic text might proceed.

Explanation and the Dramatic Text

Just as with other fictive texts we are concerned with explaining the parts of the texts and their relationship to one another, so in dramatic texts we are concerned about explaining how the events in the texts specify conflict, struggle and resolution. We are then looking to describe or define these parts in terms of the events, and to discover the causes that connect the events to one another. We will now return to *Romeo and Juliet* and consider how we might explain it.

An inspectional reading of *Romeo and Juliet* will lead us to suspect strongly that the play fits the action-type "tragedy." The play concludes with the death of the two lovers by their own hands. Their first meeting at the masked ball offers the possibility that the play would fit the pattern of the romantic comedy; that expectation is soon dashed and the end of the play makes a convincing argument in favor of the tragic pattern. So we begin to examine the play on the supposition that its action-type is tragedy. We would, then, look at the events in the light of the tragic structure: conflict which presents the play world in disorder; a struggle of the principal persona because of that disorder; and a resolution in which the principal personae pay a significant price for the restoration of order.

At the end of the play order is restored to the city, the feud dissolved, but the lovers pay what might seem to be an exorbitant price. Only with their deaths is order restored. We might well feel that the price was too high, that the lovers did not deserve this treatment. But the conclusion follows resolutely on the beginning and the middle of the plot; tragedy never promises us a rose garden. In any event, we can summarize the plot of *Romeo and Juliet* this way:

1. Confrontation/Conflict: Scions of two feuding families, Romeo and Juliet, fall in love and determine to marry in spite of the feud.
2. Struggle: Romeo, newly married to Juliet, becomes actively embroiled in the feud when he kills Tybalt, a kinsman of Juliet's, and is exiled.
3. Resolution: The couple commits suicide when the father-confessor's intrigue fails and subsequently the families are reconciled.

It is plain how this summary specifies the action-type of tragedy. We see what kind of conflict initiates the plot and how that conflict results in the struggle of the protagonists and, finally, what kind of resolution follows. By using the tragic action-type as a heuristic, we are able to specify the events of the plot of *Romeo and Juliet* and to explain how they are related to one another.

Another illustration of the use of action-type as heuristic might be helpful here. Edward Albee's *Who's Afraid of Virginia Woolf?* is a play that does not announce itself as belonging to one action-type or another. Whereas *Romeo and Juliet* is included explicitly among the "tragedies of William Shakespeare" in all the editions, the title page of *Who's Afraid of Virginia Woolf?* simply says: "A play by Edward Albee." Armed with our conventional pre-understandings about action-types, we can consider the events of the play.

In an inspectional reading of *Virginia Woolf* we can describe the beginning, middle and end in this summary way:

> Beginning: George and Martha, husband and wife, give a party to which they invite another couple.
> Middle: In the midst of the party, Martha decides that their marriage is over.
> End: After the guests leave, George and Martha are reconciled.

This outline of the principal events suggests that the play fits the action-type of romantic comedy: boy meets girl, boy loses girl, boy gets girl.

When we set about explaining the relationship between George and Martha, especially the obstacles that create the separation, we discover that the party situation conceals as much as it reveals. The activities which describe the status of their relationship are the games they play with the guests at the "party." There are four games which the two couples play, two which precede the separation of George and Martha and two which follow. Martha invents games one and three and George, games two and four. We may summarize the games as follows:

> Game 1: Humiliate the host. In this game, Martha makes it clear that George is a failure in his profession. He is "in the History Department, not the head of the History Department." Even though he has married the college president's daughter, he has not gotten ahead in his chosen profession.
> Game 2: Get the guests. George garners information about the guests, Nick and Honey, a new faculty couple at the college. He discovers that Nick married Honey because she had an hysterical pregnancy and that, moreover, Honey is afraid to bear children. George gets Nick to admit to a calculating ambition for advancement in the college.
> Game 3: Hump the hostess. After declaring the marriage a failure, Martha takes Nick upstairs to the bedroom. When Nick and Martha return, it is apparent that Nick has failed to perform adequately and finds himself the object of Martha's scorn and under her control.
> Game 4: Bringing up baby. George announces that he has received a telegram informing him and Martha of the death of their son. Martha insists that George cannot kill the baby without her permission. George declares that he can and did.

The games amount to a series of revelations about the relationship between George and Martha. The "obstacle" to their union is a power struggle, Martha's determination to control the relationship and George's resistance to that control.

The fourth game, bringing up baby, culminates in the revelation that their "son" is a product of Martha's imagination. With this revelation, Martha's self-image crumbles; she is no longer "Earth-Mother," the dominant female. Since this image supported her drive for power, with its destruction the obstacle to their union is removed and the play can proceed to its end: the reconciliation of George and Martha.

Viewed from this perspective, the removal of the "obstacle" is also the unmasking of an impostor. Martha is not what she appeared to be. In retrospect, we notice that Nick and Honey and George are also unmasked in the course of the play. Nick and Honey are not the happily wedded, ideal couple they appear to be; George is not the helpless, hen-pecked husband. So, along with the action-type of romantic comedy, we notice a series of events which characterize what we have called "satiric comedy." In that action-type, the society of the play includes impostors, personae who pretend to a position in society which they do not in fact hold. The events of a satiric comedy unmask the impostors, show them up for what they are, and either exile or reconcile them. In the possible world of *Virginia Woolf* the revelations about the obstacles to George and Martha's relationship amount to unmaskings. We can, then, view the events of the play as combining the action-types of romantic and satiric comedy.

1. Conflict: George and Martha "meet" at the party and initiate a series of games that result in revelations.
2. Complications: George and Martha separate because of the revelations of the first two games.
3. Resolution: George and Martha reconcile because of the revelation of the two concluding games.

This structure of events outlines the general movement of the plot within the framework of the two action-types—romantic and satiric comedy.

Dramatic Action-Types as Heuristic

Describing the plot of a given play as "tragic" or as "romantic-satiric comedy" provides us with a framework for considering specific features of the play. They effectually organize our investigation and explanation of dramatic texts. To say that a play is a tragedy is to say only that it has the typical tragic plot structure as described above. The rest of our explanation of the dramatic texts leading on to understanding of the whole requires us to fill in specific details relative to the personae, the attitudes they represent and the choices they make.

The Cultural Dimension

To this point we have investigated general characteristics of dramatic plot structure, what happens in a play. We have divided the events into three parts: Conflict, Complication and Resolution. We have looked at different kinds of conflict-complication-resolution and classified them under the conventional headings of comedy and tragedy. Our grasp of the various action-types and our application to a given play provide us with an outline of the plot and a general framework for examining specific features of a given play. We are now ready to deal with those specifics:

1. Where the personae are;
2. Who the personae are;
3. What the personae think;
4. What choices the personae make.

It is important to remind ourselves that, because there is no storyteller in the dramatic text and because the personae only speak for themselves, we discover what they are doing, where and who they are, what they think and choose by examining what they say. In our examination of the events of *Romeo and Juliet* and *Who's Afraid of Virginia Woolf* we analyzed what the personae were doing. Now it remains to examine the other features of the possible world of the play.

The Cultural Situation

First, we must recollect that the possible world of a dramatic text, as it is a fictive world, is unmoored in time and place. The events in *Romeo and Juliet* take place in the city of Verona. This city may be easily located on a map of Italy, but the Verona of the play is located only in the possible world of the text. To underscore this point, the scene of the events in *Who's Afraid of Virginia Woolf* is New Carthage, a city we will not be able to locate on any map of the United States. At the same time, the possible worlds of these two plays contain references to places and times in the actual world of experience and, as we have seen, to other texts. For instance, the Verona of the Montagues and the Capulets is governed by a duke who holds absolute authority in the city. When Mercutio says, "A plague o'both your houses," he is not asking for a visitation of termites upon two edifices, but rather visiting a mild curse upon two dynastic families. Juliet's father obviously expects obedience of his daughter in the matter of selecting a husband. When Juliet remarks that Romeo "kisses by the book," and that his speeches are couched poetically in the form of sonnets, the principle of intertextuality points us to the sonnets of Petrarch and his Italian and Elizabethan successors. We may note that Edmund Spenser, Phillip Sidney, Samuel Daniel and Shakespeare himself, all major poets of the Elizabethan period, wrote sonnet sequences which describe the lover's conduct towards and relationship with his beloved. All of these details of the possible world of *Romeo and Juliet* indicate that the cultural setting of the play is Elizabethan England, that the scene—where the personae are acting out the events—is a vehicle for the presentation of concerns, issues and values of late Elizabethan England.

The cultural setting of *Who's Afraid of Virginia Woolf?* is so familiar that we take its references for granted. George and Martha invite a new faculty couple to their home after a faculty party; the cocktail party and "the games that people play" are standard features of contemporary upper-middle-class American society. The references to art, movies and books reflect the interests and values of this social stratum. Thus the cultural setting of *Who's Afraid of Virginia Woolf?* is contemporary American with the customs, conventions, issues and values that permeate this society.

The situation then of the personae is constructed by those references in the play that specify customs, conventions, institutions according to which the personae are doing what they do. The situation is not identical with "the scene" because it is a situation in a possible, not an actual, world. The scene of *Romeo and Juliet* is Verona, Italy; the cultural situation, however, refers us rather to Elizabethan England. The scene of *Death of a Salesman* is Brooklyn; the cultural situation refers to lower-middle-class American society in the twentieth century. The scene of *Virginia Woolf* is "New Carthage"; the situation is an upper-middle-class intellectual milieu. The first aspect of the cultural dimension is this situation in which the personae act out the events of the plot.

Personae as Representative Types

A second important feature of the cultural dimension in the possible world of the dramatic text is the identification of the personae. It is essential that we know who the personae are, that is, what they represent. We have already discussed the notion of persona as representative type in Chapter Fifteen of this volume; in fictive texts that have a storyteller often the type is explicitly described. For instance, in *A Rose For Emily* Homer Barron is identified explicitly "a Yankee foreman." In a dramatic text the characters do not often introduce themselves: "Good afternoon, my name is Willy Loman and I am a failed salesman." Rather, Willy first appears carrying his sample cases and his opening dialogue tells us that he has returned prematurely from a selling trip. So we recognize his type; he is a travelling salesman. In her first speech to her sister, Antigone refers to the problem of their unburied brother. Whatever else we discover about her, our first introduction to Antigone is as a family member. Willy Loman, the dialogue discloses, is also a husband and father; Antigone is also a citizen of Thebes. But Willy is first and foremost the salesman of the title and Antigone is a kinswoman. In identifying the representative type we rely on our grasp of the cultural situation and our identification reciprocally confirms that situation. The "travelling salesman" is an American type; we would be surprised to discover Willy Loman in Thebes or in Verona. Identifying the personae as representative types particularizes the events of the play in cultural terms. When Willy Loman commits suicide, it is a salesman who kills himself. When Antigone buries Polynices, it is a sister burying her brother.

We also must consider the possibility that in the course of events in the play, the personae change from one type to another. For instance, in *Romeo and Juliet* when Romeo first comes on the scene, he describes himself as a man "in love, but out of favor." The object of his affection at the beginning of the play is one Rosalynn who has disdained his suit. He languishes for her love and this attachment consumes his attention and his energies to the point that Mercutio jibes him about his devotion. When he attends, incognito, the masked ball of the Capulets, he transfers his affections totally and at first sight to Juliet before he even knows her name. His address to her, as we have noted, takes sonnet form and he uses conventional imagery from the sonnet tradition. These characteristics mark Romeo as a common type of that period: "the courtly lover." He follows the conventions of this type: singing his lady's praises, "sighing to his mistress' eyebrow," pledging his undying devotion to her. Romeo is not only a nobleman of the House of Montague but, in the first instance, a courtly lover as defined by sixteenth-century courtesy books.

At her first appearance Juliet is identified as the object of Romeo's affection and a noblewoman of the House of Capulet. As the lady to whom he pledges himself, she is complementary to Romeo's courtly lover. As we have noted, Juliet recognizes Romeo's approach as conventional; he is acting according to the book. She is, however, not only the ideal and unapproachable lady of the sonnet, but also a marriageable young woman who is moved by Romeo's devotion. When, in the balcony scene, Romeo pledges his love, Juliet wishes to make sure that he is not simply playing the game of courtly love; she wants to go beyond the world of romance to a marriage commitment. At the end of the second act the couple—courtly lover and beloved—change radically when they marry secretly in Friar Lawrence's cell.

The other personae in the play are identified in terms of their relationship to the pair of lovers. Mercutio is a courtier of the House of Montague with an earthy view of women and a skeptical view of romance; Benvolio, as his name implies, is a well-intentioned Montague inclined to promote peace between the two houses; Tybalt is a fire-eating Capulet who is affronted by the very presence of a Montague. Juliet's father treats his daughter patriarchally, following the convention of the day in choosing a husband for her. The Duke represents authority in the city and attempts to constrain the warring factions. Friar Lawrence is father confessor to the couple and an herbalist-scholar who performs in all these capacities on behalf of the lovers. The only significant change in status or type among the personae is the conversion of Romeo and Juliet from courtly lovers to husband and wife, but this change is critical to the direction of events in the drama.

Our perception of who the personae are in *Virginia Woolf* is critical to an explanation of events in the play. At the outset of the drama Martha and George both appear to be conventional American types. Martha comes on as the brassy, aggressive, dominating female who has her husband under her thumb. She describes herself as Earth Mother, the goddess of fertility. George, on the other hand, is, to all appearances, an ineffectual intellectual incapable of managing either his wife or his career. He is in short the egghead. As types, Nick and Honey contrast sharply with George and Martha. Nick is the rising young professional with driving ambition and few moral scruples; he dominates his wife whose character registers features of the "dumb blonde." These initial impressions are drastically altered through the events of the play. After "bringing up baby" Martha is shown to be barren and acquiescent, dependent on George's cooperation for her fantasies. Nick's image as the young virile professional is reduced, by his failure to satisfy Martha, to the status of "houseboy." Honey is afraid of adulthood and childbirth. Finally, George is in total control of the situation, comforting and sustaining Martha in her now-evident insecurity. These changes are the result of the unmasking which goes on in the games.

Establishing where the personae are and what types they represent specifies the cultural references in the text and provides the grounds for determining the significance of the plot-events. Once we have located the cultural situation of the play and who the personae represent we can examine what the personae are thinking and what choices they make. And these two aspects of the text will define specific issues and values on which the events of the play turn. These two features—"thought" and choices—complete the cultural dimension.

At this point we must remind ourselves that we know what the characters think and choose and do because we know what the characters say. In fact, a plot-event is made up of what the personae are thinking, choosing and doing and we know what they are thinking, choosing and doing because of what they say. Our explanation of the event, finally, will include 1) its causes and 2) its probable or necessary consequences as we discover what the personae are thinking and what they choose.

Thought: Reasons and Attitudes

When we consider the aspect of "thought" in what the personae say, we find that we can divide their statements into two categories. 1) statements that are appropriate to the type in the situation and 2) propositions that a given culture holds as self-evident. For instance, in *Oedipus the King* the personae make it clear that it is a major crime against kinship to kill one's father and marry one's mother. This is a general truth that the text vigorously maintains. In *Antigone* the conflict between Antigone and Creon pivots around two conflicting general truths: 1) that the gods have decreed that kinsmen are responsible for burying kinsmen; 2) that the gods have decreed that citizens should obey the commands of legitimate authority in the *polis*. Antigone, whose brother lies outside the gates unburied, speaks for the first general truth and Creon, newly elevated to the leadership of the *polis,* speaks for the second general truth. In *Death of a Salesman* Willy Loman insists that his goal is "success"; it is a general truth of the play that American society can be adequately divided into those who succeed and those who do not. Willy utters statements which are appropriate to his type: "If you are well-liked, you will never want"; "The world is an oyster, but you don't crack it open on a mattress." These "general truths" specify the values at issue in play. The criminal who has killed his father and married his mother must be sought out and punished if the city is to be saved. Loyalty to the family must be squared with loyalty to the city. The American dream must somehow account for those devotees of success who never succeed.

The general truths or cultural assumptions that function in *Romeo and Juliet,* as we might expect, put the events of the play in perspective. The feud between the houses is not a private matter. After the encounter in the first scene between members of the two households, the Duke enunciates the "general truths" that this feuding disrupts the harmony of the city and that, as the one responsible for keeping the peace, he must impose penalties on those fostering the feud. Juliet's father enunciates the traditional position that a daughter should accept her parents' arrangement for her marriage. Romeo, as we have noted, proceeds with his courtship in ways appropriate to his type and Juliet responds in the same vein. Friar Lawrence, as suits his type, warns Romeo, the lover, that he should keep his passions under control and counsels marriage at the first opportunity. These accepted truths suffice to provide rationales for the progression of events. Taken together, what the personae think about their situations and what they enunciate about their assumptions create the value system of the play.

What the personae think about their situation in *Virginia Woolf,* the assumptions they make, are fairly familiar to us. When George deprecates faculty parties, Nick replies he rather appreciates them, "meeting everyone, getting introduced around, getting to know some of the men." Parties serve a practical purpose; they are ways of getting to know colleagues or neighbors or business associates. The situation in *Virginia Woolf* is, as we have noted, a party and the two couples in attendance get to know one another all too well. Another general truth of the cultural dimension that emerges from the dialogue is the proposition that children hold a marriage together; when Martha is describing their relationship with their son, she sees the child between them, each holding a hand. A childless marriage is presumably less fulfilled than a marriage that produces children. The personae, in the dialogic exchanges of the play, adopt positions suitable to their types. George speaks for history, its unpredictability, its focus on pluralism and variety, its potential for progress, and he impeaches what he describes as Nick's destructive scientism, the attempt to control nature, culture and environment. Martha proclaims the centrality of the woman, the Earth Mother; sexuality and fertility provide an energy source that draws the male population into her circle of influence. The party games are struggles for serious stakes and words are weapons, winner take all. The "thought" manifest in the dialogue of *Virginia Woolf* unmasks the party in these ways, that is, as a conflict and a power struggle. It also affirms the traditional attitudinal set that children create a bond between husband and wife. Thus these positions create the issues and values which the personae present and the plot examines.

Choices

The final aspect of the cultural dimension is the choices which the personae make. The first thing to note about these choices is that, generally, like the thoughts that the persona expresses, choices are appropriate to the type. It is equally important to note that the options of the personae in any given drama are not infinite. Because their choices are consistent with the persona-type, they are limited by that type. Oedipus the King, for instance, determines to seek out the cause of the plague in Thebes. Other personae try to persuade him to give up the search, the prophet Teresias, his wife Jocasta and the chorus of citizens. Because he is king, Oedipus cannot simply choose to resign and go to the seashore. As king, it is his responsibility to solve the crime which is causing the plague, or to cease being king. Determining to discover the criminal is a choice that Oedipus makes, but it is a choice that is necessary if he is to remain Oedipus the king. Similarly, Willy Loman cannot simply stop being a salesman; he must pursue his goal to the end. Were he, say, to accept Charlie's offer of a job or if he were to become a carpenter, these choices would be inappropriate to his type. He would cease to be a salesman and there would cease to be a play. Again, Antigone chooses to hang herself because she cannot accept an authority in the city that does not honor the laws of kinship; for her suddenly to recognize the legitimacy of Creon's position would be to turn her back on the values her type represents.

Another way of making this point about the choices personae make is to say that the personae exist for the sake of the plot and not the other way around; it is their choices within the chain of events that move the plot along. Plays are not psychological case studies; we only know as much about the personae as the text reveals to us and their motivation is often determined solely by the type they represent. So in one sense, Oedipus chooses to seek out the murderer of Laius; in another sense, his identity as king makes it *necessary* that he seek him out. If Willy Loman is to be true to his type, he cannot but follow the star of success to the very end, for good or ill. The choices of the personae serve the plot by providing the motivation for its progression.

The movement of the events in *Romeo and Juliet* follow on a number of choices made by the personae. These choices are obviously appropriate to the types they represent. Romeo and Juliet decide to marry secretly; Romeo's decision to intervene between Mercutio and Tybalt is the result of his marriage and his decision to revenge his kinsman Mercutio who is killed because of that intervention leads to his exile. Juliet's determination to protect her marriage commitment to Romeo leads to her accepting Friar Lawrence's plan and potion and thus to the deathlike coma which deceives Romeo. These choices and commitments based on them determine the progress of the plot from the initial meeting of the lovers through the marriage of the couple to their separation and final destiny.

Not all the events of the play are determined by choices of the personae. Romeo's suicide is an outcome influenced by happenstance. The brother carrying Friar Lawrence's message to Romeo about the potion administered to Juliet is not able to deliver the message because he is quarantined in a plague-stricken town. Romeo therefore does not know of the strategem and so, when he comes on Juliet in the tomb, he despairs and kills himself. This piece of ill fortune has a decided impact on the outcome of the plot and such happenstance should be noted and, if possible, explained. For instance, in the possible world of *Romeo and Juliet* plagues, like feuds, can occur beyond the control of the lovers and so affect their destiny. "Accidents" in the dramatic text can have significance.

The choices of the personae in *Virginia Woolf* are strong indicators of situational control. Martha chooses to invite the guests after the official party and George chooses to acquiesce. Martha sets the rules of games 1 and 3; George chooses the rules for "bringing up baby." Nick and Honey do not have much to say about the proceedings of the evening; their choices occur within the context established by Martha and George. The choices of the games lead to the revelations that unmask the personae and George's decision to "kill the baby" leads to the reconciliation of the couple. Charting their choices in the course of the play defines the progress of the plot.

Summary: The Cultural Aspect

After we have identified the events of the plot and divided them into three phases: conflict, complication/struggle, resolution, and identified them with an action-type, we examined the causes and motivations of the events by describing the cultural aspect in terms of:

1. Where the personae are;
2. What types the personae represent;
3. What the personae think about their situation;
4. What choices the personae make in the situation.

The analysis of these parts and aspects of the play allow us to view the drama as a whole, that is, to see the events of the plot as making up a single action with beginning, middle and end.

Action and Insight

We are by now well accustomed to the notion that, when we speak of understanding the text, our understandings are always of the text as a whole. We consider the events of the drama as narrative, as having a beginning, middle and end, we assume that they make a whole, that is, we consider them as one complete action. To understand the play as an action, then, is to grasp how the events are related to one another through their rationale (thought) and motivation (choice).

We can now juxtapose our division of the events with a tagmemic analysis as a way of summarizing our explanation and exploring possible insights into the action.

Tagmemic analysis of *Romeo and Juliet:*

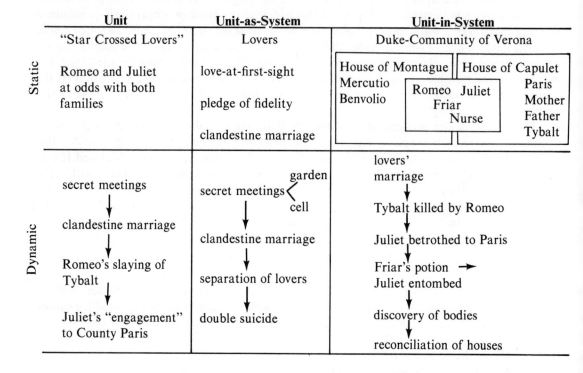

	Unit	Unit-as-System	Unit-in-System		
Static	"Star Crossed Lovers" Romeo and Juliet at odds with both families	Lovers love-at-first-sight pledge of fidelity clandestine marriage	Duke-Community of Verona House of Montague Mercutio Benvolio	Romeo Juliet Friar Nurse	House of Capulet Paris Mother Father Tybalt
Dynamic	secret meetings ↓ clandestine marriage ↓ Romeo's slaying of Tybalt ↓ Juliet's "engagement" to County Paris	secret meetings ⟨ garden / cell ↓ clandestine marriage ↓ separation of lovers ↓ double suicide	lovers' marriage ↓ Tybalt killed by Romeo ↓ Juliet betrothed to Paris ↓ Friar's potion → Juliet entombed ↓ discovery of bodies ↓ reconciliation of houses		

The tagmemic divisions of the text begin with the unit of the couples as courtly lovers and as members of rival houses. The unit as system makes it clear that the lovers are engaged in a private and clandestine relationship, that they inhabit a private universe made up of themselves, Friar Lawrence, and, peripherally, the nurse. When we look at the unit-in-system, we notice that their relationships with other personae are divided into the membership of the two houses; Romeo has no traffic whatsoever with Juliet's parents or the County Paris or, except for the duel, with Tybalt. Juliet does not meet with any of the Montagues except Romeo himself. Looking at the unit of the lovers dynamically, we see instances of their alienation from their respective families. The dynamic view of their relationship as a system moves us from the lovers' secret meetings to their clandestine marriage to the separation imposed by Romeo's exile and intensified by Juliet's coma to their death together. These events which encompass the lovers' destiny do not directly involve any of the other personae from the world of Verona at large. When, however, we consider these events and the couples' relationship as a dynamic unit-in-system, we discover those events which have a public face: Romeo kills Tybalt; Juliet is betrothed to Paris; Juliet is entombed; their bodies are discovered; after Friar Lawrence's narration, the families are reconciled. This arrangement of the personae and their relationships provides the ground for our understanding that the couple moves between two different spheres in the possible world—the sphere of their romantic relationship and clandestine marriage and the sphere of the public life of the city and their houses.

If we were to write up our understanding of the play, our topic might develop into a thesis this way. *Romeo and Juliet* is about a pair of "star-crossed lovers"; in this case the lovers are star-crossed because of the ongoing feud between the two houses. In this society a marriage which does not take place with the knowledge and approval of the whole community can lead to disaster; the marriage of the lovers cannot come to good. Our own contemporary view of marriage as essentially a private contract between two individuals is not the view taken in this dramatic text. The private nature of their marriage commitment leads on to the complications of Romeo's exile and Juliet's drinking of the Friar's potion. In a possible world where marriage must integrate the couple not only with one another, but also with the fabric of society, the lovers pay a high price for their commitment. Because of their deaths the two houses are finally reconciled. What might have been a lyric love story becomes, by virtue of the feud in the city, a tragedy of notable proportions.

Romeo and Juliet is about constant love in two different modes. It is about the experience of romantic love and courtship and this mode contrasts sharply with the second mode, married love. Romantic love is the nightingale and moonlight, a private world which the lovers can create. Married love is the lark and sunlight, and acknowledgement of the larger world with which the lovers must contend. Both modes are contrasted with the "thought" and attitudes expressed by Mercutio and the nurse. Mercutio is cynical about women and marriage; "love" is an itch to be scratched. For the nurse one husband is as good as another and Juliet should take the County Paris and not pine over her lost Romeo. Neither lover subscribes to these views; both will be faithful to their commitment. Finally, neither can live without the other; the marriage commitment that grew from their courtship defines their identities so that one cannot live without the other. Since the disorder of the feud does not permit them to publish their marriage, their love leads them to self-destruction.

If we were to write up our understanding of *Virginia Woolf,* we might note that it is also about a pair of star-crossed lovers of a very different stripe. In this case they are star-crossed because of Martha's fantasy about herself. She and George also have a private world in which Martha is fertile, the mother of a son. On the basis of this fantasy she can play the aggressive, dominant and sexually attractive female who is in control of her society. She establishes in front of Nick and Honey, that George is a failure as an academic, an author and a husband. Nick accepts this appraisal; he says to George: "You ineffectual sons of bitches! You're the worst." George is pegged as the ineffectual egghead whose wife wears the pants. George turns the tables on the guests by revealing that Nick is an ambitious climber who married his wife for her father's money. Honey turns out to be child-like, afraid of pregnancy and adulthood. And finally Martha, who has characterized herself as Earth Mother, is revealed as barren and dependent. This final unmasking reveals George as truthteller, as the one really in control of this society. He saves Martha from her destructive fantasy and lays the ground for their final reconciliation. The unmaskings of the action and the destruction of the "baby" lead to a comic resolution, the incorporation of the imposter (Martha) into a newly harmonized society.

Virginia Woolf is about love also, "love" as a bulwark against isolation and self deception. The "baby" separates, rather than unites the pair; presumably even a "real" baby would not draw them together. When Martha admits that she is "afraid of Virginia Woolf," she is acknowledging that the relationship between herself and George must stand on its own ground, that no external agency—real or imagined—can save their marriage. Though this conclusion falls far short of celebration, George and Martha are reconciled on the basis of self knowledge and so the society of the play is harmonized.

Summary: The Dramatic Heuristic

Drama offers us a possible world in which human action is represented through the words of the personae. What happens in the text, as we discover it by examining what the personae say and what they do, is the basis of our explanation of the events of the plot and, as we grasp the whole of the plot, provides the basis for our understanding of the action. When we know what happens and why, we come to insight about the play's meaning.

We can outline, then, the progress of our explanation of a given play in the following way.

The Dramatic Heuristic

Preunderstanding

Do a preliminary reading of the dramatic text.

Examine what the text *says:*
what happens in the text
what the personae are saying (supply the spectacle)
what the personae are doing
catalogue the events of the plot

Explanation

Divide and arrange the events according to action-type:
Romantic comedy
Satiric comedy
Melodramatic comedy
Tragedy

Examine the cultural dimension
Where the personae are—cultural situation
Who the personae are—representative types

Rationale for events	What the personae think—"thought"; general truths of the culture, attitudes and values appropriate to the personae
Motivation for events	What the personae choose—decisions, commitments

Understanding

Consider what the text *means*

View the play as a single complete action with beginning, middle, and end

Validate action-type

Consider causes [rationale and motivation] for movement of plot

To understand a play is to grasp the meaning of a single, complete human action in its causes and its consequences. Seeing or reading a play tells us the story without the intervention of the storyteller; it allows us to draw our own conclusions about the significance of the events presented, about the meaning of the action. In writing about a play, we develop a thesis out of these conclusions and explain it in terms of the dramatic text through the application of the narrative heuristic. The possible world of the play points to our own experience as human beings and the action patterns show us what it means to belong to a society or to suffer the consequences of past events or to illustrate how we come to self-knowledge and knowledge of our world.

We now have left, for our consideration, one final instance of fictive self-expression. We have looked at the fictive narrative: short story and novel; we have investigated the drama as a form of narrative; it remains for us to consider the poem. If poetry is another mode of fictive self-expression, how do we approach it and how does it relate to prose fiction and to drama? These are the questions we will address in the next chapter.

Chapter 18
Poetry

On my way home from work in the evening, I regularly encountered a small blond, blue-eyed boy playing in the front yard of his home. We gradually struck up a nodding acquaintance; I waved to him and, when he was not too preoccupied with his solitary games, he would wave back and smile. His most usual preoccupation was playing cowboy. He had a small white broad-brimmed hat with a chin cord and a chrome capgun with simulated pearl handle. He would trot down the driveway, waving his six-gun or gallop solemnly about the yard on his stickhorse. Occasionally, I imagined that he would like to consider me an Indian, but our acquaintance never grew to that level. I became accustomed to seeing him at play and, on those evenings when he was absent, there was a small hole in the day's routine. Then, he was not there for a week on end and I began to wonder if the family had moved. Suddenly, shockingly, a wreath in black and purple appeared on the door of the little boy's house. In the interim he had died; I would never see him play cowboy again.

This narrative is fairly straightforward in its presentation of a series of events; it also conveys a sense of regret and loss on the part of the narrator. It hints, without much elaboration, at what the narrator feels about the death of the boy. In short, we know what happened and how the narrator feels at least generally, but we do not necessarily, from the text, have the same feelings ourselves.

The fictive text which is a poem presents us with an experience which not only tells us what happens, but also and principally makes us *feel* the experience. For instance, the narrative on the death of the little boy might come out this way in a poem.

Buffalo Bill's Defunct

<pre>
Buffalo Bill's
defunct
        who used to
        ride a watersmooth-silver
                                    stallion
and break onetwothreefourfive pigeonsjustlikethat
                                                    Jesus
        he was a handsome man
                            and what i want to know is
        how do you like your blueeyed boy
        Mister Death
</pre>

At first reading, it may not be clear exactly what this poem is about. It is easy enough to say it is about the death of Buffalo Bill, or the death of an American hero. What is clear on first reading is the admiration the text expresses for the hero and the urgent and bitter turn in the accusatory last line. "How do you like your blue-eyed boy Mr. Death?" has a biting and sarcastic tone that contrasts sharply with the rest of the poem.

Even before we can quite make sense of the text, we have had a feeling about it which explanation can illuminate. That is, we experience the text as a whole emotionally before we can explain in detail its parts. In fact, however, our explanation of the text is a way of coming to understand the grounds for our feeling. A crucial issue in this explanation is the relation between Buffalo Bill and the blue-eyed boy. Are they one and same or are they two different personae? Why is the last line so bitter in tone if the subject of the poem is the unsurprising demise of a man in his seventies?

At this point, the canny reader will suspect that there is a connection between the narrative text about the death of the little boy and the experience of the poem about Buffalo Bill. If the little boy playing cowboy in the narrative is also the Buffalo Bill of the poem, then there is quite sufficient ground for the anger and sarcasm in the last line of the poem. All the qualities of the American hero—poise, confidence, and dexterity—are potential in the "blue-eyed boy." He may grow into "a handsome man" in every respect. The ease of accomplishment on a "water-smooth silver stallion" and the sharpness of aim, "one-two-three-four-five-pigeons-just-like-that," are the child's fantasy and, in the eyes of the adults who observe him, his promise. All of this promise and potential is sharply cut off by "Mr. Death." A child's death is pointless; it profits no one. It is felt as a personal attack by a malicious aggressor, Mr. Death.

This explanation of the poem proceeds on two assumptions: (1) that there is a narrative of some kind implicit in the poem and (2) that the images created by the poem carry its emotional freight.

The Buffalo Bill poem includes an explicit narrative: Buffalo Bill in the Wild West show, riding around the ring and destroying clay pigeons with his six-shooter, and, in this interpretation, an inferred narrative, a "blue-eyed boy" playing cowboy, galloping about performing imaginary feats of marksmanship. Buffalo Bill is defunct; the little boy is dead. Both these narratives may occur in the same space and are, as it were, superimposed, one on the other.

The imagery of the poem conveys the quality of the experience. The "water-smooth silver stallion" offers fluid motion, ease and grace characteristic of horse and rider; "one-two-three-four-five-pigeons-just-like-that" couples dexterity with power and the same sort of ease. "Jesus" proclaims sincerity and a quasi-religious awe that underscores "he was a handsome man." The two figures draw together and Jesus and Buffalo Bill were both "handsome men." The impact of all these admirable qualities generated by the images resonate in the bitter rhetorical question, "How do you like your blue-eyed boy, Mr. Death?"

The poem is about Buffalo Bill; it is about a "blue-eyed boy"; it is about death. Our explanation deals with the relationship among these three terms as they imply a narrative and as they generate a specific emotion. When we consider the poem as a whole, as an experience in a possible world, we see that the narrative depends on the images which create the emotion. Our admiration and awe reinforce the bitterness of our disappointment. It is clear that no explanation of the poem can produce the kind of impact that the poem itself conveys. It is also clear that it is the words of the text as they call up concrete and particular images ("water-smooth silver stallion," "blue-eyed boy") that trigger the emotion of the poem.

It is time to confess that the story about the little boy playing in his front yard was an invention that served only as illustrative narrative for "Buffalo Bill's Defunct." The assumption that a poem which is not obviously a narrative may contain an implied or inferred narrative is a heuristic for framing the text and, finally, for relating the images of the text to one another. Another way of stating the case is to say that we may view the sequence of the images in the poem as moving from beginning to middle to end the way the events of a narrative do. And also that this sequence of images organizes the emotional resonances of the poem.

We need to test this heuristic on a poem that seems to have no implied or inferred narrative and in which the emotion is not as sharply etched or as vividly intense as that of Buffalo Bill. Consider then the following:

> Let me not to the marriage of true minds
> Admit impediments. Love is not love
> Which alters when it alteration finds,
> Or bends with the remover to remove.
> O, no! it is an ever-fixed mark
> That looks on tempests and is never shaken;
> It is the star to every wand'ring bark,
> Whose worth's unknown, although his height be taken.
> Love's not Time's fool, through rosy lips and cheeks
> Within his bending sickle's compass come;
> Love alters not with his brief hours and weeks,
> But bears it out even to the edge of doom.
> > If this be error, and upon me proved,
> > I never writ, nor no man ever loved.

Our inspectional reading of the poem tells us quickly enough that the poem is about love. In fourteen lines the word "love" appears four times and "it," referring to love, appears twice. The last word of the poem is "loved," an action form of the word. We can expect, then, that any explanation of the poem will include a description or definition of "love."

The first four lines which, the rhyme scheme tells us, make up a stanza, contain general statements about love. The love which this text is addressing is, first of all, "the marriage of true minds." Love here is imaged as a marriage, calling up the picture of man and woman making a solemn commitment to each other and it is a marriage that is faithful to that commitment. And, the text insists, it does not admit impediments; this kind of "marriage" does not allow for reservations or conditions on the commitment. ("Impediments" has a legal flavor in that reservations or conditions, according to church law, make a marriage invalid.) Given this marriage of true minds, the resultant love does not change when it encounters change nor does it fade because of physical separation. The firm purpose established by the marriage of true minds is unconditional, without reservation, and will endure in the face of life's changes.

The second stanza, the next four lines, describes two kinds of difficulties that the friends will encounter in their life together. They will face "tempests," storms around them which they cannot control. Their love will be "a mark," that is, a steadfast quality or characteristic that will keep them unshaken in the face of these storms. Their life will be a journey whose destination they will control and their love will be a star that will guide them safe to port. Though they can calculate the position of the star ("take its height"), they cannot ever calculate its value for them. Love, then, helps them through stormy times and provides them with guidance on their journey through life together.

The third stanza deals with a major change which all lovers must face, the attrition of time. Rosy lips fade and cheeks wither; physical attractiveness wanes. The lover is not subject to time. Love stretches out beyond time even to judgment day. ("Doom" here has its older meaning of "judgment.") Whatever other changes a marriage of two minds may suffer, the changes effected by the passage of time are inevitable and even those changes love suffers without itself changing.

These three stanzas take the image of the friends from "marriage" through to judgment day. Though the implied narrative does not present specific incidents or events, it does outline the course of a life together, through difficulties and decisions through old age and beyond. The love which is the result of the marriage of true minds is the constant factor which holds them together through thick and thin. The implication is clear that, if difficulties, trials, disagreements or time separate them, then there was no marriage of true minds in the first place.

The imagery of these three stanzas conveys the impression of calm and steadfastness. "Marriage" offers the image of the bridal couple exchanging vows without reservation; the true minds that make this exchange are clear-eyed. The love they profess in that moment will not change or bend in the future. Love is an ever-fixed mark, a stamp on their souls which is not shaken by storms. It is a star guiding a small boat that wanders through the waves. Time is imaged with a scythe that cuts the stalk at harvest. But love is not a jester whose job it is to minister to time. Love does not cavort or jest to suit the moods and changes of time. "Brief hours and weeks" are balanced against the burden love bears even into eternity. The anxieties and uncertainties that images like "tempests" and "wandering barque" and "time's bending sickle" trigger are counterbalanced by and contrasted with the "ever-fixed mark" and "star" and "the mastery of time." A calm certainty based in the unchanging nature of love prevails in the poem.

The final couplet is a comment on this view of love as a marriage of true minds. If it can be shown that love is not the mark or the star or that love is time's fool, then this poem was never written and there is no such thing as love. This is the firmest kind of affirmation that can be mustered because it proposes a palpable contradiction. If the above is not true, then this poem was never written at all. And the love that is affirmed in the above three stanzas does not exist on land or sea. The final two lines of text then confirm the foregoing sections and underscore the validity of the emotion its images engender.

Explanation of the poetic text is based on (1) a discovery of the frame narrative and (2) an analysis of the imagery of that narrative. This heuristic brings us to a consideration of the poem as a whole, that is, to our understanding of its meaning. Nevertheless, statements about the general sense of the two texts we have considered fall short of encompassing the experience of reading those texts. For instance, we might say that "Buffalo Bill's Defunct" is about the waste of potential that the death of a child involves or that "Let Me Not to the Marriage of True Minds" is about love as a rational and constant commitment of friends that survives trials, provides guidance, and overcomes the passage of time itself. Such paraphrases are accurate enough as far as they go. But the feelings which the poems arouse are integral to the experience of reading them and the paraphrase *can never successfully reproduce the feelings*. Moreover, when we try to express the feelings generated by the text, we are forced to deal in generalities. To say that "Buffalo Bill" produces admiration and awe followed by bitterness and outrage has no specific sense except as these emotions refer to the network of imagery in the poem. The shadings of emotion that the images provoke are specific to the text of the poem itself and no exposition or explanation is adequate outside the context of the poem itself. Our understanding of poetic texts, then, as they are an experience of the whole, must be articulated in terms of the poem as imagery.

One heuristic for dealing with the poetic text may be summarized as follows:

(1) Preunderstanding: we recognize the text as fictive and poetic through the conventional signs of rhythmic and imaged language accompanied, on occasion, by rhyming patterns. Our inspectional reading will generally yield a theme for the poem; that is, "Buffalo Bill's Defunct" is about death, and "Let Me Not to the Marriage of True Minds" is about love.

(2) Explanation: we examine the progression of the poem for a narrative frame, a story which the text discovers to us. The narrative may be specific like that of "Buffalo Bill"; it may be more

general like the narrative implied in "The Marriage of True Minds." (It is also important to note that not all poems will easily yield to this method of analysis, but narrative will serve to illustrate one heuristic method for analyzing poetry.)

We then consider explicitly the imagery of the poetic text, the way in which the various images relate to one another and to the implied narrative. For example, "onetwothreefourfive" images the reports of Buffalo Bill's six-shooter and "pigeonsjustlikethat" explodes the clay disks for us. These images, as we noted, give us a sense of the cowboy hero's power and ease of performance.

We can then attempt to characterize the feeling of the poem by describing the emotions it engenders. The emotional response we can tie to the arrangement of the images.

(3) Understanding: considering the poem as a whole, we can see how the experience of the text specifies, through its progression of images, the feeling of the experience. "Buffalo Bill's Defunct" combines awe and admiration with a bitter sense of loss. This specific feeling emerges from the images of the cowboy hero and the blue-eyed boy as the vague, Latinate word "defunct" moves to the blunt Anglo-Saxon word "death." The mark and the star, fixed and unbending, characterize the love of the marriage of true minds. The specific emotion that is attached to love in this text is elaborated by these images. Our insights about the poems encompass both the progression of the events and the emotional freight their images carry.

Narrative Poetry

We began by looking at poetic texts which were not obviously narrative. Poems can, however, tell a story directly or indirectly, through dialogue or monologue or direct narration. We will find that, as these poems are narratives, they share many of the characteristics of prose narratives that we have discussed above. Some narrative poems also have dramatic qualities; they are monologues or dialogues delivered by personae. For all that, the narrative poem is a poem with concentrated and imaged language, rhythm and, occasionally, rhyme.

We might now look at a few instances of narrative poetry to see what we can make of them.

Lord Randall

Where have you been to, Randall my son?
Where have you been to my pretty one?
I've been to my Sweetheart's, Mother,
I've been to my Sweetheart's, Mother.
Make my bed soon, for I'm sick to the heart,
And I fain would lie down.

What have you been eating, Randall my son?
What have you been eating, my pretty one?
Eels and eel broth, Mother,
Eels and eel broth, Mother.
Make my bed soon, for I'm sick to the heart,
And I fain would lie down.

What will you leave your Mother, Randall my son?
What will you leave your Mother, my pretty one?
My lands and houses, Mother,
My lands and houses, Mother.
Make my bed soon, for I'm sick to the heart,
And I fain would lie down.

"Lord Randall" from *Reading Poems* by anonymous author (Wright Thomas and Stuart Gerry Brown, ed.).

What will you leave your brother, Randall my son?
What will you leave your brother, my pretty one?
My horses and cattle, Mother,
My horses and cattle, Mother.
Make my bed soon, for I'm sick to the heart,
And I fain would lie down.

What will you leave your sister, Randall my son?
What will you leave your sister, my pretty one?
My gold and silver, Mother,
My gold and silver, Mother.
Make my bed soon, for I'm sick to the heart,
And I fain would lie down.

What will you leave your Sweetheart, Randall my son?
What will you leave your Sweetheart, my pretty one?
A rope to hang her, Mother,
A rope to hang her, Mother.
Make my bed soon, for I'm sick to the heart,
And I fain would lie down.

An inspectional reading of "Lord Randall" might yield the following preunderstandings: the text is broken into stanzas; it is a dialogue between mother and son; the stanzaic pattern is highly repetitive; it is about a young lord grown sick who is making his will. If we have had some experience with narrative poetry, we might recognize the form of the poem as a folk-ballad, a narrative poem written to be sung.

The story that the poem presents is encapsulated in an event that approximates what we have called the culmination of a fictive narrative. We might summarize the events of the ballad this way:

1. Lord Randall goes to visit his sweetheart;
2. Lord Randall eats a meal of eels and eel-broth during his visit;
3. he returns home sick;
4. he tells his mother of the visit, his meal and his sickness and makes his will;
5. [Lord Randall dies.]

In the final stanza of the ballad we find the detail that knits the rest of the events together. He leaves his sweetheart "a rope to hang her." It is his sweetheart who has poisoned him and he consigns her to hell for this treachery.

It is noteworthy that this mother recognizes the situation; once she determines the dinner fare, she asks him to dispose of his property. He is her son, her "pretty one," whom she understands clearly enough is doomed. The focus of the ballad, however, is not on the mother's concern, but on the son's fate and the sweetheart's treachery.

The imagery of the poem is straightforward. The young Lord's possessions are presented in succeeding stanzas and in parallel form: "my lands and houses," "my horses and cattle," "my gold and silver." Against these possessions, clearly substantial gifts to his family, we have the stark image of "a rope." And that image is balanced not by another object as in earlier stanzas, but by a purpose, "to hang her." This set of images—the rope and the treacherous sweetheart—add a special significance to the refrain: "Make my bed soon, for I'm sick to the heart,/And I fain would lie down." "Sick to the heart" in the earlier stanzas can be read as a physical illness. With repetition the refrain comes to imply sadness at the loss of possessions along with the physical disease; then, in the final stanza, disgust and despairing disappointment and outrage at his sweetheart's perfidy.

The total experience of the poem ties together the poison working in the young Lord's body with the poison working in his mind and affections. He would fain lie down; his life and his reason for living are running out. The heaviness and weariness that this lying down communicates is tempered by a flash of outrage—a rope to hang her. The narrative gives us the events; the images relate them to one another and offer us the whole experience of "Lord Randall."

We might visualize this total experience of the poem using a tagmemic analysis. If we take the refrain of the ballad as our unit, our explanation of the poem might look like this:

	Unit: Refrain of Lord Randall	Unit-as-System	Unit-in-System
S T A T I C	Make my bed soon, for I'm sick to the heart And I fain would lie down	Weariness [undifferentiated] Physical distress Psychological distress	Refrain/Visit to Sweetheart Eels in eel broth—poison Making his will A rope to hang her [death]
D Y N A M I C	Make my bed soon ↓ I'm sick to the heart ↓ And I fain would lie down	Physical weariness—"all the day" ↓ Physical distress—"eels in eel broth" ↓ Psychological distress ↓ Loss of possessions ↓ Sweetheart's betrayal	Visit to sweetheart ↓ Poisoning ↓ Making his will—a rope to hang her ↓ Disgust/Outrage ↓ [Death]

In viewing the refrain as system, we describe a series of psycho-physical states that can be inferred from the refrain as it is a conclusion of a particular stanza. For instance, Lord Randall has been gone "all the day," visiting his sweetheart. The result of that visit is encapsulated in the refrain: he wants to retire; he is sick to the heart. We gather, from this, that he is "weary" in some general way. This unspecified weariness becomes more specific as the stanzas accumulate. Considering the refrain in a system, we can see how the events that we infer from the poem are reflected in the refrain. By comparing the dynamic relationship of Lord Randall's emotional states (unit-as-system) and the dynamic relationships of the events (unit-in-system) we gather a sense of how the whole poem works.

In "Lord Randall" there are two speakers, two personae, who tell the story; we also encounter poems in which there is only one speaker, a single persona in a monologue. In this kind of poem, the single speaker not only tells us what happened, but how he or she feels about the events; the images of the poem, taken together, convey the speaker's emotional response to the happenings of the poem.

The following poem, as will be obvious, employs a single persona responding to a set of events.

My Last Duchess

FERRARA

That's my last Duchess painted on the wall,
Looking as if she were alive. I call
That piece a wonder, now; Frà Pandolf's hands
Worked busily a day, and there she stands.
Will't please you sit and look at her? I said
'Frà Pandolf' by design, for never read
Strangers like you that pictured countenance,
The depth and passion of its earnest glance,
But to myself they turned (since none puts by
The curtain I have drawn for you, but I)
And seemed as they would ask me, if they durst,
How such a glance came there; so, not the first
Are you to turn and ask thus. Sir, 'twas not
Her husband's presence only, called that spot
Of joy into the Duchess' cheek; perhaps
Frà Pandolf chanced to say, 'Her mantle laps
Over my lady's wrist too much,' or 'Paint
Must never hope to reproduce the faint
Half-flush that dies along her throat.' Such stuff
Was courtesy, she thought, and cause enough
For calling up that spot of joy. She had
A heart—how shall I say?—too soon made glad,
Too easily impressed; she liked whate'er
She looked on, and her looks went everywhere.
Sir, 'twas all one! My favor at her breast,
The dropping of the daylight in the West,
The bough of cherries some officious fool
Broke in the orchard for her, the white mule
She rode with round the terrace—all and each
Would draw from her alike the approving speech,
Or blush, at least. She thanked men,—good! but thanked
Somehow—I know not how—as if she ranked
My gift of a nine-hundred years-old name
With anybody's gift. Who'd stoop to blame
This sort of trifling? Even had you skill
In speech—which I have not—to make your will
Quite clear to such an one, and say, 'Just this
Or that in you disgusts me; here you miss,
Or there exceed the mark'—and if she let
Herself be lessoned so, nor plainly set
Her wits to yours, forsooth, and made excuse—
E'en then would be some stooping; and I choose

"My Last Duchess" from *Poems* by Robert Browning. Oxford University Press, Inc.

Never to stoop. Oh, sir, she smiled, no doubt,
Whene'er I passed her; but who passed without
Much the same smile? This grew; I gave commands;
Then all smiles stopped together. There she stands
As if alive. Will't please you rise? We'll meet
The company below, then. I repeat,
The Count your master's known munificence
Is ample warrant that no just pretense
Of mine for dowry will be disallowed;
Though his fair daughter's self, as I avowed
At starting, is my object. Nay, we'll go
Together down, sir. Notice Neptune, though,
Taming a sea-horse, thought a rarity,
Which Claus of Insbruck cast in bronze for me!

An inspectional reading of "My Last Duchess" yields a number of preliminary understandings. It is a poetic text with a single speaker, the Duke of Ferrara who is reminiscing to an attendant lord about his former wife. The occasion for this reminiscence is the Duke's unveiling of a portrait of the Duchess, presumably hanging in his art gallery. Given these preliminary understandings, we may proceed to investigate the narrative features of the text.

There are in fact two narratives in the poem, one direct and immediate and the other imbedded in the first. Since the poem has a dramatic aspect, that is, the text is spoken by a single persona, we may draw on the dramatic technique of "supplying the spectacle." The poem begins with the Duke standing before a portrait of the Duchess and commenting on its qualities. It is only clear whom he is addressing toward the end of the poem when he says: "the count your master." The addressee is, then, a go-between from another nobleman whose mission it is to arrange another marriage for the Duke. Physical events of the text are as follows:

1. The Duke invites the ambassador to sit down.
2. The Duke draws the curtains which cover the portrait.
3. The Duke describes the qualities of the portrait.
4. The Duke discusses the qualities of the Duchess and their life together.
5. The Duke invites the ambassador to rise.
6. The Duke and the ambassador descend from the gallery as the Duke remarks on another object of art.

These are the immediate events which the text presents or implies.

The other narrative imbedded in the text is the history of the Duke's relationship with his former Duchess. Though the Duke's comments about the Duchess are general statements with illustrations, there is an embryonic chronology in his narrative. We might summarize the events of their relationship as follows:

1. The Duke remarks a democratic tendency on the part of the Duchess, her open and generous spirit.
2. The Duke becomes displeased with the Duchess' lack of appreciation of him.
3. The Duke's displeasure grows and the Duchess does not mend her ways.
4. The Duke commands her removal.
5. "All smiles stopped together."

This narrative does not make clear what happened to the Duchess, what the Duke's commands were and why exactly the smiles stopped, but it does indicate clearly the end of their relationship. The Duke follows this brief history with a reference to the negotiations he is conducting to acquire another wife.

The first incident in the direct narrative is the Duke's identification of the portrait and his critical appraisal of it—"I call that piece a wonder now." Presumably, the portrait resembles the Duchess to the life and also catches a characteristic quality: the "spot of joy" on her cheek. The Duke admires the artistry of the monk and takes pride in his possession of the canvas. He invites his listener to sit and "look at her."

To the portrait on the wall of the gallery the Duke adds his own portrait of the Duchess and, in so doing, a portrait of himself. The images that depict the Duchess may be catalogued thus:

The depth and passion of its [her] earnest glance
The spot of joy [on] the Duchess' cheek
A faint half-flush that dies along her throat
A heart . . . too soon made glad
The approving speech, or blush
Smiles

She finds all her experiences pleasurable and a joy and responds to life around her: the Duke's favor at her breast, sunsets, the gift of a bough of cherries, her favorite mule. These images describe an openhearted, gracious young woman who appreciates nature, accepts compliments modestly and responds spontaneously to every occasion.

The portrait of the Duke, on the other hand, which may be sketched from his description of the Duchess, contrasts sharply with hers. The compliments of the Friar are "stuff," not courtesy. One's heart should not be too soon made glad or be too easily impressed; distance and detachment are the Duke's response to any experience. He is amazed that "my favor at her breast" should receive much the same response as a sunset, a gift of cherries or an afternoon ride. Her appreciation of these moments is, for the Duke, a "sort of trifling." His gift of a nine-hundred years old name is ranked with "anybody's gift." The Duke will not correct her nor even call explicit attention to his displeasure because it "would be some stooping; and I choose/Never to stoop." His word for the Duchess' "trifling" is "disgust." These images come together in a portrait of the Duke. He is cold, proud, unbending, imperious, with a cruel edge to his character. He closes this discussion of the portrait with a snap: "Will't please you rise?" After disavowing his skill in speech, he returns to the subject at hand—the arrangement of a future marriage—a carefully phrased and syntactically complex statement: "The count your master's known munificence/Is ample warrant that no just pretense/Of mine for dowry will be disallowed;/Though his fair daughter's self, as I avowed/At starting is my object." The focus is on "dowry" and his demurer about the daughter is an afterthought. Having dispatched his last Duchess, he is cold-bloodedly making arrangements for the next. And as he called the ambassador's attention to the portrait of the Duchess, now he asks him to notice a bronze sculpture. The equation is clear: the portrait of the Duchess and the Duchess herself and the statue of Neptune are all his possessions to be displayed or dispatched as he wills.

The experience of the poem as a whole then focuses on the contrast between the Duke and the Duchess within the framework of the events. In dealing with drama, we remarked that the personae in the drama serve the plot; in this poetic text the events serve to fill out the portraits of the personae by imaging the qualities of their characters.

The Duke views people as objects, as possessions. He is a man of highly cultivated tastes and considerable intelligence. He articulates his attitudes with precision, and because he is a gentleman of refinement, the total absence of any emotional involvement with or feeling for his last Duchess is all the more chilling. This impression of the Duke is sharper because of the qualities of the Duchess: her open, affectionate modest and joyful demeanor. The text presents this contrast through the narrative and its images.

Image, Metaphor and Symbol

Earlier in this chapter we remarked that describing the narrative in a poetic text provides a way of arranging a sequence of images; in poetry the narrative exists for the sake of the network of images rather than the other way around. This is the case because it is the images taken together that specify the experience of the poem. Viewing the poem as narrative, then, is the heuristic which allows us to arrange the images in sequence and to discover the relations among them.

By "image" in a poetic text we mean those words which call up a physical referent; objects, qualities, actions, allusions. "Watersmooth-silver stallion" is an image because it refers to a physical object, "stallion" with two descriptors, "watersmooth" and "silver." In the same poem "rides" and "shoots" are images because they refer to actions. "Mr. Death" functions as an image in the poem because, although death is a negation (absence of life), the descriptor "Mr." personifies and objectifies the expression. The referent is an allusion—an anthropomorphic figure with traditional characteristics, cloaked in black with a skull for a head. The descriptors may also qualify actions as well as objects. Buffalo Bill shoots "onetwothreefourfive pigeons justlikethat"; running the numbers together creates an impression of suddenness and reproduces a sound—the rapid report of pistol shots. These images carry, along with their reference, sensory association that appeals to the eye, the ear, the touch. These associations have the power to evoke strong emotional responses.

We can test this power by summoning up images associated with emotional experiences of our own. The heavy scent of hothouse flowers might remind us of funerals, the acrid smell of pipe smoke might recall our grandfather's lap, sparkles of frost might recall the excitement of winter mornings. Such sensory stimuli summon up emotions directly and they come unbidden to us. The word-images of a poem function with the same immediacy. The accumulation of these word-images and the network they create constitute the emotional dimension of the poem.

Networking the Images

When we consider the way in which images relate to one another in the course of a poetic text, we can begin by drawing on the topos of antecedent/consequence. The narrative frame we have established for the text provides a temporal sequence for the images. So in the sonnet "Let Me Not to the Marriage of True Minds" the principal images are arranged chronologically: marriage, mark, star, Time's fool. The mark is ever fixed and the star a constant light, so that as a consequence love is not time's fool. Two sets of images that follow on this statement: "rosy lips and cheeks" and "bending sickle's compass" contrast with the unchanging mark and star and explain the image of Time's fool in that the sickle of time passing will cut down rosy lips and cheeks. Time is the grim reaper, but its passage will not destroy that love which is a marriage of true minds. The temporal order in which the poem presents these images conveys the progress of true friendship through a life-course.

Metaphor

Once we establish an order of images in the poem on the basis of an explicit or implicit narrative, we are prepared to deal with relations among the images of the poem. As we have noted, the images have specific physical references: objects, qualities, actions and allusions. The poems we have already considered make it clear that a poem is not simply a description of a physical object or a set of physical objects or actions. They introduce experiences which are not principally physical; experiences like love, death, betrayal. They generate an emotional response to a situation or a person. When words work this way, they link the object or the person or the situation with an image or set of images. This linkage identifies person, situation or condition with an image. The resulting statement is a metaphor. "Happiness is a warm puppy." "Love is the marriage of true minds." "John Brown was a lion in the fight." In each of these statements one whole is linked to and identified with another whole. In each case the predicate contains a word or a phrase which has a physical object or situation as referent. To explain how a metaphor works requires considerable articulation. We can only describe the metaphor in a clumsy paraphrase. For instance, "happiness is a warm puppy" might be explicated this way. Happiness is a quality or condition of the human person; the feeling of being happy is identical with the feeling of a small child holding a warm puppy. A more technical description of happiness might describe it as "a psychological state of well-being characterized by relative permanence and dominantly agreeable emotion ranging in value from mere contentment to deep and intense joy in living." If we have never experienced happiness, this definition is not particularly helpful and, indeed, reading it does not communicate the emotion. In terms of creating the *feeling* associated with happiness, "warm puppy" is more effective. We must also admit that making the metaphor is a mysterious performance of the mind. On the face of it a metaphor is a lie in that John Brown is not, and never was, a four-footed, carnivorous feline. On the other hand, language allows us to express an identity which John Brown and a lion share. This identification draws on the image "lion" to describe John Brown in battle. This metaphoric use of language is central to the way words work in a poetic text.

We have already enumerated a series of metaphors in the sonnet "Let Me Not to the Marriage of True Minds." We have also arranged those metaphors in a chronological sequence. Love is a marriage of true minds; it is an ever-fixed mark; it is a guiding star; it is not Time's fool. Each metaphor contributes to a definition of love, from the controlling metaphor of marriage through the negation of Time's fool. The associations that these linkages present are effectively the definition of love in this poetic text. In "Buffalo Bill's Defunct" the controlling metaphor is the identification of Buffalo Bill and the blue-eyed boy. The terms that describe Buffalo Bill are associated with the boy whom death has taken and this association effects the emotional freight of the poem. The metaphorical use of language in "Lord Randall" we find in the ambiguity of the refrain "I'm sick to the heart." It is, as we pointed out, a physical sickness deriving from poisoned food; it is also a psychological sickness at his sweetheart's treachery. Similar use of physical detail in a metaphorical vein is the Duke's statement in "My Last Duchess": "I choose never to stoop." The Duke will not bend to accommodate anyone on any level. Explaining himself to the Duchess, communicating to her as an equal is "stooping." So we see how, within the context of the narrative frame, the metaphor works to create analogues and allusions.

The metaphoric use of language can also include reference to other literary texts. A poetic text can be made up of metaphoric language referring not only to physical objects or persons but also to allusions from other texts. An allusion is a word or phrase or name that occurs in another text and which carries with it the meaning and emotional freight which it has in that text. The experience of reading that text can be recalled by inserting a key word image or phrase in a new text. Now we will examine a poetic text that makes use of metaphor and metaphoric allusion.

Sweeney Among the Nightingales

ωμοι πεπληγμαι καιριαυ πλγσην εσω

Apeneck Sweeney spreads his knees
Letting his arms hang down to laugh
The zebra stripes along his jaw
Swelling to maculate giraffe.

The circles of the stormy moon
Slide westward toward the River Plate
Death and the Raven draft above
And Sweeney guards the horned gate.

Gloomy Orion and the Dog
Are veiled; and hushed the shrunken seas;
The person in the Spanish cape
Tries to sit on Sweeney's knees

Slips and pulls the table cloth
Overturns a coffee-cup
Reorganized upon the floor
She yawns and draws a stocking up;

The silent man in mocha brown
Sprawls at the window-sill and gapes;
The waiter brings in oranges
Bananas figs and hothouse grapes;

The silent vertebrate in brown
Contracts and concentrates, withdraws;
Rachel *nee* Rabinovitch
Tears at the grapes with murderous paws;

She and the lady in the cape
Are suspect, thought to be in league;
Therefore the man with heavy eyes
Declines the gambit, shows fatigue,

Leaves the room and reappears
Outside the window, leaning in,
Branches of wistaria
Circumscribe a golden grin;

The host with someone indistinct
Converses at the door apart,
The nightingales are singing near
The Convent of the Sacred Heart,

And sang within the bloody wood
When Agamemnon cried aloud,
And let their liquid siftings fall
To stain the stiff dishonored shroud.

This poem, like the others we have examined, has a narrative frame which provides a context for its word-images. Sweeney is sitting at his ease, laughing. A person in the company tries to sit on his knees and slips off, sprawling on the floor; a man looks in at the window and a waiter brings fruit to the table. At this point our inspectional reading yields this information: Sweeney is sitting in a tavern and the people around him, the person in the Spanish cape and the silent man in mocha brown, are not necessarily friendly; they have some designs on Sweeney. The man in the window withdraws and a third member of the company devours grapes the waiter has brought. Then the man with heavy eyes, presumably Sweeney, because he thinks Rachel and the lady in the cape are up to no good, leaves the room and reappears outside the window, grinning among the wistaria. The host of the tavern is in conversation apart from the rest of the company, presumably not involved in the intrigue or perhaps in collusion with it but not actively taking part in it. In any event, Sweeney has left the room and grins through the open window. It is by no means clear that he is out of danger, but the grin indicates at least a qualified victory.

This rudimentary and dimly sketched narrative provides a context for the word-images of the poem. We can divide these word images into two categories: those related directly to the narrative and those that are indirectly related. The images directly related to the narrative include descriptions of the persona and their actions: Sweeney is apeneck, his jaw is zebra striped and swells to maculate giraffe. He is also the man with heavy eyes who has a golden grin. The other personae are the woman in the Spanish cape who slips off Sweeney's lap and is reorganized upon the floor, drawing a stocking up; the man in mocha brown, a silent vertebrate, sprawls at the window sill and snakelike, contracts and concentrates; Rachel *nee* Rabinovitch has murderous paws. The animal imagery that characterizes Sweeney is balanced against similar connotations in the descriptions of the personae: the silent vertebrate and murderous paws. The descriptive imagery that does not deal directly with event involves sets of allusions. The circles of the stormy moon slide westward toward the Plate, a river in South America. Death and the Raven, the bird of ill-omen, hover above; "the horned gate" is the gate in the sixth book of Virgil's *Aeneid* through which true dreams issue into the upper air from the underworld. This moonscape creates an atmosphere of impending disaster. If Sweeney is half-dreaming, his dreams are premonitions of disaster; if his dreams come through the horned gate, then his premonitions are true. He cannot however read the specifics of his fate in the stars; Orion and the Dog star are veiled and the tides are not running. This landscape works within the context of the narrative to specify both a general atmosphere and Sweeney's psychological state.

The final six lines of the poem are also indirectly related to the narrative, though they do not seem like the earlier indirect reference, to be encapsulated by it. Rather, they seem to be a choric comment on the narrative itself. We are presented here with two very different associations relative to nightingale: the Convent of the Sacred Heart, and the bloody wood where Agamemnon was murdered. Taking the nightingale itself as an allusion, in folk literature it announces a season of romantic love; it is the harbinger of May and of midsummer night. In English romantic poetry the nightingale sings of summer and the tender night. Its song, in this intertextual sense, is a call to romance and new love. The association with the Convent of the Sacred Heart introduces an image of quiet nuns praying and working in seclusion, motivated by a sacred love of which Christ's bleeding heart is the emblem. To this set of allusions is contrasted the nightingales who sang in the bloody wood of Agamemnon's murder. The Greek epigraph of the poem establishes a referent for Agamemnon in that this is the cry he utters when struck down by his wife in Aeschylus' play *Agamemnon.* So the nightingales that sang within that wood are imported from Greek literature.

The nightingale itself also appears in the legend of Philomela, a maiden who is raped by a relative, whose tongue is cut out so that she cannot inform on him and who is then transformed into a nightingale. In the context of this legend the nightingale sings of adulterous wrong. The wrong referred to is double: Agamemnon, the Greek general, returns from the Trojan War with a captive Trojan consort Cassandra; his wife Clymnestra has herself, in Agamemnon's absence, taken a lover. Both are adulterous, though Clymnestra takes the wrong to the outer limits by murdering her husband. In any event, the nightingales' song in this stanza describes a world, not of romantic and sacred love, but a world of betrayal and sudden death.

The singing of the nightingales constitutes an allusion which functions metaphorically in the poetic text. By virtue of its intertextual significance the nightingale sings of a world that combines the possibility of love with the possibility of the betrayal of that love. The birds who sing are in the last two lines of the poem are themselves defilers. They sing of romantic love and adulterous wrong; their droppings stain the shroud of the murdered hero. The contrast of the ethereal song with the earthy droppings heightens the different aspects of the world which the nightingale represents.

If we arrange the images and events of the poem tagmemically around the central figure of Apeneck Sweeney, our explanation of the poem might look like the example on the following page.

In surveying the images and actions of the poem thus layed out, we cannot help but notice how pervasive the animal imagery is. Sweeney is apenecked, zebra striped and spotted like a giraffe. Raven and The Dog brood over his revery. Among the conspirators the man in mocha brown is a vertebrate whose actions are snakelike; Rachel attacks the hothouse grapes with murderous paws. These animal images suggest that the personae are operating on instinct rather than intellect. With the introduction of the nightingale the animal imagery moves from brute to bird and the allusions that define the nightingale's significance suggests a broader awareness than could be attributed to any of the personae in the poem.

The metaphorical function of the nightingale can be articulated thus: the nightingale is romance, devotion and treacherous violence, past and present. Because this image does move beyond the descriptive function of metaphors like apeneck or silent vertebrate, it also works symbolically. To say "Sweeney is an ape" or "the man in mocha brown is a snake" puts these metaphors on a descriptive level. The nightingale sings of a world, not of a person or a specific situation. When we spoke of symbol earlier in this text, we said that a symbol is an object in one order of reality which points to a reality in a different order (p. 149). Here the nightingale is a word-image that points, as we have said, to a new level of awareness.

Finally, then, we can try a description of the experience of the poem. On first reading, the poem conveys impressions of danger and impending violence. The Greek epigraph, the images of "stormy moon," "death and the Raven," "murderous paws," "the stiff dishonored shroud" foster that impression. The narrative of the poem may be summarized:

1. Sweeney is sitting at his ease in a tavern
2. He spurns a casual attempt at seduction by the person in the Spanish cape
3. He was observed by the silent man in mocha brown at the window who then withdraws
4. Because he suspects that there is collusion between Rachel and the woman in the cape, he leaves the room
5. He appears at the window and grins

	Unit	Unit-as-System	Unit-in-System
S T A T I C	*Sweeney* Apeneck arms hanging laughs zebra stripes maculate giraffe heavy eyes fatigue golden grin	Sweeney premonitions—horned gate stormy moon River Plate Death and The Raven suspicion about person in Spanish cape departure from room grin surrounded wistaria	man in mocha brown- vertebrate person in Spanish Cape — Rachel nee Rabinovitch— murderous paws Ape-neck Sweeney host—someone indistinct nightingales near Convent of the Sacred Heart nightingales in the bloody wood
D Y N A M I C	Ape-neck zebra stripes along jaw → laugh → maculate giraffe ↓ heavy eyes → shows fatigue ↓ golden grin	Sweeney laughing ↓ premonitions of danger ↓ lets the person in the Spanish cape slip off his knees ↓ is observed by the silent man in mocha brown from outside the window ↓ leaves the room ↓ grins through the window	Sweeney relaxing in tavern ↓ attempted seduction by person in Spanish cape conspiracy — threat of silent man Rachel ↓ Sweeney leaves, grins from outside nightingales — sing of romantic and sacred love sing of adulterous wrong, stains Agamemnon's shroud

The narrative is inconclusive; it is not clear what finally happens to Sweeney at the conclusion of this episode. The implications are that the person in the Spanish cape, the silent man and Rachel are plotting against Sweeney, that the host, if not a party to the conspiracy, is at least indifferent to it (he converses with someone indistinct apart) and that Sweeney is well advised to get out of the situation.

The animal imagery works through the narrative to create a network of metaphors that describe the personae. Sweeney is an ape, a zebra and a giraffe; a silent man is a snake; Rachel is a monkey or a cat. All these personae are all acting on brutish instinct and cunning. For all practical purposes, the room is a jungle; the River Plate of Sweeney's premonitions underscores this impression. The nightingales of the final stanzas symbolize a world in which the romantic and the spiritual are intermeshed with the possibility of treachery and violence. Before the bird sings of romance and devotion, it sang of adulterous wrong. Though the last image of the narrative, "the golden grin," bespeaks Sweeney's escape from this particular deadfall, it is clear that his escape (if indeed he does escape) is only temporary. Sweeney remains "among the nightingales" and because he has nothing but instinct and cunning to protect him, he is likely to come to Agamemnon's end. On the basis of these features, we may conclude that the poem is about the imminence of violence in a world where animal cunning predominates and that the emotional freight of the poem is a sense of impending disaster.

Poetic Uses of the Narrative Heuristic

With this poem, as with the others we have examined, it is important to remember that our techniques for explanation remain heuristic and that the experience of the poem will always defy precise formulation. What the poem means always turns back on what we have described as the emotional freight or feeling of the poem. Because the metaphor will always remain something of a mystery and its analysis defies the logician, no interpretation contains the final word about a poetic text. The poem, more than the short story or the novel or the play, speaks to immediate experience and organizes the text around the feelings that the experience engenders. So, "Buffalo Bill's Defunct" deals with the experience of the death of a small boy; "let me not to the marriage of true minds" embodies the experience of longterm friendship; "My Last Duchess" the experience of listening to an autocratic, renaissance Duke who has put away his wife. Consider how each of these experiences might be presented as exposition or as argument or even in fictive prose narrative. To confirm this statement, reread the opening paragraph which treats the death of the small boy as prose fiction. The poem, through its use of word-images, renders the emotional freight of the experience directly.

Our explanation of the poetic text begins with an examination of a narrative frame, direct, implied or inferred. The poem may tell a story, but not for the sake of the story. The narrative elements in the poem establish a framework for the imagery working in the text. Even in a narrative poem like "Lord Randall," the narrative is sketchy, indeed. We know very little about the relationship between Lord Randall and his mother or between Lord Randall and his sweetheart. We do experience the intensity of his feeling when he leaves to his sweetheart "a rope from hell to hang her." In "Sweeney Among the Nightingales" we do not even know, with any certainty, what happens to Sweeney. He may have escaped this particular deadfall; he may have been cut down as Agamemnon was. The poem does not provide us with information that other narratives would ordinarily include. So the narrative framework provides us with a context for the imagery of the poetic text, a method of arranging that imagery in time.

The aggregate of images, arranged in this narrative framework, produce the emotional weight of the poem. The words that refer to physical objects, descriptive of sensate qualities like colors, smells, sounds and textures, make up the imagery of the poem. The way in which these images are linked together is metaphorical, that is, the poem is a galaxy of images that explode like shooting stars. "Love is a star that guides the wandering bark"; "the Duke is a man who choses never to stoop." Love is not literally a celestial body nor is the Duke a man who never bends from the waist. These word-images work metaphorically to produce an emotional impact. There are word-images and metaphors also in prose narratives; there the images serve the narrative by coloring the persona and the events, whereas in the poem the narrative highlights the images to produce the emotional freight of the experience.

Finally, here is a poem about poetry. It raises appropriate questions about what a poem "should" be while presumably giving answers to those questions. It is a series of images with metaphorical function that describe a poem.

Ars Poetica

A poem should be palpable and mute
As a globed fruit,

Dumb
As old medallions to the thumb,

Silent as the sleeve-worn stone
Of casement ledges where the moss has grown—

A poem should be wordless
As the flight of birds.

A poem should be motionless in time
As the moon climbs,

Leaving, as the moon releases
Twig by twig the night-entangled trees,

Leaving, as the moon behind the winter leaves,
Memory by memory the mind—

A poem should be motionless in time
As the moon climbs.

A poem should be equal to:
Not true.

For all the history of grief
An empty doorway and a maple leaf.

For love
The leaning grasses and two lights above the sea—

A poem should not mean
But be.

If the impression that this poem makes runs counter to what we have said about narrative framework (and it seems to), it reinforces what we have said about word-images, the use of metaphor and the experience of the poem. We would certainly agree that a poem does not "mean" in the same way a short story or novel or essay mean, but we may not accept the notion that a poem is an object in its own right. In any event, through our use of the narrative frame, we have come to see that the images of a poem carry the emotional burden of the experience the poem presents and that this experience cannot be adequately rendered except by the poem itself.

Chapter 19
The Literate Mind

Literacy, in common parlance, means being able to read and write. Since the Phoenicians invented the alphabet, literacy has been a mark of the elite in any society. The ability to interpret written texts makes available to us the collective wisdom of society; the ability to compose meaningful texts enables us to contribute to that wisdom. There is obviously a broad spectrum of literate capabilities, from reading street signs and writing notes to the mailman to reading the classics of Western civilization and writing commentaries on them, and everything in between. The larger literacy we have been discussing in this book deals with capabilities at the more sophisticated end of the spectrum; our assumption is that, if we can read and write more sophisticated texts, we will be capable of dealing with those less sophisticated. This larger literacy, then, empowers us to learn by reading and writing.

All the activities in which we have been engaged, reading and writing, analyzing and interpreting, inventing and composing, are directed towards acquiring this larger literacy. What we have been pursuing is the development of mental capabilities, of certain qualities of mind. We will have garnered information along the way and we will have come on insights relative to given texts, but our major accomplishment cannot be measured simply in terms of information or insight. What we have acquired (hopefully) is a set of qualities of mind and an awareness of the power those qualities can deliver. We are now in a position to explore those qualities or characteristics of the literate mind in more detail.

In his *Autobiography,* Ben Franklin sets out a list of virtues or habits he wished to acquire. He listed each virtue and described it in some detail. Then he went about developing them systematically by keeping a record of his failures to practice the virtue on which he was concentrating. We will follow Franklin's example in listing those characteristic qualities or habits which distinguish the literate mind.

1. The literate mind is **reflective.** The word "reflective" comes from a Latin stem which means to "bend back." When faced with a task or a problem, the reflective mind does not, like the desperate messenger, mount his horse and ride off in all directions. Being reflective means taking stock of the task, thinking about the problem. On a superficial level, it means reading the directions for an examination and making sure we understand them. More pointedly, it means, when we have a reading or writing task, reflecting on the rhetorical situation it involves. It means checking our preunderstandings about the task, the problem or the text. Rushing off with little or no reflection can mean that we do not see the forest for the trees. Taking time to size up the task, to consider the problem, to garner preunderstanding about the text will save wasted motion and energy in the long run. The literate mind is reflective.

2. The literate mind is **methodical.** Method is, as we have seen, a way of getting where we are going. Applying appropriate methods to the task, the problem or the text gives us control over our material and ensures progress towards our goal. We have described and applied a series of

heuristic methodologies throughout this book. The two general methodologies—the topoi and tag-memics—can help organize our analysis of a given text and help us explore ways of organizing our writing on a given topic. The Toulmin Model of argument offers a way of approaching argument and argumentation. The narrative heuristic offers a method for analyzing history, biography and fiction. Internalizing these methods, making them our own, make habitual the orderly exploration of data. Control of these methods will help us to add others as need dictates. The literate mind is methodical.

3. The literate mind is **inventive.** Invention or discovery is, as we know, crucial to any self-expression. Because our methodologies are heuristic, they are aids to discovery. The literate mind casts about for novel ways of arranging data, of expressing an insight, of elaborating a thesis. Although Mr. Edison thought that invention was one percent inspiration and ninety-nine percent perspiration, we can not underestimate the importance of that one percent. Reflection and the use of method create propitious conditions for the visitation of inspiration. Often an hour of perspiration must precede the flash of discovery. Arranging and rearranging the data encourages that moment of invention, that eureka of insight. The literate mind is inventive.

4. The literate mind is **curious.** The most insistent word in the vocabulary of young children is "why." Human beings as a species want to know; this desire has sent us out on uncharted seas and off into the stratosphere. It urges us to track the infinitesimal particles of the atom. It leads us into the labyrinthine ways of the human psyche, into the thickets of the law and up the long stretches of philosophy. We want to know why this title for this text, why these grounds for this argument, why this order of narration in this story. The habit of asking "why?" is a habit that the literate mind can not resist.

5. The literate mind is **flexible.** Flexibility, in this instance, is obviously a metaphor. That is flexible which bends, but does not break. As a quality of the mind, flexibility means openness to new ideas, willingness to suspend judgment until the evidence is in, a tolerance of ambiguity. The arch enemy of learning is an inflexible adherence to our own preunderstandings. We learned it *this* way at the office or in the army or in grammar school or at our mother's knee and we are unwilling to reconsider the matter. Here we have looked at arguments pro and con, we have discovered that the actual world can be problematic, we have investigated possible worlds with values and institutions that do not resemble our own. All these investigations contribute to that flexibility which makes us open to further learning about ourselves, others and the world. The literate mind is flexible.

6. The literate mind is **confident.** To be confident is to put trust in something. In what does the literate mind trust? First and foremost, in its own capabilities: the ability to distinguish the whole from its parts, to explore and explain the data methodically, to come to some insights on the basis of that exploration and to express those insights in clear, convincing and interesting ways. We can trust ourselves to make sense of a task or a problem or a text no matter how daunting it may at first appear. We have methods and strategies at our disposal and those we can apply toward a solution or a conclusion. This is what it means to "think for ourselves." We come to our own conclusions with a conviction that they are reasonable and that we can explain them. The literate mind is confident.

The final two qualities of the literate mind are specific to the experiences described in this book. They can be considered problematic and so open to debate. We will not find them in most catalogues of intellectual virtues, but they are distinctively relevant to the habits of mind inculcated by the processes described here.

7. The literate mind is **recursive.** "Recursive" means "to run over again." There are valuable and useful "minds," that is aggregates of mental qualities or habits, that view the world as a set of problems to be solved definitively. This type of mind puts its trust in algorithmic methods, settling one issue after another without ever looking back. It is intolerant of ambiguity and strives purposefully for as much univocity as possible. The literate mind, on the other hand, makes progress by running back over ideas and texts already explored. Insights and understandings garnered by one trip around the hermeneutic circle become preunderstandings for another round leading to new insights and expressions. The same text can be read three times in three different ways— as exposition, as argument, as self-expression—and those three readings can coalesce in a fourth reading and a fifth and so on. The fourth rewrite of our paper is the final one only in the sense that we have run out of time and that we are satisfied that we have met the exigency of the rhetorical moment. We can take the paper out of our drawer at some later time and rewrite it again in response to a different exigency. Each turn around the circle enriches our understanding of parts and whole and renders these understandings more available to ourselves and our audiences. The literate mind is recursive.

8. The literate mind is **dialogic.** To this point, all the qualities or habits which distinguish the literate mind belong to the tagmemic category unit-as-system. In the aggregate they are a description of that mind. The dialogic quality of the literate mind belongs also in the tagmemic category unit-in-system. The literate mind carries on a dialogue, first, with its own insights recursively. It dialogues with the texts it reads and with the texts it writes. It carries that dialogue across a range of disciplines and interests. The participants in the dialogue are all those texts that bear on a given topic or thesis, the range of previous insights brought to bear on the topic. But the dialogue also engages other communities. The literate mind can, and often must, engage what we have described as the algorithmic mind. In fact, to some degree, we all have to entertain both minds within the same skull. When we look at unit-in-system, there are a plurality of minds making up the dialogue. And the literate mind must entertain all of them. The dialogue ensures that we will not mistake the literate mind and its capabilities for the totality of mental capabilities and the world of the literate mind for the entire cosmos. And if our academic major or our chosen profession requires that we foster algorithmic habits and attitudes, it is critical to our intellectual balance that we not let the qualities of the literate mind atrophy. It is never a case of either/or; it is appropriately a case of both/and. The literate mind is dialogic.

An End and a Beginning

We have omitted one of Ben Franklin's virtues from our list relative to the literate mind: "Industry." This omission is appropriate because industry is a moral rather than an intellectual virtue. The difference between a quality and a habit is that a quality may come and go while a habit is a *permanent* quality. We have to exercise the qualities of the literate mind in order to acquire them as habits. So the end of the book is also a beginning. In dealing with texts henceforward, during our formal education and after, we will be able to apply the principles we have learned here and to develop these habits forever in our reading and our writing. We will not necessarily need Ben Franklin's examination book to remind us, but an occasional review of these qualities and our methods would not hurt. The effort expended will be worthwhile as we continue to cultivate the literate mind.

Index